A Different Justice

Reagan and the Supreme Court

A Different Justice

Reagan and the Supreme Court

Elder Witt

Congressional Quarterly Inc.
1414 22nd Street N.W.
Washington, D.C. 20037

Congressional Quarterly Inc.

Congressional Quarterly Inc., an editorial research service and publishing company, serves clients in the fields of news, education, business and government. It combines specific coverage of Congress, government and politics by Congressional Quarterly with the more general subject range of an affiliated service, Editorial Research Reports.

Congressional Quarterly publishes the *Congressional Quarterly Weekly Report* and a variety of books, including college political science textbooks under the CQ Press imprint and public affairs paperbacks on developing issues and events. CQ also publishes information directories and reference books on the federal government, national elections and politics, including the *Guide to Congress,* the *Guide to the U.S. Supreme Court,* the *Guide to U.S. Elections* and *Politics in America.* The *CQ Almanac,* a compendium of legislation for one session of Congress, is published each year. *Congress and the Nation,* a record of government for a presidential term, is published every four years.

CQ publishes *The Congressional Monitor,* a daily report on current and future activities of congressional committees, and several newsletters including *Congressional Insight,* a weekly analysis of congressional action, and *Campaign Practices Reports,* a semimonthly update on campaign laws.

The online delivery of CQ's Washington Alert Service provides clients with immediate access to Congressional Quarterly's institutional information and expertise.

Cover: Robert Redding
Art: p. 41, Robert Redding; pp. 57, 69, George Rebh
Photo Credits: pp. 5, 23, 25, 49, 77, 79, 89, 91, 96, Supreme Court Historical Society; pp. 15, 17, 21, Library of Congress, p. 38, *New York Times,* George Tames; p. 42, *New York Times;* pp. 137, 155 (left), Sue Klemens; p. 155 (right), Karen Ruckman

---

Printed in the United States of America

Library of Congress Cataloging in Publication Data

Witt, Elder:

A different justice.

Bibliography: p. 199
Includes index.
1. United States. Supreme Court. 2. Judicial power—United States. 3. Reagan, Ronald. 4. Executive power—United States. I. Title.
KF8742.W57   1986   347.73'26 '   85-29160
ISBN 0-87187-367-2   347.30735

Contents

Preface

There is no perfect time to write a book about the Supreme Court. The Court does not stand still to have its portrait painted.

The Supreme Court — the individual justices and the institution itself — is always changing. The issues before the Court change. The cases change: much-publicized cases shrink into obscurity as they are decided on technical points of law; obscure cases catapult into the lawbooks as the Court uses them to announce major new principles.

If there is no ideal time to write a book about the Court, there are good times. If a definitive portrait of the contemporary Court cannot be produced, then a good set of photographs will serve to illuminate the characters of the justices and the Court at a particular point in history. That is the intent of *A Different Justice*.

The midpoint of Ronald Reagan's presidency provides an apt point to take a close look at the contemporary Court and the effect of Reagan's campaign to reshape American society by persuading the Court to redirect the course of American law, to espouse a different brand of justice. Chapter 1 introduces the characters and themes that figure in this Reagan campaign.

Chapter 2 sets President Reagan's effort in context, examining the relationship between presidents and the Court over nearly 200 years.

The path that brought Sandra Day O'Connor to the Supreme Court is outlined in Chapter 3, which examines her background, the process of her selection and nomination and her confirmation by the Senate. Chapter 4 analyzes the impact of her appointment on the Court, her votes and, more important, her views.

Chapter 5 profiles the other members of the contemporary Court, drawing upon their own words to provide a clear understanding of the men in the black robes.

Chapter 6 begins the narrative of Reagan's other campaign — the effort to change the mind of the Supreme Court on key issues such as antitrust, abortion, affirmative action, criminal law and matters of church and state. The chapter describes the opening of this campaign in 1981 and its disappointing results for the administration in 1982.

The groundwork done in 1983 and the stunning conservative victories of early 1984 are related in Chapter 7, followed by a description of the period in 1985 when the Court rebuffed the administration's effort to capitalize on the rightward shift of the previous term.

Chapter 8 looks to the future. Framed by the constitutional debate set off this summer by Attorney General Edwin Meese and taken up by Justices William J. Brennan Jr. and John Paul Stevens, the chapter examines key issues facing the Court in the next several years. It also provides thumbnail sketches of the individuals thought most likely to be in the running for Reagan's next nomination — should he have a second opportunity to name a justice.

The text of the Constitution, the recent speeches by Meese and Brennan and biographical sketches of the justices are provided in the appendix.

Finally, a word of thanks — to David Tarr, who proposed this book be written; to Carolyn Goldinger, whose careful editing and gentle guidance improved the final product while leaving it my own; to Martha Angle, the editor who has guided my weekly coverage of the Supreme Court for the *Congressional Quarterly Weekly Report;* and finally to my family, without whose support none of this would have been possible.

Elder Witt
November 1985

1

A Time of Change

Ronald Reagan came to Washington January 1981 convinced that it was time for a change in the way the American government related to the Americans governed. The election returns from November 1980 were his mandate for that mission.

The U.S. Supreme Court was a major target of Reagan's crusade. For a generation, the Court had operated as a liberalizing force in American life. Its decisions had accelerated the civil rights movement, ignited a reapportionment revolution, reformed police procedures and curtailed state powers over controversial matters such as school prayer and abortion.

Not only did Reagan disagree with the substance of most of these decisions, but also he objected to the judicial activism that the Supreme Court had by 1980 thoroughly imprinted on the entire federal court system. By example and by directive, the Court had encouraged federal judges to intervene to an unprecedented degree in matters heretofore left to other branches of the government, involving themselves in drawing electoral maps, desegregating school systems and operating prisons.

As president, Reagan had two ways to influence the Court: the opportunity to appoint, which is a matter of chance, and the power to argue, which is a routine, but vital,

administration task. Within his first year in office, Reagan wielded the appointment power to great advantage. By selecting Sandra Day O'Connor, the first woman justice, Reagan set the stage for the long-awaited judicial reaction to the liberal activism that had characterized the Court since the tenure of Chief Justice Earl Warren.

The first signs of this judicial reaction had come a decade earlier. The Court had strictly limited the power of federal judges to interfere in state court proceedings. It had begun to make it more difficult for taxpayers and public interest groups to challenge government practices in federal court, and it adopted narrower views of some of the key criminal law rulings of the 1960s. By the latter years of the 1970s, however, the Court had moved back to a more moderate stance. And by 1981 commentators were writing about the judicial counterrevolution that didn't happen.

Although O'Connor made quite a impact, she alone could not bring about the different justice Reagan sought. The president also used the power of argument, directing the solicitor general to intervene in key cases and to urge the Court to rethink its positions on issues of particular concern to the administration.

Within months of O'Connor's arrival at

Supreme Court Terms

By law the Supreme Court begins its annual term on the first Monday in October of each year and continues it until the first Monday in October of the next year. The term that began on Oct. 7, 1985, is called the October 1985 term — although it extends well into 1986. The Court usually recesses for the summer early in July, just before the Fourth of July holiday.

Because of the overlap between years, another way in which a particular term is labeled is by the two years' dates — hence the October 1985 term is also known as the 1985-1986 term.

the Court in September 1981, it was clear that the immediate significance of her appointment was not that she was the first woman justice but that she was this particular Court's fourth conservative vote. An immediate ally of the most conservative justices — Chief Justice Warren E. Burger, William H. Rehnquist and, usually, Lewis F. Powell Jr. — O'Connor tilted the Court more and more toward judicial restraint and into a new posture of deference to Congress and the White House, the political branches of the government.

This shift did not immediately produce a spate of conservative rulings. Indeed, the Reagan administration suffered some painful defeats at the hands of the Court in 1982 and 1983. By the summer of 1984, however, the counterrevolution had begun. In a dramatic sequence of rulings, the Court approved Reagan administration initiatives to modify key Warren Court rulings on criminal rights, to limit the use of affirmative action, to lower the wall of separation between church and state and to lighten the burden of government regulation of the business community.

Then, in the term that bridged the first and second Reagan administrations, from October 1984 through June 1985, the Court moved back toward the moderate center and away from the unremitting conservatism of the previous term. By May 1, 1985, for example, criminal defendants had won more victories from the Court than during the entire previous term. Overall, in civil liberties cases, individuals had won more than half the cases reaching the Court during the term, a sharp change from the previous term, when individuals lost four of every five such cases.

If the October 1984 term was a moderate interval, the October 1985 term seemed likely to test the Court's commitment to some of the liberal landmarks of the past. Already on the docket were cases in which states once again sought more leeway to regulate abortions, in which white employees protested lay-off rules favoring black employees with less seniority and in which cities sought more power to restrict obscene or offensive entertainment.

The Court's decisions in these cases will show whether the October 1983 term marked a true change in course or merely a minor zigzag in constitutional history.

Activism and Restraint

During Earl Warren's tenure as chief justice, (1953-1969) the Supreme Court had led the nation into a period of unprecedented activity by federal judges. Espousing James Madison's view that the federal courts were "in a peculiar manner the guardians of those rights" set out in the Bill of Rights, the Warren Court did not hesitate to exercise its power.

In less than two decades, the Court declared racial segregation unlawful in public schools, required a wholesale redrafting of the nation's electoral districts, extended the guarantees of fair treatment to criminal suspects apprehended by state and local police and demanded that police adhere to the spirit and the letter of those guarantees.

The result was a judicial reformation of American life and an established expectation that federal judges, the Supreme Court in particular, would continue to take a leading role in the nation's effort to realize the ideals set forth at its founding.

Not everyone found this a congenial vision. Among the most important critics of this active use of judicial power were Richard Nixon, elected president in 1968, and Burger, whom Nixon selected as Warren's successor the following year. However, no Warren Court landmark toppled during the first decade of Burger's tenure. The Court refused to enlarge upon such landmarks and, in some cases, began to undermine them, but none were actually dismantled.

Nixon had named three more justices to the Court by December 1971. After two unsuccessful efforts, Nixon nominated a modest, able and hardworking appeals court judge named Harry A. Blackmun to succeed the brilliant and ill-fated Abe Fortas, who had resigned from the Court under a cloud in May 1969.

To replace the feisty veteran Hugo L. Black, Nixon chose Powell, a courtly and highly respected Virginia lawyer. At the same time he picked Rehnquist, a young assistant attorney general from the Justice Department, to succeed the gentle and dignified John Marshall Harlan.

Although Nixon made a point of selecting "strict constructionists," the Court through the 1970s did not wander far from the path set out by the Warren Court. Russell W. Galloway Jr., law professor at the University of Santa Clara, outlined in his 1982 book, *The Rich and The Poor in Supreme Court History,* a useful framework within which to place the work of the contemporary Court. Galloway divided the

Court's history into two major liberal and two major conservative periods, each alternating with the other.

He dated the first conservative period from the Court's establishment in 1790 to the end of the tenure of Chief Justice John Marshall in 1835. The first liberal era began with the accession of Chief Justice Roger B. Taney, Andrew Jackson's choice, and extended until 1890.

The second conservative era — during which the Court, for example, held an income tax unconstitutional — began in 1890 and lasted until the New Deal turnaround in 1937. The second liberal era began in 1937 when Franklin D. Roosevelt made the first of his nine appointments to the Court and extended through Warren's tenure.

Galloway views 1969 as a transition year and 1970 as the beginning of the third conservative era. He points to the Burger Court's rulings making it more difficult for plaintiffs to bring their complaints into federal courts, requiring federal judges to refrain from intervening in matters before state courts and narrowing the reach of landmark decisions in criminal procedure and civil rights.

But in 1976, after President Gerald R. Ford replaced liberal maverick William O. Douglas with John Paul Stevens, a judge of equally independent intellect and character, the Court adopted a more moderate stance on many issues.

No Counterrevolution

By 1976 only four of the sitting justices had been members of the Warren Court and two of them, Byron R. White and Potter Stewart, had disagreed with many of its major decisions. And yet, while the Court adopted a narrow view of many of the Warren Court's most significant rulings, it had not overturned any of its landmarks.

Conservative and Liberal

In this book, the description "conservative" is used to describe a person, vote or opinion that generally supports government authority rather than an individual's claim.

As might be expected, the description "liberal" is used to describe a person, vote or opinion that generally backs an individual's claim of a right or freedom, rather than the government's argument in opposition to that claim.

Indeed, it erected quite a few of its own, some in response to extraordinary claims from the executive branch — as in the Pentagon Papers and Watergate tapes cases — and some in response to social changes, particularly in the area of women's rights, where the Warren Court had a scanty and conventional record.

In 1983 Yale University Press published a collection of essays entitled *The Burger Court: The Counter-Revolution that Wasn't.* In the foreword, *New York Times* columnist Anthony Lewis, a former Supreme Court reporter, wrote that "there has been nothing like a counterrevolution" during the 1970s at the Court.

"It is fair to say, in fact, that the reach of earlier decisions on racial equality and the First Amendment has been enlarged. Even the most hotly debated criminal law decision, *Miranda,* stands essentially unmodified," Lewis observed.

But while Lewis was making this statement, change was under way. Bruce Fein, a close observer of the Court from both inside and outside the federal government, attributed the onset of the long-awaited change at the Court to a single person: Sandra Day O'Connor.

A Surprising Retirement

O'Connor's impact on the Court stems in part from the character and philosophy of Potter Stewart, whom she replaced. From December 1975, when Stevens took his seat, until July 1981, there had been no change in the Court's membership. President Jimmy Carter had left office in January 1981 the only full-term president with no opportunity to select a member of the Supreme Court.

The Court in 1981 consisted of men selected by five presidents, going back to Dwight Eisenhower. His nominees were Stewart, born 1915, and William J. Brennan Jr., born 1906. President John F. Kennedy selected White, who was born in 1917. President Lyndon Johnson named Thurgood Marshall, born 1908. The Nixon nominees were Burger, born 1907; Blackmun, born 1908; Powell, born 1907; and Rehnquist, born 1924. President Ford chose Stevens, born 1920.

To the surprise of those expecting one of the older justices to retire, the relatively youthful Stewart announced he would leave the Court after 23 years. He died Dec. 7, 1985.

A Voice of Moderation

Stewart was known as a "swing vote" because he voted sometimes on the liberal side of an issue and sometimes on the conservative side. This was a pragmatic position, particularly at the time of his arrival at the Court in 1958. The Court tended to divide, on a wide variety of issues, into a liberal bloc of four justices led by Warren and a conservative bloc of four led by Justice Felix Frankfurter.

Stewart approached each case and each issue as unique, without preconception as to the desired result. One of his former clerks, Terrance Sandalow, dean of the University of Michigan Law School, wrote in 1981, "Shades of gray may not be per-

The members of the U.S. Supreme Court: seated, from left to right, Thurgood Marshall, William J. Brennan Jr., Chief Justice Warren E. Burger, Byron R. White and Harry A. Blackmun. Standing, from left to right, John Paul Stevens, Lewis F. Powell, William H. Rehnquist and Sandra Day O'Connor.

ceptible to everyone, but ... Justice Stewart inhabits a world in which moral and political choices, and therefore legal decisions, are made in gray areas. Both emotionally and intellectually, he appreciates that cases that reach the Supreme Court rarely present a simple contest between the forces of light and the forces of darkness."

Justice Powell described Stewart's role as "a voice of moderation ... both during the expansive years of the Warren Court and the more traditional years of the Burger Court."

Reagan's New Justice

The October 1980 term ended July 3, 1981. Four days later, Reagan introduced Sandra Day O'Connor, 51, as his choice to succeed Stewart. Confirmed with ease, O'Connor took her seat Sept. 25, 1981.

O'Connor quickly became a fully participating member of the Court, providing a consistent vote and an articulate voice for the Court's conservative wing. It was clear she was not a swing vote. With notable steadiness during her first three terms, she voted with Burger, Powell and Rehnquist, her former law school classmate. She also provided a persuasive voice for the conservatives' views — both in public and in conference. As a result, the conservatives were increasingly successful, winning the support of the two remaining swing votes — White and Blackmun.

Only seven years earlier O'Connor had been majority leader of the Arizona State Senate. The skills of persuasion and articulate expression honed in that chamber stood her in good stead in the conference room at the Court.

Despite their long period of shared

service, the justices in the late 1970s seemed to be in chronic and worsening disagreement on a number of important issues. Even when they concurred on *what* to do in a particular case, they frequently disagreed on *why* they were doing it.

In 1981 the *Harvard Law Review* pointed out that since Burger became chief justice in 1969, there had been more plurality decisions — those in which fewer than five justices agreed on the reasons for the Court's decision — than there had been in the entire previous history of the Court. O'Connor's arrival seemed to provide the Court with some sort of philosophical glue to mend this splintering bench.

O'Connor is an effective conservative advocate. Her majority opinions are cogent, well reasoned and effective. Since her arrival on the Court, the conservative wing has been able to attract the critical fifth vote with notable regularity. But it is in dissent that O'Connor expresses herself most forcefully. Because it is possible that O'Connor will be joined on the Court by other Reagan appointees, creating a solid conservative majority, her dissenting opinions may provide a road map to the future.

One of the best examples of O'Connor's strength is her incisive dissenting opinion written in 1983 when the Court reaffirmed *Roe v. Wade,* its 1973 decision legalizing abortion. With unwavering logic, O'Connor pointed out a potentially fatal flaw in the logical structure of *Roe v. Wade.* She put the *Roe* majority on notice: if they wished to preserve *Roe* as a viable constitutional landmark, they had best begin building it a new foundation. *(Details, Chapter 4)*

Reagan's New Advocate

By naming O'Connor to replace Stewart, Reagan set the stage for change, but he did not stop there. Through his first solicitor general Reagan also presented the Court a

script that encouraged the justices to disavow any active role in certain areas of life and to leave decisions about matters such as abortion, civil rights and criminal law to legislators and prosecutors.

"There is no question," said an attorney able to observe closely both the workings of the Court and the administration, "that the Reagan administration is more willing than some to use litigation as an instrument of policy."

To make full use of that instrument before the Supreme Court, Reagan chose as his solicitor general — the government's voice before the Court — Rex E. Lee, dean of Brigham Young University Law School. Lee, like Reagan, believed firmly in judicial restraint. The modern Supreme Court, he thought, had overstepped its proper role in the system and intruded into the territory of the legislature, particularly with its rulings on school prayer and abortion.

These rulings "vest in the judiciary the license to roam at will through the territory of legislative policymaking," Lee warned. He urged that judges adopt an attitude of restraint, "upsetting the legislative judgment only in those instances where the error is quite clear and where the balance scales quite clearly disfavor the policymakers' judgment."

The Solicitor General's Office

The office of the solicitor general, which is part of the Department of Justice, screens and coordinates the government's appeals of adverse lower court rulings to the Supreme Court. Its highly professional staff of some two dozen attorneys argues the government's cases before the Court.

The solitictor general's office includes some of the most experienced and ablest Supreme Court advocates in the country. These attorneys have ample opportunity to practice because the government participates in almost half of the cases argued, either as a party or as friend of the court, *amicus curiae.*

There were, until the Reagan administration created a new post, four deputy solicitors general, each of whom — in addition to handling cases — supervises briefs and arguments by staff attorneys in certain areas of the law.

To ensure that its political philosophy was effectively communicated to the ranks of civil service personnel who *are* the federal government, the Reagan White House made a concerted effort to have politically appointed people placed in key second-level slots in government departments and agencies. This move was regarded with some concern by the career staff of the solicitor general's office, who pride themselves on their professionalism and their non-political character. They view their task as representing the institutional interests of the executive branch, not the policy preferences of a president.

A compromise was worked out by creating a new position for a fifth deputy attorney general, which carried the additional title of counselor to the solicitor general. Paul Bator of Harvard Law School was the first occupant of this office. Unlike the other deputies, Bator was considered part of the policy structure. Having won the political approval of the White House, he was viewed as an emissary of the administration's beliefs in a way that the other deputies were not — and felt that they should not be.

Bator, who served from December 1982 through December 1984, when he returned to Harvard, displayed notable skill in arguing the administration's case before the Court.

When Bator left, Charles Fried, another Harvard Law faculty member, took his place. Fried, a member of Reagan's task force on regulatory reform, had served as an adviser to the Reagan administration, both

in the White House office of policy development, the Department of Transportation and the Department of Justice. Fried eventually replaced Lee as solicititor general.

Presenting Reagan's Views

With firm backing from the White House, Lee took advantage of almost every opportunity to present the Reagan administration's views to the Supreme Court. In addition to the cases in which the government was a party, Lee chose to file amicus curiae briefs in a number of others.

Among them was a case from Minnesota in which the state defended as constitutional its state income tax deduction for tuition, textbook and transportation expenses for elementary and secondary school students. Others included a case from Akron, Ohio, in which key provisions of a model anti-abortion ordinance had been held unconstitutional; a case from Pawtucket, R.I., where city officials had been judicially rebuked for including a crèche in part of the city's holiday display; and a case from Alabama where a federal court had held unconstitutional the state law permitting a daily moment of silence for voluntary prayer or meditation in each public school classroom.

In almost every case, the administration's argument was a variation on the theme of judicial restraint. Without directly challenging the landmarks already established in each area — the original school prayer decision, for example — the brief filed by the solicitor general's office characterized the lower court ruling of which it complained as judicial excess, as activism, as intrusion into areas better left to the discretion of the political branches.

Early Efforts. For the first two years of the Reagan presidency, the Court rebuffed most of the administration's arguments for change, although usually ruling in the government's favor when the solicitor general defended the status quo. In October 1981, only weeks after O'Connor had begun her first term, the justices stepped into the long-simmering dispute between private schools that discriminated against black students and the Internal Revenue Service, which denied such schools tax-exempt status. The justices granted review of two cases, *Bob Jones University v. United States* and *Goldsboro Christian Schools v. United States*.

In both cases, the solicitor general's office had urged the Court to uphold the IRS policy, which had been in effect for more than a decade. Early in 1982 the administration reversed course, telling the justices that the IRS would no longer follow this challenged policy and suggesting that the Court dismiss these cases.

This announcement touched off a storm of criticism. Recognizing the massive political damage it had inflicted on itself with this move, the administration later reversed itself to the extent of eventually telling the justices that they should resolve the pending cases. However, the administration persisted in its refusal to defend the challenged IRS policy before the Court.

All the twists and turns in this case delayed its argument until October 1982. In the meantime, perhaps because of its preoccupation with the *Bob Jones* case and perhaps because it was Lee's first term as solicitor general, the administration's push for Supreme Court approval of policy change was slow in getting under way.

Lee argued four cases before the Court in the October 1981 term; he won three of them. In two of the three, his position was an institutional one, not a policy one. He was fulfilling the traditional role of the solicitor general, defending the institutional prerogatives of the executive branch and of Congress.

In the first case, Lee persuaded the Court that the organization Americans United for Separation of Church and State did not have standing to come into federal court to challenge the government's practice of transferring surplus government property to schools, including church-related schools.

In the second case, the Court agreed that the federal law barring sex discrimination by federally aided schools and colleges reached not only discrimination among students but that among employees as well.

Lee lost his third case, defending the new system of bankruptcy judges set up by Congress in 1978. The Court held the system unconstitutional, setting off a three-year effort on the part of Congress to revise it.

In the fourth case Lee argued for the administration, he urged the Court to uphold anti-busing initiatives approved by California and Washington State voters. The Court upheld California's initiative, finding that it did no more than tell state courts they could not go beyond the actions of federal courts in desegregating schools, leaving school boards free to do as they wished. But the Court struck down Washington's initiative as infringing too far on individual rights and the authority of the local school board.

Resistance. In the October 1982 term the administration's push for change at the Court moved into high gear but got nowhere. In half a dozen cases the Reagan administration urged the justices to sanction dramatic changes in national policy. In all but one, the Court rejected or sidestepped such requests.

The Court seemed to be giving new meaning to a statement Justice Robert Jackson made the year before his appointment, that the Supreme Court "is ... the check of a preceding generation on the present one." The solicitor general's office won its usual quota of victories at the Court, but those came primarily on cases involving institutional issues — like the legislative veto — not policy questions. Despite the Reagan administration's call for change, the Court upheld the policies of earlier administrations and laws passed by previous Congresses.

In May 1983 the Court dealt the administration a resounding defeat in *Bob Jones,* reaffirming, 8-1, the nation's commitment to ending racial discrimination in education — and upholding the IRS policy of denying tax favors to discriminatory schools. Only Justice Rehnquist dissented, agreeing with the administration position that Congress must by law authorize the IRS to adopt such a policy.

The administration, in the Akron abortion case, had urged the Court to bow out of that controversy, leaving the issue to elected officials. To the contrary, the Court, 6-3, reaffirmed a woman's right to an abortion free of state and local interference until late in pregnancy.

The Court struck down as arbitrary and capricious the administration's effort to rescind a requirement that all automobiles have passive restraints — air bags or automatic seat belts. The Court told the administration that, to rescind a regulation, it must have reasons that were just as good as the reasons for adopting it in the first place.

The Court sidestepped two cases, at least until the next term. In one the administration sought a major exception to the "exclusionary rule," which denies prosecutors the use of evidence that police have obtained by improper methods. In the other, the administration asked the Court to limit the use of affirmative action.

The Court accepted one of the administration's arguments in support of a state tuition tax deduction benefiting patrons of parochial schools. But the Court did so in a way that imposed large practical obstacles to the enactment of such a federal policy.

A Change in the Wind? Then came the 1983-84 term. In the months between October 1983 and July 1984, the administration convinced the Court to shift its position on a number of key issues. By early 1985 it seemed clear that the Court had indeed changed course, turning firmly away from the judicial activism committed to enlarging individual rights to a new position of conservative restraint.

The Reagan administration, far more solicitous than its predecessors of the concerns of American business, won Court approval for its relaxed enforcement of federal antitrust laws — and its redefinition of key terms in federal environmental laws. Redefining terms would have the effect of lightening the burden of regulation.

A majority of the justices seemed to discard the view that the First Amendment mandates a strict separation of church and state and to espouse the view that history dictates a policy of accommodation between religion and government.

On individual rights issues, the Court agreed with the administration's narrow view of the reach of the federal ban on sex discrimination in federally aided schools and colleges. The Court also voted to limit the reach of affirmative action to preserve the jobs of recently hired minorities.

In the area of criminal law, the Court for the first time in almost two decades, carved out major exceptions to the exclusionary rule and to the *Miranda* rule barring use of any statements made by suspects not formally warned of their constitutional rights.

A Judicial Pause. The following term was a disappointing sequel for the Reagan administration. Particularly in the area of church-state matters, the administration was firmly rebuffed as the Court struck down Alabama's moment-of-silence law permitting voluntary silent prayer in the classroom. The Court also struck down New York City and Grand Rapids, Mich., programs of state aid to students attending parochial schools and Connecticut's Sabbath-off law, which had required employers to permit devout employees to take their Sabbath day off.

Attorney General Edwin Meese criticized these rulings as "bizarre" and far from the original intent of the First Amendment clause barring establishment of religion.

However, the administration won a notable share of victories in the criminal law area. And administration officials must have found pleasing the Court's renewed emphasis on deference to the decisions of the more political branches of the government, a deference particularly in evidence on questions of environmental regulation, labor law, and military or national security.

A Different Justice

Earl Warren left the Court in 1969, but for the next dozen years he continued to be its dominant presence. By 1976 Black, Harlan and Douglas also were gone, but it took five more years and the departure of one more veteran — Potter Stewart — before the Warren Court era came to an end.

O'Connor's appointment marked the end of that era and the beginning of another. Yet, four years after her arrival, the precedents set by the Warren Court were still the law of the land. The Supreme Court of 1985 was disinclined to tear down these major landmarks in American law, although it might approve exceptions and modifications, even occasional renovations.

Today's Court sees itself as very different from the Warren Court. Its landmarks will reflect that self-image and stand in sharp contrast against the landscape shaped by *Brown v. Board of Education,* decreeing

an end to state-imposed racial segregation in public schools; *Miranda v. Arizona,* setting out rules for police to follow in dealing with an arrested suspect; *Baker v. Carr,* permitting federal judges to enter the political thicket of legislative reapportionment; and *Engel v. Vitale,* denying state officials the power to prescribe prayer for public schools.

In those rulings, the Warren Court assumed for itself and for federal judges across the country a role in reshaping American social and political life unlike that claimed by the judiciary since the days of John Marshall and the initial shaping of the nation's government. Today's justices by and large find such a role inappropriate and uncomfortable. They are willing to foster and encourage change, but they prefer to do so by deferring to the initiative of the political branches of government, by accepting the solicitor general's arguments, by clearing the way for Congress to act, by upholding executive decisions and legislative enactments.

They see themselves as proscriptive, warning Congress and the president when constitutional bounds are overstepped. It is not the Court's task, its more conservative members say, to tell the other branches what to do once they step back inside constitutional bounds.

The Reagan administration continues to press its campaign for a different justice — for a more traditional role for federal courts in general and the Supreme Court in particular. The administration responded to the disappointments of the 1984-85 term with a quick succession of aggressive moves. In a speech to the American Bar Association July 9, 1985, just a week after the end of the Court term, Attorney General Meese criticized what he called the Court's "jurisprudence of idiosyncracy."

The Court's work, Meese said, reflected "a greater allegiance to what the

Court thinks constitutes sound public policy than a deference to what the Constitution — its text and intention — may demand." This was a mistaken allegiance, Meese emphasized, and one the Reagan administration was committed to change.

The Court should adopt a "jurisprudence of original intention," he contended. The justices should "resurrect the original meaning of constitutional provisions and statutes as the only reliable guide for judgment." *(Text, p. 171)*

The implications of Meese's speech are clear if one looks at the government's arguments to the Court in the summer of 1985 on two controversial issues — abortion and affirmative action. In one, the government urged the Court to overturn a landmark, the 1973 decision forbidding states to ban abortion. In the other, the government argued that the Court should return to the original meaning of another major judicial milepost — the 1954 school desegregation ruling — and declare highly suspect all affirmative actions plans favoring minorities at the expense of the majority. Both sets of arguments were volunteered to the Court in friend of the court briefs filed by Charles Fried, who was the acting solicitor general.

Not since Roosevelt in 1937 threatened to pack the Court with new justices, had a president mounted such a full-scale campaign to change the Court's mind on a variety of issues. Modern presidents, from Truman to Nixon, felt the sting of loss at the hands of the Court, but they did not respond with an assault on the Court itself. And Roosevelt's attack was in response to decisions striking down the economic recovery program he had proposed and Congress approved.

The Reagan campaign is different. Many of the positions the administration wants the Court to adopt have been rejected by Congress. Perhaps it will be easier to convince nine justices than the necessary majority of a 535-member Congress. Perhaps not.

Both the power to appoint and the power to argue have limits. Use of the one can enhance or diminish the effectiveness of the other. The administration's new initiatives in the summer of 1985 may reflect frustration that President Reagan has had only one chance to appoint a member of the Court, despite continuing predictions of impending retirements of some of the aging justices.

The Court in September denied Fried the opportunity to participate in the oral arguments on abortion or affirmative action. At least one close observer read that denial as a signal to the administration that it was pushing too hard for change in these areas. In October two justices, Brennan and Stevens, spoke out to take issue with Meese's call for a return to the literal view of the Constitution. *(Brennan speech, p. 183)*

Their remarks served as a reminder that the balance of power between the Supreme Court and the sitting president is a fragile one. The president can appoint and he can argue, but the Court alone decides.

At the end of the 1984-85 term some Court-watchers speculated that its surprisingly moderate tone was the justices' demonstration of independence from the label of the "Reagan Court." Whether that was the case we are unlikely ever to know, but it is clear that the relationship of president and Court is one that should not — for the good of both — be subjected to continuous strain.

A decade ago Justice Powell delivered such a warning: "Repeated and essentially head-on confrontations between the life-tenured branch and the representative branches of the government will not, in the long run, be beneficial to either."

2

Presidents and the Court

"One of the many marks of genius which our Constitution bears is the fine balance struck in the establishment of the Judicial Branch, avoiding both subservience to the supposedly more vigorous Legislative and Executive Branches, on the one hand, and to total institutional isolation from public opinion, on the other," Justice William H. Rehnquist said in October 1984.

"The performance of the Judicial Branch . . . for . . . nearly two hundred years has shown it to be remarkably independent of the other coordinate branches," Rehnquist continued.

"Yet the institution has been constructed in such a way that the public will, in the person of the President of the United States . . . have something to say about the membership of the Court, and thereby indirectly about its. decisions," the justice added.

Appointing Justices

There are no constitutional qualifications for Supreme Court justices, except that they be nominated by the president and confirmed by the Senate. They need not be native-born; they need not be attorneys; they need only be approved by the person who sits in the Oval Office and a majority of the members of the Senate.

The absence of rules governing the selection of justices gives presidents free rein in choosing whomever they wish. Politics invariably plays a major role in such decisions.

There is nothing wrong with a president trying to "pack" the Court, when vacancies occur, by appointing people who are sympathetic to his political or philosophical principles, Rehnquist said. Virtually every president has recognized this opportunity to influence the Court as one aspect of his broad power.

A president serves a limited term of four or eight years; the man or woman he chooses as a Supreme Court justice may serve for a lifetime. John Adams was president for four years. The man he appointed chief justice, John Marshall, served for 34 years, from 1801 until 1835. Andrew Jackson served eight years as president; Roger B. Taney, whom he selected as chief justice, served nearly three decades.

Supreme Court justices are long-lived. Amid all the talk about the age of the current members of the Supreme Court, five of whom are over 75 in 1985, it is worth noting that both Marshall and Taney served until their death. Marshall was within three months of his 80th birthday when he died in 1835; Taney died at 87. In this century, Justice Oliver Wendell Holmes Jr. served on the Court until the age of 90 and lived to be 94.

General Success

Every president has his own ideas about how the government should operate. Appointing Supreme Court justices who agree with his views on this basic issue is one way he can try to ensure that his values play a part in government decisions for as long as possible.

Most of the time presidents succeed in this effort. President Adams' nomination of Secretary of State Marshall as chief justice in 1801, barely two months before Adams left the White House, had more impact on the course of the nation's history than any other single action of Adams' four years in the White House.

Marshall was the nation's chief justice for 34 years, exerting federalist influence on the shape of the new nation long after the Federalists passed from power as a political force. One of the most able and forceful men ever to head the Court, Marshall was its dominant figure throughout his tenure, establishing firmly in American law both the Court's power and the broad power of the national government.

In similar fashion, Jackson's selection of Secretary of the Treasury Taney as Marshall's successor extended Jackson's own strong democratic and states' rights views far beyond his tenure in the White House. Taney, who took his seat in 1836, served until 1864 — 28 years. Jackson's influence on the Court was reinforced by the five other justices he selected, of whom three, in addition to Taney, served well into the Civil War era.

In the 20th century, President Franklin D. Roosevelt had notable success with his nine appointments in turning the Court in a new liberal direction, permissive of federal regulation of economic life and critical of government's treatment of the individual. Roosevelt's most far-reaching judicial appointments were his first, Justice Hugo L. Black, who served from 1937 until 1971, and his third, Justice William O. Douglas, who served longer than any justice to date, from 1939 until 1975.

Earlier in the century, and generally less noticed, President Warren G. Harding shaped the Court firmly into a conservative institution by his selection of four men, including three rock-ribbed conservatives — former president William Howard Taft, George Sutherland and Pierce Butler. When Taft came to the Court in 1921, he joined two of his own appointees there — Willis Van Devanter and Mahlon Pitney.

Occasional Failure

Occasionally, however, even the most carefully chosen justice proves a disappointment to the president who selected him. This was the case with President Abraham Lincoln and his chief justice, Salmon P. Chase.

Lincoln, who served only a single term before his assassination in 1864, appointed five men to the Supreme Court. The first three, Noah Swayne of Ohio, David Davis of Illinois and Samuel F. Miller of Iowa, all men instrumental in Lincoln's election, were appointed early in his term.

Blockade Vote. For a short time, which was a particularly critical period for Lincoln and a nation at war, Lincoln's justices voted the way he had hoped. The votes of Swayne, Davis and Miller in favor of Lincoln's position were crucial in 1863 when the Court, 5-4, upheld the president's power to institute a blockade of Southern ports even before Congress authorized such an act of war.

The legality of the blockade was the major war issue resolved by the Court dur-

John Marshall

Roger B. Taney

ing the war years. Had the Court voted against Lincoln in these *Prize Cases,* all of his wartime actions would have been called into question, seriously undermining his ability to lead the nation in the conflict.

The long-term effect of Lincoln's appointments, however, was not as he had hoped. In 1863 Congress expanded the size of the Court to 10 justices, and Lincoln named his fourth justice, Stephen J. Field of California, one of the most colorful men ever to serve on the Court.

Legal Tender Acts. The next year, after Taney died, Lincoln chose Chase, who had just resigned the post of secretary of the Treasury, to be the nation's chief justice. Chase was chosen in part because Lincoln felt certain that he would vote to uphold the constitutionality of the Legal Tender Acts, which had been passed to finance the war by permitting the use of paper money as legal tender. These laws were being challenged as unconstitutional by banks, creditors and others who wished to take payment only in gold.

Although Chase was a member of his Cabinet, Lincoln was aware that it would be inappropriate to ask him directly how he would vote on this or any other issue. Lincoln confided in a friend that "we wish for a chief justice who will sustain what has been done in regard to emancipation and the legal tenders. We cannot ask a man what he will do, and if we should, and he should answer us, we should despise him for it. Therefore, we must take a man whose opinions are known."

Lincoln had good reason to anticipate that Chase would vote to uphold these laws as constitutional. As secretary of the Treasury, Chase had been one of the architects of the legislation.

The first legal tender case, *Hepburn v. Griswold,* took a long time to resolve. It was placed on the docket in 1865, was argued in 1867 and again in 1868. Finally, in 1870, five years after Lincoln's death, the Court ruled.

By a 4-3 vote the Court held the Legal Tender Acts unconstitutional. Chief Justice Chase wrote the Court's opinion, holding invalid the law he had helped to draft. Justice Field agreed with Chase; the other three Lincoln nominees dissented. It was only the third time that the Supreme Court had held a major act of Congress unconstitutional.

Chase explained that the Court viewed the acts as an inappropriate exercise of congressional power in light of the "losses of property, the derangement of business, the fluctuations of currency and values, and the increase of prices ... and the long train of evils which flow from the use of irredeemable paper money."

"Chief Justice Chase's vote in the legal tender cases," Justice Rehnquist has observed, "is a textbook example of the proposition that one may look at a legal question differently as judge than one did as a member of the Executive Branch.

"There is no reason to believe that Chase thought he was acting unconstitutionally when he helped draft and shepherd through Congress the greenback legislation, and it may well be that if Lincoln had actually posed the question to him before nominating him as Chief Justice, he would have agreed that the measures were constitutional.

"But administrators in charge of a program, even if they are lawyers, simply do not ponder these questions in the depth that judges do, and Chase's vote in the legal tender cases is proof of this fact," Rehnquist concluded.

Grant: A Quick Reversal

Ironically, Lincoln's failure on the legal tender issue led directly to one of the most successful "Court-packing" efforts in history. Two new justices were sworn in just a few months after the decision that greenbacks were not legal tender, and a year later the Court reversed itself to uphold the use of paper money.

Even as Chase was reading his opinion striking down the legal tender acts, President Ulysses S. Grant was sending the Senate his nominations of two new justices — Joseph P. Bradley and William Strong. In their legal practice both Strong and Bradley had represented railroads, which were among the strongest advocates of the use of paper money, along with borrowers of all varieties who were hoping to repay their debts with greenbacks, rather than gold.

Strong and Bradley were quickly confirmed. Less than two weeks later, the Court announced that it would hear two more legal tender cases and would review its decision striking down the laws. On May 1, 1871 — 15 months after holding the Legal Tender Acts unconstitutional — the Court resurrected those laws, ruling 5-4 that they were proper. Strong wrote the Court's opinion in this second legal tender case, *Knox v. Lee*. Joining him were Bradley and the three dissenters from *Hepburn v. Griswold*.

Strong emphasized the deference which the Court should display in reviewing acts of Congress, asking rhetorically: "Is it our province to decide that the means selected were beyond the constitutional power of Congress, because we may think other means to the same ends would have been more appropriate and equally efficient? ... The degree of the necessity for any congressional enactment, or the relative degree of its appropriateness ... is for consideration in Congress, not here."

Scholars still debate whether Grant intended by his appointments to bring about such a quick reversal on this particular issue. But intentional or not, it worked.

Roosevelt: Old Court, New Deal

"The Court is almost never a really contemporary institution," wrote Robert H. Jackson in 1941, the year he moved from a seat in Franklin Roosevelt's Cabinet to the Supreme Court. "The operation of life tenure in the judicial department, as against elections at short intervals of the Congress,

Abraham Lincoln

Salmon P. Chase

usually keeps the average viewpoint of the two institutions a generation apart," Jackson continued.

"The judiciary is thus the check of a preceding generation on the present one; a check of conservative legal philosophy upon a dynamic people, and nearly always the check of a rejected regime upon the one in being."

Never was that point more forcefully illustrated than by the Court's concerted efforts in 1935 and 1936 to smash into constitutional smithereens key elements of Roosevelt's New Deal program for economic recovery. That effort brought about the textbook example of a president's attempt to pack the Court — one that fell flat in the short term and succeeded beyond all hopes over the long term.

The New Deal. Roosevelt took office in March 1933 amid the greatest economic crisis the United States had ever known. Unemployment had reached 12 million, pro-

duction had fallen to half of its 1929 level, and the entire banking network was on the verge of collapse. The concomitant social crisis brought about a major political upheaval as well as Roosevelt's election by an impressive margin.

Within the now-legendary first Hundred Days of his term in office, Roosevelt pushed through Congress a dozen major new laws, through which federal power was exerted to restructure and resuscitate the nation's ailing economy.

Central to Roosevelt's plan were the Agricultural Adjustment Act (AAA) and the National Industrial Recovery Act (NIRA). The AAA was designed to raise agricultural prices by retiring farm acreage from production and subsidizing the price of the commodities grown on the remaining acreage. The NIRA was intended to restore industrial production and reduce unemployment by encouraging cooperation between manufacturers and their employees. It provided for the establishment of "codes of fair competition" to govern wages, prices and trade practices in different industries. If industry representatives agreed on these codes and the president approved them, they had the force of law.

Both these laws and many of the other New Deal measures reflected a revolutionary idea of federal power to regulate economic matters that had been left largely to state and local authority since the nation's founding.

The Old Court. As constitutional challenges to these new laws reached the Supreme Court, that body proved to be unreceptive to revolution. Four of the sitting justices were staunch conservatives: Van Devanter, named by Taft; James C. McReynolds, nominated by President Woodrow Wilson; and Sutherland and Butler, both named to the Court by Harding.

Two — Louis D. Brandeis, a Wilson selection, and Harlan Fiske Stone, the nominee of President Calvin Coolidge — tended to take a more liberal view on questions of federal power.

The three most junior justices had been chosen by Roosevelt's predecessor, Herbert Hoover: Chief Justice Charles Evans Hughes, a former associate justice considered liberal in his earlier time on the Court who became progressively more conservative; Owen Roberts, a conservative attorney from Pennsylvania; and Benjamin Cardozo, a liberal and well-respected legal scholar and judge.

By 1935, five of the justices — Hughes, Van Devanter, McReynolds, Brandeis, Sutherland — were over 70 years of age, and the remaining four were 60 or older. President Roosevelt was 53.

Cases challenging the constitutionality of the New Deal's legislative underpinnings began to appear at the Court in late 1934. Between January 1935 and June 1936, the Supreme Court ruled against the New Deal in seven out of nine major cases. Only

emergency monetary legislation and the measure creating the Tennessee Valley Authority were upheld.

—On Jan. 7, 1935, the Court struck down a key provision of the NIRA providing for a "code of fair competition" to govern the production of oil and petroleum products. By a vote of 8-1, the Court held that this gave the president too much "legislative" power (*Panama Refining Co. v. Ryan,* the "Hot Oil" case).

—On May 6, 1935, the Court struck down the Railroad Retirement Act, which created an industry-wide pension system. The Court divided 5-4 to find this matter outside the power of Congress to regulate interstate commerce (*Railroad Retirement Board v. Alton Railway Co.*).

—On "Black Monday," May 27, 1935, the Court unanimously struck down another key portion of the NIRA, expanding its ruling in the Hot Oil case to hold that Congress was delegating too much legislative authority to the president when it authorized the development of these "codes of fair competition" and provided that the president's approval would give the codes the force of law (*Schechter Poultry Corp. v. United States*).

—The same day the unanimous Court struck down, as unfair to creditors, the Federal Farm Bankruptcy Act, another measure enacted during the Hundred Days (*Louisville Joint Stock Land Bank v. Radford*).

—On Jan. 6, 1936, the Court, 6-3, struck down the AAA as an unconstitutional intrusion of federal authority into agriculture, an area traditionally left to state regulation (*United States v. Butler*).

—On May 18, 1936, the Court held, 6-3, the Bituminous Coal Conservation Act, the New Deal measure to control and regulate coal production, unconstitutional as an invasion of state's rights (*Carter v. Carter Coal Co.*).

The Politics of Picking a Justice

Presidents almost always choose Supreme Court justices from their own political party. In part this tradition dates from the early days of the nation when the Court sometimes became an open political battlefield as competing political parties sought to impose their ideology on the government of the new nation.

The practice of looking to one's own party for Court nominees also reflects simple recognition of the correlation between political party membership and beliefs about the proper way the government should operate.

Political affinities are still an important consideration in a president's choice of a new justice, but the political element has become less openly partisan as the Court has become an equal and independent branch of the federal system.

Republicans have been more likely than Democrats to deviate from strict party loyalty in selecting Court nominees. Republican presidents, beginning with Lincoln, have selected nine Democrats, but Democratic presidents have named only three Republicans. Personal friendship often has played a role in "cross-over" selections.

Whig president John Tyler in 1845 was the first to choose a nominee from a different party, but that pioneer effort was born of desperation. Tyler sent six Court nominations to the Senate; only one, Samuel Nelson, was confirmed. Nelson, a well-respected New York judge, was a Democrat and Tyler's third nominee to fill a particular vacancy.

President Abraham Lincoln selected Democrat Stephen J. Field to fill a new 10th seat on the Court in 1863 — after Lincoln had placed three Republicans on the Court. Thirty years later President Benjamin Harrison nominated Democrat Howell E. Jackson, a friend from Harrison's days in the Senate.

All the other cross-over nominations have come in the 20th century. President William Howard Taft, a Republican and later himself chief justice, appointed six justices during his term in office — three Democrats and three Republicans. The three Democrats were Horace H. Lurton, a personal friend and former colleague on the federal appeals court; Edward D. White, a sitting associate justice whom Taft promoted to chief justice, and Joseph R. Lamar, a Georgia attorney and golf partner of Taft's.

Woodrow Wilson became the first Democratic president to select a Republican when he nominated Louis D. Brandeis in 1916. Republican president Warren G. Harding named Pierce Butler, a Democrat; Republican Herbert Hoover named Democrat Benjamin Cardozo.

During World War II, Democratic president Franklin Roosevelt promoted Associate Justice Harlan Fiske Stone, a Republican, to chief justice. Within that decade, President Harry S Truman chose Republican Harold H. Burton, a former Senate colleague, to fill another vacancy.

Republican presidents Dwight D. Eisenhower and Richard Nixon both placed Democrats on the Court — William J. Brennan Jr. in 1956 and Lewis F. Powell Jr. in 1971.

Judicial Selection: Politics Aside

Although political considerations often override all others when a president selects a nominee for the Supreme Court, other factors — experience, friendship, geography, religion and ideology — do come into play.

Almost all justices have had some prior record of public service. Some have held Cabinet positions or other executive appointments. Thurgood Marshall was the nation's solicitor general at the time of his nomination to the Court. William H. Rehnquist was an assistant attorney general, and Byron R. White, deputy attorney general.

Many justices have served as state or federal judges. William J. Brennan Jr. and Sandra Day O'Connor were state court judges; Warren E. Burger, Harry A. Blackmun and John Paul Stevens served as federal appeals court judges.

While judicial experience would seem to be the ideal background for a justice, many distinguished members, including eight chief justices, never had served as judges before coming to the Court. They include Chief Justice Earl Warren and Justices William O. Douglas, Abe Fortas, Lewis F. Powell Jr., White and Rehnquist.

Personal friendship was an important factor in several Supreme Court nominations earlier in the 20th century, but in recent times this factor seems irrelevant. President Lyndon B. Johnson prevailed on his friend Abe Fortas to accept a Supreme Court nomination, but the unfortunate end of Fortas' Court career may have caused later presidents to avoid nominating their friends.

Geography was a major consideration in selecting justices in the early part of the nation's history — primarily because each justice rode circuit, serving a particular area of the country. Justices have come from 31 states. New York has been home to the most, 15. For two extended periods, from 1806 until 1893, and from 1925 until 1971, there was a "New York" seat on the Court. There has not been a justice from New York since John Marshall Harlan retired in 1971.

Although geography is a minor consideration today, the Court continues to reflect demographic shifts. In 1985 the Court, so long dominated by justices from the East and South, consists primarily of Westerners and Midwesterners. Rehnquist and O'Connor are from Arizona, White from Colorado, Burger and Blackmun from Minnesota and Stevens from Illinois. Brennan is from New Jersey, Marshall is from Maryland and Powell from Virginia.

For most of the 20th century there has been a Catholic seat and a Jewish seat on the Court, a way of acknowledging the role of these influential religious minority groups in the life of the nation. Justice Brennan currently holds the Catholic seat, which has been occupied by a Catholic since 1894, except the period 1949-1956. There was a Jewish member of the Court from 1916, when Louis D. Brandeis was sworn in, until 1969 when Fortas resigned.

As religious and regional concerns fade, it seems likely — now that the Court has both a black justice and a female justice — that for the foreseeable future there will be some effort to assure that each of those groups is represented.

—A week later the Court, 5-4, held the Municipal Bankruptcy Act an unconstitutional invasion of state's rights (*Ashton v. Cameron County District*).

The Challenge. The standoff seemed complete. President Roosevelt did not mince words in describing the impact of the Court's rulings. "Is the United States going to decide . . . that their Federal Government shall in the future have no right under any implied or any Court-approved power to enter into a solution of a national economic problem, but that national economic problems must be decided only by the States?" he asked the country.

"We thought we were solving it, and now it has been thrown right straight in our faces. We have been relegated to the horse-and-buggy definition of interstate commerce."

In November 1936 Roosevelt was reelected by a landslide. Members of Congress began to propose that the Court's power to block legislation be curtailed either by limiting its jurisdiction or by requiring a two-thirds vote to declare an act of Congress unconstitutional. It was also proposed that the Constitution be amended to permit Congress to override a Court decision by a two-thirds vote of both houses, just as Congress can override a presidential veto.

But the power punch of the counterattack came from Roosevelt himself. On Feb. 5, 1937, he proposed to Congress that it approve a judicial reorganization. Roosevelt suggested increasing the number of seats on the Supreme Court by creating one new seat for each justice, who, upon reaching the age of 70, declined to retire.

By this point, six of the current justices were 70 or older. Had Congress approved Roosevelt's plan, he could have appointed six new justices and the Supreme Court would have found itself with 15 members.

On the matter of aging judges, Roosevelt was forthright: "The modern tasks of

Franklin D. Roosevelt

judges call for the use of full energies. Modern complexities call also for a constant infusion of new blood in the Courts. . . . A lowered mental or physical vigor leads men to avoid an examination of complicated and changed conditions. Little by little, new facts become blurred through old glasses fitted, as it were, for the needs of another generation; older men, assuming that the scene is the same as it was in the past, cease to explore or inquire into the present or the future."

Roosevelt's proposal was not well received by Congress or the country. Within a matter of weeks, it was clear, as one of his Cabinet members commented, that the president now had another "first-class fight" on his hands.

Roosevelt was not deterred. On March 9, 1937, he addressed the issue in a radio broadcast. The American form of government, he said, was like a "three-horse team provided by the Constitution to the American people so that their field might be plowed. The three horses are, of course, the three branches of government — the Congress, the Executive, and the Courts. Two of the horses are pulling in unison today; the third is not.

"The Court has been acting not as a judicial body, but as a policy-making body. When the Congress has sought to stabilize national agriculture, to improve the conditions of labor, to safeguard business against unfair competition, to protect our national resources . . . the Court has been assuming the power . . . to approve or disapprove the public policy written into these laws. . . .

"The Court . . . has improperly set itself up as a third House of the Congress — a super-legislature, as one of the Justices has called it — reading into the Constitution words and implications which are not there, and which were never intended to be there.

"We have, therefore, reached the point as a Nation where we must take action to save the Constitution from the Court and the Court from itself," Roosevelt continued. By adopting his plan, Congress could "save our national Constitution from hardening of the judicial arteries."

Acknowledging the criticism of his plan as one to "pack the Court," Roosevelt conceded that if Court-packing meant "that I would appoint . . . Justices . . . who understand . . . modern conditions — that I will appoint Justices who will not undertake to override the judgment of the Congress on legislative policy — that I will appoint Justices who will act as justices and not as legislators — if the appointment of such Justices can be called 'packing the Courts,' then I say that I and with me the vast majority of the American people favor doing just that thing — now."

The Rebuttal. Roosevelt was wrong. The public still regarded the Court as aloof

from politics, and Roosevelt's plan was seen as destroying the Court's independence and integrity. Public opinion opposed the plan. The Democrats in Congress were so badly divided that Republicans just stood aside and let them battle the matter out.

Chief Justice Hughes wrote a letter to the Senate opposing the proposal, emphasizing that the Court was fully able to keep up with its work, despite the age of its members. "An increase in the number of Justices . . . apart from any question of policy, which I do not discuss, would not promote the efficiency of the Court. . . . There would be more judges to hear, more judges to confer, more judges to discuss, more judges to be convinced and to decide. The present number of Justices is thought to be large enough so far as the prompt, adequate and efficient conduct of the work of the Court is concerned," he wrote.

Congress began formal consideration of Roosevelt's plan. But first, in a move that would prove crucial, it separated out and enacted a new Supreme Court Retirement Act providing that Supreme Court justices could retire and continue to receive full salary, just as other federal judges could already do. This measure became law in March, a month after the Court-packing bill had arrived on Capitol Hill.

Judicial Turnabout. Unknown to any but the justices themselves, however, a judicial about-face was under way even as the Senate Judiciary Committee turned to Roosevelt's proposal. The Court had already decided to abandon its conservative attempt to protect business from government regulation, state or federal. This change was signaled by a decision that was reached even before Roosevelt made his proposal.

On March 29, 1937, the Court ruled, 5-4, to uphold Washington State's minimum wage law. Implicit in *West Coast Hotel Co. v. Parrish* was the willingness of a majority of the justices to accept government author-

The Supreme Court in 1937. Seated, left to right, George Sutherland, James C. McReynolds, Chief Justice Charles E. Hughes, Louis D. Brandeis and Pierce Butler. Standing, left to right, Benjamin Cardozo, Harlan F. Stone, Owen J. Roberts and Hugo L. Black.

ity to act to protect the general welfare of society and to discard the Court's role as censor of economic legislation.

The same day, it unanimously upheld two New Deal statutes: a second farm bankruptcy act, virtually identical to the one struck down on Black Monday, and provisions of the Railway Labor Act encouraging collective bargaining. Two weeks later, on April 12, the Court voted, 5-4, to uphold the National Labor Relations Act, which guaranteed the right to organize for collective bargaining.

On May 18 the Senate Judiciary Committee recommended to the full Senate that it reject Roosevelt's proposal to enlarge the Court. Almost simultaneously, Justice Van Devanter, aged 78, informed Roosevelt that he would retire when the term ended. The new retirement plan was thought to have

facilitated Van Devanter's decision.

Less than a week later, the Court confirmed the completeness of its turnabout, upholding the unemployment compensation and old-age benefits programs of the Social Security Act.

A New Era. Roosevelt's Court-packing plan, already doomed, quickly shriveled and died in the Washington summer of 1937. At the same time, the way opened for Roosevelt to pack the Court through replacing retiring members.

With Van Devanter's retirement, Roosevelt finally had the chance to place a man of his own choice on the Supreme Court. Many had expected him to reward "Joe" Robinson, the Senate majority leader who had led the ill-fated fight for the Court-packing plan. But Robinson died of a heart attack July 14. Roosevelt selected Sen. Hugo Black of Alabama, a staunch supporter of New Deal legislation. Black, confirmed in August, served for 34 years, retiring a week before his death in September 1971.

Black's arrival at the Court in October 1937 marked the beginning of a new era. The Court, having resigned its role as arbiter of the wisdom of economic legislation, turned its attention to questions of individual rights and liberties. In so doing, it set off a social revolution that reshaped life in the United States just as dramatically as the New Deal reshaped economic reality.

During the next six years, Roosevelt named seven more justices and elevated an eighth — Harlan Fiske Stone — to chief justice. The men he placed on the Court were, with a few exceptions, young enough to be the sons of the men they succeeded. Black, for example, was 51 when he replaced the 78-year-old Van Devanter.

What Roosevelt had tried to do through legislation was eventually accomplished through the simple powerful passage of time. Late in 1937, Justice Sutherland, 75, retired and was succeeded by Solicitor General Stanley F. Reed, 54. In 1938, Justice Cardozo died and was replaced by Roosevelt's close friend and adviser, Felix Frankfurter, then a professor of law at Harvard. Reed served 19 years on the Court; Frankfurter, 23.

Brandeis retired at age 82 in 1939 and was succeeded by the 40-year-old chairman of the new Securities and Exchange Commission, William Douglas. Douglas would serve on the Court until 1975, the longest-serving justice in history.

Late in 1939 Justice Butler died at the age of 73. He was replaced by Attorney General Frank Murphy, 50, who served for a decade. With Murphy's arrival in January 1940, Roosevelt nominees made up a majority of the Court. Their numbers were further augmented by Roosevelt's nominations

of James F. Byrnes, Wiley B. Rutledge and Attorney General Robert Jackson in the early 1940s.

The Roosevelt Court, as it could well be called, then turned its attention away from economic matters to questions of individual rights and liberties, laying the groundwork for the Warren Court and its liberal reformation of American life.

Disappointing Justices

"Nothing is more striking in the history of the Court than the manner in which the hopes of those who expected a judge to follow the political views of the President appointing him are disappointed," wrote historian Charles Warren in 1922.

And indeed, despite their best efforts to name persons to the Court who share their views, presidents have at times been severely disappointed. Once on the Court, justices tend to display an independence that can diverge widely from the political philosophy of the president who appointed them.

Justices defend this sort of behavior as necessary to maintain the independence of the Supreme Court. When asked if a person changed his views once he became a Supreme Court justice, Frankfurter is alleged to have responded "If he is any good, he does!"

And Earl Warren, whose liberal views flowered after he left a career in politics to become chief justice in 1953, looked back on his 16-year term and commented that he saw no way that "a man could be on the Court and not change his views substantially over a period of years . . . for change you must if you are to do your duty on the Supreme Court."

Chase's vote against legal tender after the Civil War is the classic example of such a change in views and the way the change frustrates a president's hopes in selecting a particular justice.

The Supreme Court in 1952. Seated, left to right, **Felix Frankfurter, Hugo L. Black, Chief Justice Fred M. Vinson, Stanley Reed and William O. Douglas. Standing, left to right, Tom C. Clark, Robert H. Jackson, Harold H. Burton and Sherman Minton.**

Antitrust and Bananas

In 1902 President Theodore Roosevelt felt sure he was selecting for the Supreme Court a man whose views were compatible with his own when he chose Oliver Wendell Holmes Jr., then chief justice of the Massachusetts Supreme Court. Not only was Holmes a lifelong Republican, but he had set out his views on a myriad of issues in more than 1,000 opinions written during his 20 years on the state court.

Nevertheless, when the Roosevelt administration's effort to dissolve a major railroad conglomerate, the Northern Securities "trust," came before the Court in 1904, Holmes voted against it. The administration still won, 5-4, but Holmes' dissenting vote left Roosevelt irate. Roosevelt is reported to have said that he "could carve out of a banana a Judge with more backbone than that!"

Holmes, who had thereby demon-strated the strength of his spine, later remarked to another critic of his vote in that case: "What you want is favor, not justice. But when I am on my job, I don't give a damn what you or Mr. Roosevelt want."

That independent jurist served on the Court until 1932 when he resigned at the age of 90, the oldest man ever to serve as a Supreme Court justice.

Curmudgeons and Closet Liberals

The gentle idealist Woodrow Wilson must have been dismayed at the opinions and behavior of his nominee James C. McReynolds. Not only did McReynolds prove to hold views antagonistic to Wilson's on almost every question, but his prejudices, particularly against Jews, resulted in flagrant discourtesy to Brandeis and Cardozo, his two Jewish colleagues on the Court.

To fill the first Court vacancy during his term, President Coolidge, a conservative

Republican, selected Attorney General Harlan Fiske Stone, the man who chose J. Edgar Hoover to head the new Federal Bureau of Investigation. Despite Stone's Republican credentials and his service in the Coolidge administration, one of the nation's more conservative periods, he quickly allied himself with the liberal Holmes-Brandeis wing of the Court.

The Steel Seizure Case

President Harry S Truman, who named four men to the Court and then found himself forcefully rebuffed when he attempted to take over the nation's steel mills, stated flatly that "packing the Supreme Court simply can't be done.... I've tried and it won't work.... Whenever you put a man on the Supreme Court he ceases to be your friend."

When Truman had the opportunity to name a Supreme Court justice, he selected nominees from his friends and colleagues. Two, Harold Burton and Sherman Minton, had served in the Senate with Truman. The other two, Fred Vinson — named chief justice in 1946 — and Tom C. Clark, had served in Truman's Cabinet as Treasury secretary and attorney general, respectively.

So when Truman found himself before the Court in May 1952, defending his decision to seize the nation's steel manufacturers to avoid a strike and disruption of production during the Korean conflict, he probably expected the Court to look favorably upon his side of the case. Not so. On June 2 the Court ruled against Truman, 6-3. The president had exceeded his authority in attempting to take over the steel mills, wrote Justice Black for the majority. Congress had not authorized such action by law, and no explicit or inherent constitutional authority sanctioned it.

Truman's four nominees were evenly divided. Burton and Clark voted against him, Vinson and Minton for him.

Eisenhower's 'Mistakes'

President Dwight D. Eisenhower also named four men to the Supreme Court; he had a radical change of heart about two of them. But in 1953 Eisenhower's selection of Earl Warren as the new chief justice made perfect political sense. Warren, who had served three terms as a popular governor of California, had delivered that state's delegates to Eisenhower at the Republican convention in 1952.

Warren's record as governor was progressive, but not liberal. In fact, by placing him on the Court and removing him from the political scene, Eisenhower did a favor for more conservative California Republicans, Vice President Richard Nixon and Senate Majority Leader William F. Knowland.

Under Warren's leadership, however, the Court commenced a "judicial revolution" that Eisenhower found distressing. Less visible but of equal importance in leading that revolution at the Court was another Eisenhower nominee, William J. Brennan Jr., whom Eisenhower promoted to the Court from the New Jersey Supreme Court in 1956.

Later, when Eisenhower was asked if he had made any mistakes as president, he responded, "Yes, and they are both sitting on the Supreme Court."

Nixon, Crime and Watergate

There has been no more ironic episode in the history of presidential efforts to influence the Court than that in which President Nixon figured prominently. Nixon campaigned against the Warren Court and promised that, if elected, he would choose his Supreme Court nominees for their hardline views on criminal law and their responsiveness to the concerns of police and prosecutors.

During his presidency Nixon had the opportunity to fill four vacancies. He chose "strict constructionists" to fill those seats. Their votes began to turn the Court in the more conservative direction Nixon espoused, curtailing the role of federal judges in social change and refusing to expand upon rights guaranteed by the Warren Court's liberal rulings.

And then Nixon found himself before those very men arguing against a special prosecutor and for the right to withhold evidence sought for use in a criminal case.

Even earlier, however, Nixon had suffered some notable setbacks from the Court. In June 1971, when only two of his nominees were yet seated there, the Court had rejected his administration's argument for an order halting publication of newspaper articles based on a classified Pentagon history of the American involvement in Vietnam.

A year after the Pentagon Papers decision, the Court rejected administration arguments for free rein in using wiretaps to keep track of domestic groups suspected of subversive activity. In this case, one of Nixon's nominees, Lewis F. Powell Jr., spoke for the majority as it refused to grant the president such broad and unreviewable discretion in such matters.

Nixon was frank in his opposition to abortion. Yet during the week of his second inauguration, the Supreme Court, in the most controversial decision of the decade, struck down state laws criminalizing abortion and established a woman's right to privacy in making that decision. Again, a Nixon nominee — Harry A. Blackmun — wrote the Court's decision.

By then the Watergate investigation was under way; a year later an impeachment inquiry began. And in July 1974, in a session extraordinary in many ways, the Supreme Court heard arguments in the case of *United States v. Nixon.*

Nixon contended that he had an absolute executive privilege to withhold certain tapes of White House conversations, even when those tapes were sought by the Watergate special prosecutor for use as evidence in the criminal trials of former attorney general John N. Mitchell and former top presidential assistants John D. Ehrlichman and H. R. Haldeman.

The Court rejected that argument. By a vote of 8-0 it ruled that Nixon must surrender the tapes. Three of Nixon's four Court nominees voted against him. Rehnquist did not participate in the decision.

The decision, which forced disclosure of evidence damning to Nixon as well as to his aides, cost the president his office. Two weeks later, on Aug. 9, Nixon resigned.

Individualism and Independence

Some presidents do succeed in shaping the Court through their appointments; of that there is no doubt. But such success is part skill and part luck.

"When one puts on the robe" of a Supreme Court justice, explained Justice Rehnquist in his October 1984 speech, "one enters a world of public scrutiny and professional criticism which sets great store by individual performance, and much less store upon the virtue of being a 'team player.'"

Rehnquist continued: "Neither the President nor his appointees can foresee what issues will come before the Court during the tenure of the appointees.... Even though they agree as to the proper resolution of current cases, they may well disagree as to future cases involving other questions....

"Longevity of the appointees, or untimely deaths ... may also frustrate a president's expectations; so also may the personal antagonisms developed between strong-willed appointees of the same President."

How a justice will vote on any given issue remains a mystery until the vote is cast: that is the lesson of history. What is certain is that Supreme Court justices reach their decisions after an independent evaluation of the issue and the situation in which they act — a situation in which the views of the man who selected them for the Court are only a single factor.

As Rehnquist concluded: "The Supreme Court is an institution far more dominated by centrifugal forces, pushing toward individuality and independence, than it is by centripetal forces pulling for hierarchial ordering and institutional unity. The well-known checks and balances provided by the Framers of the Constitution have supplied the necessary centrifugal forces to make the Supreme Court independent of Congress and the President."

3

Reagan's Justice

Sandra Day O'Connor was born a pioneer. Daughter and granddaughter of men who chose to leave more settled areas to make their living on a desert ranch in southern Arizona, Sandra Day graduated from Stanford University Law School in 1952 when women lawyers were still an oddity.

And that was only the beginning of O'Connor's own pioneer career. In 1972 she was elected majority leader of the Arizona Senate, the first woman in the nation to hold such a position. Less than a decade later, she won an unchallenged place in American history as the first woman member of the U.S. Supreme Court.

One hundred and one men had served the nation as Supreme Court justices in the 191 years of the Court's history.

O'Connor's nomination highlighted the significant political strength and professional recognition that American women had attained by the third quarter of the 20th century.

In 1873, just about the time that O'Connor's grandfather was leaving New England to push west, the Supreme Court held that Illinois could deny Myra Bradwell a license to practice law — just because she was a woman.

As one of the justices explained: "The natural and proper timidity and delicacy which belongs to the female sex evidently unfits it for many of the occupations of civil life. The constitution of the family organization ... indicates the domestic sphere as that which properly belongs to the domain ... of womanhood."

Ninety years later not much had changed. A decade after O'Connor had graduated from law school, the Court in 1961 upheld the routine exclusion of women from juries, again citing the role of women "as the center of home and family life."

O'Connor had already encountered that attitude. Freshly graduated near the top of her class at Stanford Law School, she found that in California in 1952 no private law firm would hire her. As she later recalled, "None had ever hired a woman before as a lawyer, and they were not prepared to do so." One firm, Gibson, Dunn and Crutcher in Los Angeles, did offer her a job — as a legal secretary!

But attitudes changed. In 1981 Attorney General William French Smith, one of the partners in Gibson, Dunn, recommended the woman his firm had refused to hire as an associate, for the post of associate justice, U.S. Supreme Court.

The Path to Confirmation . . .

Sandra Day O'Connor's confirmation was smooth, but so was the path to Senate approval for most of the current members of the Court.

The two most liberal members, William J. Brennan Jr. and Thurgood Marshall, encountered more difficulties during the Senate's consideration of their nominations than did any of their current colleagues.

Brennan, a member of the New Jersey Supreme Court in 1956 when he was appointed by President Eisenhower, had spoken out publicly against the tactics employed by Sen. Joseph McCarthy, R-Wis., in his effort to flush out communists from within the government. During confirmation hearings, Brennan was cross-examined for an entire day by McCarthy about his speeches on this point. When Brennan's name came to the full Senate, McCarthy cast the only vote against confirmation.

Marshall, the first black man named to the Court, had been the nation's most prominent and succcessful civil rights attorney for two decades before being named a federal appeals court judge and then solicitor general.

For five days in July 1967, several Southern senators — chief among them Strom Thurmond, R.-S.C., John L. McClellan, D-Ark., and Sam J. Ervin Jr., D-N.C. — repeatedly asked Marshall questions that he insisted he could not answer because they involved issues likely to come before him as a justice. For their part, the questioning senators insisted they could not evaluate Marshall's qualifications without his answers. When the nomination came to the Senate floor in August, it was confirmed, 69-11.

Byron R. White, deputy attorney general at the time of his nomination by President John F. Kennedy, was nominated March 30, 1962, and confirmed April 11.

The Senate forced President Lyndon Johnson to withdraw his nomination of Justice Abe Fortas as chief justice in October 1968. President Richard Nixon selected the new chief justice, Warren E. Burger, a judge on the federal court of appeals for the District of Columbia. Burger was nominated May 21, 1969, and confirmed June 9 by a vote of 74-3.

The Nomination

O'Connor's selection was a stroke of political genius.

The first woman named to the Supreme Court, in response to a decade or more of pressure from women's advocates, was not only a capable judge, but also a devoted wife and mother who made it a point to introduce her husband and three sons to the Senate Judiciary Committee as it began public hearings on her nomination.

In her opening remarks, O'Connor emphasized her commitment to traditional values, noting the "importance of families in our lives and in our country." Reading from a marriage ceremony she had written, she made her views plain: "Marriage . . . is the foundation of the family, mankind's basic unit of society, the hope of the world and the strength of our country. It is the relationship between ourselves and the generations which follow."

By linking such commitment to the

... Usually Smooth, Occasionally Bumpy

Nixon encountered historic difficulties in attempting to fill the vacancy Fortas left when he resigned in May 1969. In August Nixon named federal appeals court judge Clement F. Haynsworth, but in November the Senate refused, 45-55, to confirm him.

It was the first time in 39 years that the Senate had rejected a president's Supreme Court nomination. Allegedly based on concern about Haynsworth's sensitivity to potential conflicts of interests, the Senate's rejection in fact represented the liberals' revenge on Nixon for his administration's role in bringing about Fortas' untimely departure from the Court.

In January 1970 Nixon tried again, naming another federal appeals court judge, G. Harrold Carswell, to the empty seat. Carswell, whose qualifications for the post were mediocre at best, was rejected by the Senate in April, 45-51. Not since 1894 had a president had two Supreme Court nominees rejected by the Senate.

The third time, however, Nixon succeeded. His nomination of Harry A. Blackmun, a quiet and well-respected judge on the 8th U.S. Circuit Court of Appeals, was easily approved, 94-0, in May 1970, barely a month after Nixon sent his name to the Senate.

Nixon was more careful a year later, when Justices Hugo L. Black and John Marshall Harlan resigned just before the new term began. After several trial balloons about other nominees sank, Nixon nominated Assistant Attorney General William H. Rehnquist and former American Bar Association president Lewis F. Powell Jr. to the empty seats.

Nominated in October, both underwent close scrutiny from the Senate Judiciary Committee, but were confirmed without undue difficulty in December. Rehnquist, who had often argued the Nixon administration's case before an unfriendly Congress in his Justice Department role, was confirmed, 68-26. Only one vote was cast against Powell's confirmation.

John Paul Stevens virtually glided into the seat left vacant by William O. Douglas. Nominated Nov. 28, 1975, Stevens — a 7th U.S. Circuit Court of Appeals judge — was confirmed, 98-0, on Dec. 17.

---

traditional role of women with her record of notable accomplishment in the normally male-dominated fields of law and politics, O'Connor showed herself the unassailable nominee. Although several right-to-life groups criticized her for some of her votes as a legislator, there was never any serious threat to her confirmation.

The Pledge

When Justices Hugo L. Black and John Marshall Harlan left the Court in 1971, women's groups urged President Richard Nixon to select a woman to fill one of the empty seats. Nixon selected Lewis F. Powell Jr. and William H. Rehnquist.

In 1975, when Justice William O. Douglas retired, first lady Betty Ford urged her husband, Gerald Ford, to appoint a woman justice. He chose John Paul Stevens.

In 1980 public opinion polls showed that presidential candidate Ronald Reagan was badly trailing President Jimmy Carter among women voters. On Oct. 14 Reagan opened a press conference in Los Angeles with a denial of the charges that he was opposed to full and equal opportunities for women.

Then, after defending his record on women's rights, Reagan pledged that "one of the first Supreme Court vacancies in my administration will be filled by the most qualified woman I can find, one who meets the high standards I will demand for all my appointments. It is time for a woman to sit among our highest jurists." *(Statement, box, p. 33)*

Two weeks earlier, in an interview with the *New York Times,* Reagan had alluded to the possibility that he would name a woman to the Court. He also had said that he would choose judicial nominees whose views were broadly compatible with his own philosophy, but that he would not use a single issue — abortion, for example — as a litmus test for his appointees.

The 1980 Republican party platform urged the appointment of judges with "compassion for innocent human life," a phrase read by most as meaning an opposition to abortion. Candidate Reagan said he read the plank as broader than that, as simply reflecting that "we all ought to have compassion for innocent human life."

After pledging to name a woman to the Court, Reagan was asked whether, in choosing that woman, it would be important that she oppose abortion. Reagan again replied: "I believe . . . that you make those appointments on the whole philosophical viewpoint of the individual, not picking out individual or single issues."

The Person

Sandra Day O'Connor was born March 26, 1930, in El Paso, Texas. Her parents, Harry and Ada Mae Day, lived on the Lazy B Ranch established by her grandfather, Henry Clay Day, in 1881. The ranch straddles the border of southeastern Arizona and southwestern New Mexico. Because the

Lazy B was far from medical services, Ada Mae had returned to her parents' home in El Paso for the arrival of her first child. This house, the home of Sandra Day's maternal grandparents, Willis and Mamie Wilkey, would be Sandra's second home.

Harry Day's plans to attend Stanford University had been changed when his father died suddenly. Harry was forced to return to the Lazy B to work out severe financial problems that threatened the family with loss of the homestead.

One El Paso rancher who helped Harry in these difficult times was Willis Wilkey. His daughter, Ada Mae, was a well-traveled and well-educated young lady, who had graduated from the University of Arizona. In 1927 she and Harry were married.

Three years later, Sandra was born, followed later by sister Ann and brother Alan. Alan now runs the Lazy B Ranch in which Sandra retains a partnership interest.

Although Sandra flourished in the ranch life of the Lazy B, her parents, for whom education had always been a high priority, sent her to El Paso to live with her grandparents and attend school. Summers, however, were spent at the ranch.

In 1946 Sandra took the path her father had been unable to follow. A bright high school graduate at the age of 16, she entered Stanford University. After majoring in economics in college, she moved on to law school.

There she met two men who would figure notably in her adult life: John J. O'Connor, whom she married in 1952, and William Rehnquist, whom she later joined on the U.S. Supreme Court.

She did well in law school, serving as an editor of the *Stanford Law Review* and graduating third in the class. Rehnquist ranked first.

In December after graduation, she married O'Connor, son of a San Francisco physician, in a ceremony at the Lazy B. They returned to California so that he could

Reagan's Pledge

On Oct. 14, 1980, presidential candidate Ronald Reagan pledged to name a woman to the Supreme Court. Excerpts from his statement follow:

As you know, a number of false and misleading accusations have been made in this campaign. . . . One . . . has been that I am somehow opposed to full and equal opportunities for women in America. . . .

Nothing could be further from the truth. My entire life, public and private, has been devoted to the dignity of all people. I could never personally tolerate any kind of discrimination.

As Governor of California, I signed legislation prohibiting discrimination on account of sex in employment, real property transactions, or in the provision of accommodations and services by businesses; establishing the right of a married woman to obtain credit in her own name; revising community property to give the wife equal rights in regard to management and control of community property; extending the state unemployment disability benefits to pregnant employees; increasing the penalties for rape and for the use of firearms in a rape; providing for the development and improvement of child care centers. . . .

Now, as President, I will follow my convictions. Intelligent, committed, qualified and responsible women will be placed in important jobs in my administration.

I oppose tokenism, and I oppose setting false quotas. . . . I am also acutely aware, however, that within the guidelines of excellence, appointments can carry enormous symbolic significance. This permits us to guide by example, to show how deep our commitment is and to give meaning to what we profess. One way I intend to live up to that commitment is to appoint a woman to the Supreme Court.

I am announcing today that one of the first Supreme Court vacancies in my administration will be filled by the most qualified woman I can find, one who meets the high standards I will demand for all my appointments.

It is time for a woman to sit among our highest jurists. I will also seek out women to appoint to other Federal courts in an effort to bring about a better balance on the Federal bench.

There will be no name announced nor will I submit names to be considered until I have conducted a comprehensive search and have received the recommendations of an advisory committee of eminent legal and judicial experts.

The procedures they will be asked to follow are the same procedures I intend to establish for all judicial appointments.

I am confident that this woman, whomever [sic] she may be, and all of my other women appointees, will contribute to the goals that I seek for America.

But no matter who holds those jobs, the ends we seek to achieve will be the same: a country at peace, an economy with strength, a maximum of freedom and the renewal of a community of values.

finish law school.

Rebuffed by law firms in her hunt for a job, O'Connor went to work as deputy county attorney for San Mateo County. After John graduated from law school, he joined the Army as a member of the Judge Advocate General's Corps. The O'Connors lived for several years in Frankfurt, where Sandra found work as a civilian attorney for the Quartermaster Corps.

In 1957 they returned to Arizona, not to the Lazy B, but to Phoenix. Both O'Connors went into private law practice, John with the firm of Fennemore, Craig, von Ammon and Udall, and Sandra with one other attorney.

Their first son Scott was born in 1957, followed in two years by Brian and two years later by Jay. During the five years she was at home with her children, 1960-1965, O'Connor practiced her profession as a volunteer. She handled juvenile cases on assignment from the juvenile court judge; she served as chairman of the juvenile detention home visiting board, as a member of the county planning and zoning commission, as chairman of the local bar effort to provide legal services to the community at low cost. She also wrote bar examination questions and graded the tests.

During this time she was an active participant in local civic and Republican groups, serving as president of the Junior League of Phoenix, and as a member of the boards of the Arizona chapters of the Salvation Army, the YMCA and the National Conference of Christians and Jews.

The O'Connors resumed their friendship with the Rehnquists; William Rehnquist was also practicing law in Phoenix at the time. Living nearby was Sen. Barry Goldwater, with whom they became friends.

In 1965 Sandra O'Connor decided to return to work. Finding a job was still not easy for a woman lawyer, but she persisted in her search and finally secured a position as assistant attorney general for Arizona.

She was the first woman to hold that post in the state.

Four years later, she was appointed to fill a vacancy in the state Senate. She served on the judiciary committee and quickly made a reputation for herself. Winning a full term, she was elected majority leader of the state Senate in 1972, another "first" for Sandra Day O'Connor.

An active Republican, O'Connor was co-chairman of the Arizona Committee to Re-Elect the President in 1972. That same year she was honored as Arizona Woman of the Year.

As a legislator, she redrafted a number of laws to remove provisions that discriminated against women in areas such as property rights, working restrictions and child custody. She was known as meticulous, hard-working, intelligent, tactful and tough.

In 1974 she left the legislature for the bench, running for and winning a seat on the Maricopa Superior Court. She served there five years, hearing cases of all types from bad checks and burglary to murder.

Although friends, including Goldwater and former House Republican leader John J. Rhodes, encouraged her to run for governor in 1978, O'Connor decided to stay on the bench.

In 1979 Gov. Bruce Babbitt, a Democrat, appointed her to the Arizona Court of Appeals. Deflecting comments that he was simply removing a potential political rival from the scene, Babbitt responded that O'Connor exemplified his commitment to placing the finest available legal talent on the state bench. "Her intellectual ability and her judgment are astonishing," he added.

O'Connor served on the state appeals court for two years. There were few legal landmarks in her caseload, but she continued to develop and to demonstrate her expertise in dealing with appeals on matters ranging from bankruptcy, crime and divorce to workers' compensation.

The Philosophy

Her work as a state judge won her an invitation to a symposium in Williamsburg, Va., in January 1981, on the subject of "State Courts and Federalism in the 1980s." One of the other participants was Chief Justice Warren E. Burger, who was impressed with O'Connor and her presentation, which was subsequently published in the *William and Mary Law Review.*

At Williamsburg, O'Connor for the first time in a national forum sounded a theme which would recur in her opinions time and again: the capability and willingness of state judges to enforce the guarantees of the federal Constitution.

"State judges do in fact rise to the occasion when given the responsibility and opportunity to do so," she argued. "There is a keen awareness among state court judges in state criminal cases of the federal constitutional protections of the defendant."

Federal judges have no special ability to implement the Constitution, she continued, noting that "many appointments to the federal bench are made from state court benches. When the state court judge puts on his or her new federal court robe he or she does not become immediately better equipped intellectually to do the job."

It was perhaps for symbolic reasons that O'Connor — when she became the first state court judge in 25 years to be named to the Supreme Court — wore her state court robe for her swearing-in.

Another participant in the Williamsburg symposium was Harvard law professor Paul Bator, who would also play a significant role in the Reagan campaign to convince the Court to change the course of American policy.

O'Connor cited Bator in defending state judges: "What is really being said is that federal judges are inclined to be more receptive to *some* federal constitutional claims. Professor Bator is correct in stating what is required is a sensitivity and respon-

siveness to *all* the constitutional principles, not just *some* of them.

"There is no reason to assume that state court judges cannot and will not provide a 'hospitable forum' in litigating federal constitutional questions," O'Connor continued. She quoted from her former classmate, Justice Rehnquist: "State judges as well as federal judges swear allegiance to the Constitution of the United States, and there is no reason to think that because of their frequent differences of opinions as to how that document should be interpreted that all are not doing their mortal best to discharge their oath of office."

O'Connor urged the Supreme Court and other federal courts to uphold the decisions of state judges, so long as they had provided full and fair hearings and rulings on federal constitutional questions raised before them.

Her remarks fell upon receptive ears. Chief Justice Burger, perennially concerned about the growing caseload of the federal courts, heard a welcome invitation to shift work from the federal judiciary to state courts. Key figures in the still-organizing Reagan administration heard suggestions that fit neatly within the administration's commitment to encourage state governments to do more, and to shrink the duties and powers of the federal government.

The Selection

In March 1981 Justice Potter Stewart confided to his old Yale friend Vice President George Bush that he was planning to retire at the end of the current term. Stewart also notified Attorney General Smith of his plans.

Because of the attempted assassination of President Reagan and his subsequent hospitalization, Smith and Bush delayed telling the president. Reagan was informed of the impending resignation in April.

Reagan asked the White House staff and Smith to draw up lists of potential

The Announcement

President Reagan July 7, 1981, announced his selection of Sandra Day O'Connor as the nation's first woman justice in the following words:

Without doubt the most awesome appointment a President can make is to the United States Supreme Court. Those who sit on the Supreme Court interpret the laws of our land and truly do leave their footprints on the sands of time, long after the policies of Presidents, Senators and Congressmen of a given era may have passed from the public memory. . . .

. . . [D]uring my campaign for the Presidency I made a commitment that one of my first appointments to a Supreme Court vacancy would be the most qualified woman I could possibly find.

This is not to say that I would appoint a woman merely to do so. That would not be fair to women, nor to future generations of all Americans whose lives are so deeply affected by the decisions of the Court. Rather, I pledged to appoint a woman who meets the very high standards I demand of all court appointees.

I have identified such a person.

So, today, I am pleased to announce that upon completion of all necessary checks by the Federal Bureau of Investigation I will send to the Senate the nomination of Judge Sandra Day O'Connor of the Arizona Court of Appeals for confirmation as an Associate Justice of the United States Supreme Court.

She is truly a "person for all seasons," possessing those unique qualities of temperament, fairness, intellectual capacity and devotion to the public good which have characterized the 101 "brethren" who have preceded her.

I commend her to you and urge the Senate's swift bipartisan confirmation so that as soon as possible she may take her seat on the Court and her place in history.

nominees, reminding them of his pledge to place a woman on the Court. By the time Stewart made his plans public on June 18, 1981, the White House and the Justice Department had each drawn up lists. O'Connor was on both.

Although O'Connor was little known outside Arizona and judicial circles, some of those who did know her were both powerful and well-placed. Goldwater, a long-time friend and neighbor, had sent just one name to the White House — hers. Chief Justice Burger was impressed with her, and, when queried by the White House, Justice Rehnquist added his endorsement.

Five days after Stewart had made his announcement, a Justice Department attorney arrived in Phoenix to gather additional information on O'Connor. The last week of June, two more government attorneys came to Phoenix to talk with her. FBI investigators were already at work compiling a detailed report on the potential nominee.

On June 29, O'Connor flew to Washington. She met first with Attorney General Smith, and then with top White House aides Edwin Meese, James Baker, Michael Deaver and Fred Fielding. On July 1 she met with Reagan at the White House. Then she returned to Phoenix. She would not know the outcome of her interviews for five more days.

On July 1, the *New York Times* reported that the White House had a "tentative short list" of potential nominees, including Judge Cornelia G. Kennedy of the U.S. 6th Circuit Court of Appeals and Judge Joan Dempsey Klein of the Superior Court in Los Angeles County. O'Connor was not mentioned.

But the very next day, the *Washington Post* ran a front-page story: Woman Tops List for Court. The story read: "Sandra D. O'Connor, a prominent Arizona jurist with Republican political credentials, has emerged as a leading candidate for the Supreme Court vacancy that will be created Friday when Justice Potter Stewart retires."

Less than a week later on July 7, the president made his announcement: O'Connor was his choice. She had learned of her selection the day before. O'Connor, said Reagan, "is truly a 'person for all seasons,' possessing those unique qualities of temperament, fairness, intellectual capacity and devotion to the public good which have characterized the 101 'brethren' who have preceded her." *(Full statement, box, p. 36)*

O'Connor, surrounded by her family, responded to the announcement with a brief news conference in Phoenix. She said that she was honored by the nomination, but out of deference to the confirmation process, she would not answer any questions of substance.

The Reaction

Despite her moderate-to-conservative record and the firm backing of Republican elder statesman Goldwater, O'Connor's nomination drew immediate criticism from radical conservative groups such as the Moral Majority. They criticized her support, as a state senator, of the Equal Rights Amendment and some of her votes in the legislature that they viewed as pro-abortion.

Sen. Jesse Helms, R-N.C., the leading conservative voice of the Senate, said he was "skeptical" about O'Connor. Rev. Jerry Falwell, leader of the Moral Majority, declared the nomination a "disaster."

The National Right to Life Committee pledged an all-out fight against her confirmation. "O'Connor's appointment represents a repudiation of the Republican platform pledge" to appoint judges "who respect traditional family values and the sanctity of innocent human life," said Dr. J. C. Willkie, the committee's president.

Such criticism, however, was barely heard over the chorus of praise from liberals and moderates. "If we're going to have Reagan appointees to the Court, you couldn't do much better" than O'Connor, said Rep. Morris K. Udall, D-Ariz. O'Connor, he continued, "is about as moderate a Republican as you'll ever find being appointed by Reagan."

Even Sen. Edward M. Kennedy, D-Mass., leader of the liberal wing of the Democratic party, praised Reagan's choice. Eleanor Smeal, president of the National Organization for Women, called the nomination "a major victory for women's rights."

O'Connor came to Washington again in mid-July, two weeks after her initial visit. After a public and much-photographed meeting with President Reagan in the Rose Garden, she met with White House staff members and Justice Department attorneys to begin preparing for the confirmation hearings. She spent three days on Capitol Hill, paying courtesy calls on key senators, especially the members of the Senate Judiciary Committee, including Helms.

While the FBI completed its check of her background, and the American Bar Association committee on the federal judiciary began its probe of her legal qualifications, O'Connor spent her summer combing through her own past record and studying Supreme Court history and constitutional law in preparation for the hearings.

On Aug. 19, 1981, Reagan formally

President Reagan escorts Sandra Day O'Connor through the White House Rose Garden.

sent to the Senate the nomination of Sandra Day O'Connor as associate justice, U.S. Supreme Court.

Confirmation

The Senate Judiciary Committee held three days of hearings on O'Connor's nomination — Sept. 9, 10 and 11, 1981. All were broadcast live. The committee questioned her on a variety of subjects. There was testimony in favor and in opposition to the nomination, but the outcome was never in doubt.

O'Connor had returned to Washington several days before the hearings began. She spent some time rehearsing possible questions and answers with Justice Department attorneys.

She filed a financial statement with the committee, reporting a net worth of more than $1.1 million. The O'Connors' primary assets were their home near Phoenix, John's share in his law partnership in Phoenix, and Sandra's share in the Lazy B.

Only two of the sitting justices — Powell and Burger — were wealthier. In May 1981 disclosure statements Powell reported assets from $2.5 million to $5 million; Burger, $888,000 to $1.5 million.

Before the hearings began, the ABA committee declared O'Connor "qualified" for a seat on the Supreme Court.

Atmosphere

The opening of the hearing resembled a wedding. Honored guests were seated in a large reserved area behind the witness table. Chairman Strom Thurmond, R-S.C. escorted O'Connor into the room on his arm. Both smiled to friends they recognized. As O'Connor reached the witness table, committee members rushed to shake her hand and offer congratulations.

The senators' opening remarks further enhanced the feeling of celebration. Each praised O'Connor warmly, remarking on the historic significance of the occasion.

During the hearing the committee hoped to find the answers to three major questions, said Joseph R. Biden Jr., the ranking Democratic member:

—Does she have the intellectual capacity, competence and temperament to be a Supreme Court justice?

—Is she of good moral character and free of conflict of interest that would compromise her ability to faithfully and objectively perform her role as a member of the U.S. Supreme Court?

—Will she faithfully uphold the laws and Constitution of the United States of America?

The committee was "not attempting to determine whether ... the nominee agrees with all of us on each and every pressing social or legal issue of the day," Biden added. "Indeed, if that were the test no one would ever pass by this committee, much less the full Senate."

But not all the committee's members were content with this broad general view of their purpose. Sen. Jeremiah Denton, R-Ala., made clear that O'Connor's views on abortion would determine his vote. His vote for or against her confirmation, he said, would be affected by his belief that "legalized abortion" was "a denial of the most fundamental ... national principle of this Nation."

O'Connor's Statement

"As the first woman to be nominated as a Supreme Court Justice, I am particularly honored," O'Connor told the committee, "and I happily share the honor with millions of American women of yesterday and of today whose abilities and whose conduct have given me this opportunity for service. . . .

"If confirmed by the Senate, I will apply all my abilities to insure that our Government is preserved; that justice under our Constitution and the laws of this land will always be the foundation of that Government.

"I want to make only one substantive statement to you at this time. My experience as a State court judge and as a State legislator has given me a greater appreciation of the important role the States play in our federal system, and also a greater appreciation of the separate and distinct roles of the three branches of government at both the State and the Federal levels. Those experiences have strengthened my view that the proper role of the judiciary is one of interpreting and applying the law, not making it."

O'Connor told the committee that there were limits on her ability to answer their questions: "I hope to be as helpful to you as possible in responding to your questions," she told them.

However, she continued, "I do not believe that ... I can tell you how I might vote on a particular issue which may come before the Court, or endorse or criticize specific Supreme Court decisions presenting issues which may well come before the Court again. To do so would mean that I have prejudged the matter or have morally committed myself to a certain position.

"Such a statement ... might make it necessary for me to disqualify myself on the matter. This would result in my inability to do my sworn duty: namely, to decide cases that come before the Court.

"Finally, neither you nor I know today the precise way in which an issue will present itself in the future, or what the facts or arguments may be at that time, or how the statute being interpreted may read. Until those crucial factors become known. I suggest that none of us really know how we would resolve any particular issue."

Abortion

Despite that explicit statement, some members of the committee still tried to elicit from O'Connor precisely that sort of commitment to vote against abortion. Initially, Chairman Thurmond provided O'Connor the opportunity to explain some of her criticized legislative votes as a state senator on this issue:

THURMOND: Judge O'Connor, there has been much discussion regarding your views on the subject of abortion. Would you discuss your philosophy on abortion, both personal and judicial, and explain your actions as a state senator in Arizona on certain specific matters. . . .

O'CONNOR: Very well. May I preface my response by saying that the personal views and philosophies, in my view, of a Supreme Court Justice and indeed any judge should be set aside insofar as it is possible to do that in resolving matters that come before the Court.

Issues that come before the Court

should be resolved based on the facts of that particular case or matter and on the law applicable to those facts, and any constitutional principles applicable to those facts. They should not be based on the personal views and ideology of the judge. . . .

Now, having explained that, I would like to say that my own view in the area of abortion is that I am opposed to it as a matter of birth control or otherwise. The subject of abortion is a valid one, in my view, for legislative action subject to any constitutional restraints or limitations.

O'Connor then explained that:

—In 1970 she voted in committee for a bill that repealed Arizona laws making it a felony to provide anyone the means for causing a miscarriage.

Noting that since that time she had become more knowledgeable on the subject and more aware of the issues and concerns involved in the abortion controversy, O'Connor said she thought she "would not have voted . . . for a simple repealer thereafter."

—In 1973 she supported a bill that would have established a state policy of encouraging the availability of contraceptive information. "It seemed to me that perhaps the best way to avoid having people . . . seeking abortions was to enable people not to become pregnant unwittingly," she added.

—In 1974 she voted against a proposal urging Congress to amend the Constitution to overturn the Supreme Court's landmark ruling in *Roe v. Wade* (1973) forbidding states to ban all abortions.

"It seems to me . . . that amendments to the Constitution . . . should be undertaken after a great deal of study and thought and not hastily. I think a tremendous amount of work needs to go into the text and the concept being expressed. . . . I did not feel at that time that that kind of consideration had been given to the measure," she explained.

—Also in 1974 she opposed an anti-abortion rider which the state House of Representatives added to a bill authorizing expansion of the state university football stadium. As majority leader, she said, she opposed the addition of non-germane riders to Senate bills.

O'Connor added, however, that the same year she supported a bill providing medical aid for needy persons, but denying benefits for abortions except when they were necessary to save the life of the mother or where the pregnancy had resulted from rape, incest or other criminal action. That bill became law, she noted.

The abortion issue recurred time and again throughout the three days of hearings. O'Connor was consistent in stating her personal opposition to abortion. "It is a practice in which I would not have engaged," she stated with quiet decisiveness.

She qualified that, however, with the observation that "I'm over the hill. I'm not going to be pregnant any more . . . so perhaps it's easy for me to speak." And time and again she emphasized her equally strong feeling that her personal views on that issue had no place in resolving legal cases concerning abortion.

O'Connor's care in responding to these questions frustrated some committee members. On the last day of the hearing, Denton declared, "I do not feel I have made any progress personally in determining where you stand on the issue of abortion."

Sen. John P. East, R-N.C., expressed similar frustration: "the Senate and the Congress are trying . . . to reassert their policy-making function which many feel has been eclipsed by the bureaucracy . . . or frequently by the Supreme Court and the judiciary." East wondered whether the Senate's role in the confirmation process was in fact "negated and eliminated simply because questions cannot be asked in a fairly thorough and substantive way."

He continued, "I can appreciate you cannot promise anything; I can appreciate

Woman Justice Sparks Debate

REAGAN NOMINATING WOMAN, AN ARIZONA APPEALS JUDGE, TO SERVE ON SUPREME COURT

O'Connor Is Attacked Over ERA, Abortion

REACTION IS MIXED

Senate Seems Favorable but Opposition Arises on Abortion Stands

By STEVEN R. WEISMAN
Special to The New York Times

ldwater Vows ht for Nominee

By Roberta Hornig
and Allan Dodds Frank
Washington Star Staff Writers

esident Reagan's choice of San-
D. O'Connor to fill a Supreme
rt vacancy was given a cool re-
ion by some conservatives in the
ate, but Barry Goldwater – who
ms to be the chamber's most con-
/ative member – vowed to battle
opposition to the nomination.
.iberals and moderates generally
ised the selection of the judge
m Goldwater's home state of Ari-
ia yesterday.
Goldwater, in an interview, exco-
ted the right-to-life movement
d Equal Rights Amendment oppo-
nts as "non-conservatives" who
ve been obstructing the work of
.ngress. He said they should have
) say in the consideration of O'Con-
)r's nomination.
The Arizona senator reserved his

President's Choice Sets a Precedent

By Lyle Denniston
Washington Star Staff Writer

President Reagan has broken two
centuries of national habit in choosing a woman – Sandra D. O'Connor
of Arizona – for the Supreme Court.
In announcing yesterday that he
had picked O'Connor, 51, a judge on
the Arizona Court of Appeals, the
president also stirred up a sizable
but perhaps passing political storm
over her views on women's rights.
Those views have not been spelled
out fully in public, but some of the
president's own political followers
immediately denounced her as too
liberal, particularly on abortion.
Conservative religious groups,
anti-abortion leaders and New Right
Republicans vowed to fight her
.nomination in the Senate.
It appeared that Senate liberals
and moderates, along with feminist
organizations critical of Reagan
since his election, would support
her.
The nomination will be reviewed
at hearings of the Senate Judiciary
Committee, starting perhaps later
this month. One committee aide said
he doubted that final Senate action
would come before September.
The president called for "swift bipartisan confirmation," but the
prompt outbreak of controversy
made it seem that it could be several
weeks before O'Connor's name is put
to a vote on the Senate floor.
~ummer recess and

Feelings of Betrayal and Delight

By FRANCIS X. CLINES

he National Organization
.lled the nomination a
>men's rights." Eleanor
dent of the organization,
ncreasing political pres-
n's groups and a drop in

Page A12, Column 3

Reagan Choice for Court Decried by Conservatives But Acclaimed by Liberals

By Bill Peterson
Washington Post Staff Writer

The reaction yesterday to President
Reagan's first nomination to the Su-
Court was an ironic one: he

form pledge . . . . This appointment is
a grave disappointment to the pro-life
public nationwide," said Dr. J.C.
Willke, president of the National
Right to Life Committee, which supported Reagan in the 1980 campaign.

SIDE

ails His Critics
n, in a speech pre-
»ublican gathering,
pressure on foes of
·am. Page A13.

:uted in Iran

Conservatives Feud in Wake of O'Connor Choice

By Fred Barbash
Washington Post Staff Writer

Conservatives feuded

Judge Sandra Day O'Connor at news conference

---

you could not comment upon pending cases;
but when we are told there cannot be
comment upon previous cases and previous
doctrines of substance, I query as one lowly
freshman Senator whether we are able
really to get our teeth into anything."

Sex Discrimination

O'Connor characterized the problem of
discrimination against women as "greatly
improved" since the 1950s, although she
acknowledged the statistical gap between
the earnings of men and women and the fact
that "in some instances attitudes still have
not followed along with some of the
changes" in the law.

Nevertheless, she said, "It has been
very heartening to me as a woman in the
legal profession to see the large numbers of
women who are now enrolled in the nation's
law schools, who are coming out and beginning to practice law and who are serving on
the bench. We are making enormous
changes. I think these changes are very
welcome."

Busing

Drawing on her own childhood experience, O'Connor expressed strong reservations about the usefulness of busing as a tool
for desegregating public schools.

"I grew up in a very remote part of

Justice Sandra Day O'Connor and Chief Justice Warren E. Burger. O'Connor took the oath of office Sept. 25, 1981.

Arizona," she explained, "and we were not near any school. It bothered me to be away from home to attend school, which I had been from kindergarten on. In the eighth grade I attempted to live at home on the ranch and ride a school bus to get to school. It involved a 75-mile trip each day, round trip ... and I found that I had to leave home before daylight and get home after dark.

"I found that very disturbing ... and I am sure that other children who have had to ride long distances on buses have shared that experience. I just think that it is not a system that often is terribly beneficial to the child."

During her terms in the Arizona Senate O'Connor supported legislation seeking termination of forced busing to desegregate schools.

Excluding Evidence

Asked about the exclusionary rule, applied to state courts in 1961 to prohibit the admission of evidence obtained in violation of a defendant's rights, O'Connor reflected upon her experience as a state judge.

"There are times when perfectly relevant evidence and, indeed, sometimes the only evidence in the case has been excluded by application of a rule which, if different standards were to be applied ... maybe would not have applied in that situation, for instance to good faith conduct on the part of police.

"I am not suggesting ... that I think it is inappropriate where force or trickery or some other reprehensible conduct has been used, but I have seen examples of the application of the rule which I thought were unfortunate, on the trial court."

Activism and Precedent

O'Connor distinguished between "judicial activism," of which she disapproved, and landmark Supreme Court rulings overturning settled practices, such as the 1964 decision in *Brown v. Board of Education.*

"I do not believe that it is the function of the judiciary to step in and change the law because the times have changed or the social mores have changed.... I believe that on occasion ... the Court has reached changed results based on its research of what the true meaning of that provision ... is — based on the intent of the Framers, its research on the history of that particular provision."

When asked her views on the doctrine of *stare decisis* — deciding new cases in keeping with the already-announced precedents of the Court — O'Connor again demonstrated her ability to state an opinion without tying herself to any rigid standard:

"I think most people would agree that stability of the law and predictability of the law are vitally important concepts.

"Justice Cardozo pointed out the chaos that would result if we decided every case on a case-by-case basis without regard to precedent. It would make administration of justice virtually impossible....

"... there has been some suggestion made that the role of stare decisis is a little bit different ... if the Court is deciding a case concerning the interpretation ... of a congressional act and the Court renders a decision, and if Congress feels that decision was wrong, then Congress itself can enact further amendments.... Therefore, we are not without remedies in that situation.

"Whereas, if what the Court decided is a matter of constitutional interpretation and that is the last word, then the only remedy ... is either for an amendment to the Constitution to be offered or for the Court itself to either distinguish its holdings or somehow change them.

"We have seen this process occur throughout the Court's history. There are instances in which the Justices of the Supreme Court have decided after examining a problem or a given situation that their previous decision or the previous decisions of the Court in that particular matter were based on faulty reasoning or faulty analysis or otherwise a flawed interpretation of the law. In that instance they have the power, and indeed the obligation if they so believe, to overturn that previous decision and issue a decision that they feel correctly reflects the appropriate constitutional interpretation."

Senate Action

Five days after the hearings ended, the Senate Judiciary Committee Sept. 15 voted 17-0 to recommend confirmation of Sandra Day O'Connor as associate justice of the U.S. Supreme Court. Denton abstained, citing his dissatisfaction with O'Connor's answer to his questions on abortion.

At 6 o'clock on Sept. 21, the Senate, 99-0, confirmed O'Connor as the 102nd member of the U.S. Supreme Court. Four hours were set aside for debate on the nomination, but no real debate occurred. The Senate chamber was deserted for most of that period.

Denton voted for confirmation as did Helms, who said that after talking with Reagan, he assumed that O'Connor agreed with Reagan's position on abortion — which was that *Roe v. Wade* should be overturned.

Sen. Max Baucus, D-Mont., a strong supporter of O'Connor, was in Montana and could not vote.

After the vote O'Connor appeared on the steps of the Capitol with Vice President Bush. She thanked the Senate for its vote of approval and said she was "absolutely overjoyed."

She took her seat on the Court Sept. 25, 1981.

4

O'Connor at the Court

The day Sandra Day O'Connor became a member of the U.S. Supreme Court was also the 10th anniversary of the death of Justice Hugo L. Black, Franklin Roosevelt's first Court nominee. Black's arrival on Oct. 4, 1937, marked the beginning of a new era in the Court's history. O'Connor's debut 44 years later may have marked a similar watershed, but with a significant difference.

Black was soon joined on the bench by other Roosevelt appointees — William O. Douglas, Felix Frankfurter, Stanley Reed and Frank Murphy — all within three years. The end of the Court's conservative opposition to New Deal policies, in sight before Black's arrival, then came quickly.

O'Connor was not joined by any other Reagan justices during her first four years on the bench. And yet, the period from 1981 to 1985 saw a clear conservative shift at the Court. Without doubt, one factor in that change was O'Connor herself and her own strongly held and articulated views in favor of state prerogatives, judicial restraint and deference to the political branches of government.

Another factor, however, was the philosophical difference between O'Connor and Potter Stewart, the justice she succeeded. Stewart was in many ways a classic moder-

ate who found himself a conservative in dissent from some of the Warren Court's most controversial liberal decisions and a liberal dissenting from some of the Burger Court's more conservative rulings.

During the 1970s Stewart's vote was rarely predictable. In several key cases, he provided the crucial fifth vote for a majority. Sometimes it was a liberal majority, striking down the state death penalty laws in 1972. And sometimes it was a conservative majority, as when the Court in the *Bakke* case struck down minority quota systems for medical school admissions in 1978.

O'Connor began her Court career as a committed conservative, voting far more consistently than Stewart for the government's side of an issue. Allying herself firmly with Chief Justice Warren E. Burger and William H. Rehnquist, O'Connor rarely played the "swing vote" role that Stewart played so consistently.

Stewart: Man in the Middle

When Potter Stewart, then 43, became an associate justice in the autumn of 1958, he joined a Court that frequently found itself divided right down the middle on important questions. Chief Justice Earl Warren, Justices Black, Douglas and William J. Brennan Jr. usually took the liberal view of a question, while Justices Frankfurter, Tom C. Clark, John Marshall Harlan and Charles E. Whittaker took the conservative view.

Like O'Connor's, Stewart's vote initially strengthened the conservative bloc on the Court and enabled it to prevail on a number of important issues. For example, in a set of three decisions issued in 1959 and 1961, the Court, 5-4:

—Limited the First Amendment rights of witnesses appearing before congressional investigating committees (*Barenblatt v. United States*);

—Upheld provisions of the 1950 Subversive Activities Control Act requiring the Communist Party to register with the Justice Department (*Communist Party v. Subversive Activities Control Board*);

—Upheld laws penalizing active membership in subversive organizations (*Scales v. United States; Noto v. United States*).

Conservative Among Liberals

The departure of Justices Frankfurter and Whittaker in 1962 and their replacement by Byron R. White and Arthur J. Goldberg moved the Warren Court into its most liberal period. Stewart disagreed with a number of its major rulings during the remaining years of the Warren Court. Among the decisions from which Stewart dissented were:

—*Mapp v. Ohio*, 5-4, applying the exclusionary rule to state trials (1961);

—*Engel v. Vitale*, 6-1, striking down the use of a prescribed school prayer in public schools (1962);

—*Fay v. Noia*, 6-3, enlarging the rights of state prisoners to ask a federal court to order their release (1963);

—*Malloy v. Hogan*, 5-4, extending Fifth Amendment protection against self-incrimination to state defendants (1964);

—*Escobedo v. Illinois* and *Miranda v. Arizona*, 5-4, denying prosecutors the use of confessions obtained from suspects not advised of their constitutional rights (1964, 1966);

—*Griswold v. Connecticut*, 7-2, declaring that the Constitution guarantees personal privacy in certain areas of life and that a state intruded on that right when it banned all use of contraceptives (1965);

—*In re Gault*, 7-2, extending some due process guarantees to juvenile court proceedings (1967).

But Stewart was not invariably in dissent. He joined the Warren Court in many important liberal decisions during these same years, including:

—*Baker v. Carr*, 6-2, which set off the reapportionment revolution by permitting federal judges to consider constitutional challenges to legislative districting (1962);

—*Robinson v. California*, 6-2, which declared it unconstitutional for states to make narcotics addiction a crime (1962);

—*New York Times v. Sullivan*, 9-0, which extended First Amendment protection of the press to libel suits by public officials (1964);

—*Gideon v. Wainwright*, 9-0, which required that all persons charged with serious crimes be provided the aid of an attorney (1963);

—*Heart of Atlanta Motel v. United States*, 9-0, which upheld Title II of the 1964 Civil Rights Act barring racial discrimination in public accommodations (1964);

—*South Carolina v. Katzenbach*, 8-1, which upheld the Voting Rights Act of 1965 (1966);

—*Green v. County School Board of New Kent County*, 9-0, which struck down a "freedom-of-choice" plan for desegregating schools (1968).

And Stewart was the Court's spokesman in several major rulings of the 1960s enlarging the rights of individuals. For example, he wrote the opinion in *Jones v. Mayer* (1968) making innovative use of an 1866 civil rights law to ban discrimination in the private sale or rental of housing. When the Court in 1965 held that cities could not use breach-of-peace statutes to penalize the peaceful exercise of the rights of free speech, petition and assembly, Stewart was its spokesman. Two years later, Stewart explained the Court's decision to impose constitutional restrictions on wiretapping and electronic surveillance.

Liberal Among Conservatives

After Burger became chief justice in 1969, Stewart found himself more powerful, more comfortable — and often more liberal — in the context of the Burger Court. In a dozen major rulings on issues ranging from affirmative action to capital punishment, Stewart cast the deciding vote.

In 1972 Stewart and the remaining members of the Warren Court — Douglas, Brennan, White and Thurgood Marshall — composed the five-man majority that declared all existing death penalty statutes unconstitutional. The four newest justices, all named by President Richard Nixon, dissented.

Each justice wrote his own opinion in *Furman v. Georgia,* but it is Stewart's vivid language that is quoted most often. Death sentences imposed under these laws, he explained, "are cruel and unusual in the same way that being struck by lightning is cruel and unusual." The offending laws, he said, permitted judges and juries to impose the ultimate sentence of death "wantonly" and "freakishly."

Four years later, when the Court reviewed the new death penalty statutes enacted by states to permit capital punishment without the constitutional flaw pointed out in *Furman,* Stewart again demonstrated his ability to keep to the middle of the constitutional road.

Death is not always a cruel and un-

Potter Stewart

usual punishment, he wrote, refusing to place capital punishment forever outside the bounds of the Constitution. Rather, he wrote, it is "an extreme sanction, suitable to the most extreme of crimes." But the same day Stewart, again a deciding vote, joined Brennan, Marshall, John Paul Stevens and Lewis F. Powell Jr. to hold it unconstitutional for states to make death the mandatory sentence for first-degree murder.

Stewart disagreed with the Warren Court's school prayer ruling but joined virtually every decision during his 23-year tenure in which the Court struck down state aid to parochial schools.

In 1975 the Court held that Pennsylvania could lend textbooks to non-public school students but could not lend instructional equipment or provide auxiliary staff and services to non-public schools. Burger, Rehnquist and White dissented on the first point; Brennan, Douglas and Marshall dissented on the second. Stewart wrote the opinion, since he, Powell and Harry A. Blackmun were the only justices agreeing with both holdings.

Stewart's talent for picking a path between two extremes was apparent again in the late 1970s as the Court wrestled with the issues of affirmative action and reverse discrimination.

In 1978 he was one of five justices declaring it illegal for medical school admissions officers to set aside a quota of slots in an entering class for minority students. But the very next year he was one of five justices voting to allow private employers voluntarily to adopt race-conscious affirmative action programs.

Stewart joined the Court's landmark abortion ruling in 1973, but seven years later he spoke for the five-man majority that upheld the power of Congress to forbid public funding of abortions.

The Change to O'Connor

Moving beyond O'Connor's consistent conservatism versus Stewart's middleman role on the Court, an outline can be traced of the differences between the two on particular issues. This outline must be sketchy because of the relative brevity of O'Connor's record at this point and because history teaches that a justice's first years on the Court are not always indicative of what will follow.

Justice Blackmun, who compiled such a conservative voting record in his first several terms that he was described as the Chief Justice's Minnesota Twin, had, by the time he marked his 10th anniversary on the Court, moved into alliance with its more liberal members.

It is also important to remember that O'Connor was not addressing the same cases, nor the same questions, as Stewart. Many of the issues upon which Stewart was a decisive vote have not returned to the Court and may never recur.

However, with such a caveat in mind, some comparisons can be made between Justices Stewart and O'Connor.

Criminal Law

O'Connor and Stewart are probably most similar in their views on questions of criminal law. Stewart dissented when the Court extended the controversial exclusionary rule to bar admission of illegally obtained evidence in state trials. O'Connor was part of the majority voting to adopt the "good faith" or "reasonable mistake" exception to that rule in 1984.

Stewart dissented from *Miranda* in 1966. Nineteen years later O'Connor spoke for a majority that held that an initial failure of police to advise a suspect of his rights and the suspect's unwarned admission of guilt do not so taint any subsequent confesssion given after Miranda warnings to prevent its use in court.

On the question of capital punishment, Stewart and O'Connor disagree. Since coming to the Court, O'Connor has participated in a dozen cases in which a death sentence has been challenged as unconstitutional. She voted to invalidate such a sentence in only two cases. It appears certain that had O'Connor been sitting on the Court in 1972, she would not have voted as Stewart did to strike down existing death penalty laws but would have voted with Burger, Blackmun, Powell and Rehnquist to uphold them.

Individual Rights

O'Connor and Stewart express quite different views on two key questions of individual rights — abortion and affirmative action. The depth of that difference was expected to be tested during the October 1985 term when the Court heard major cases on both issues.

O'Connor, after firmly resisting all pressure to elaborate her judicial views on abortion during her confirmation, wrote an articulate dissenting opinion in the summer of 1983 when the Court reaffirmed *Roe v. Wade*.

Although she stopped short of urging the Court to overrule that decision, O'Connor placed the majority on notice that the logical structure underlying that ruling was seriously flawed and must be rebuilt if the ruling was to stand. O'Connor's decision made clear that had she been a member of the Court in 1973 she would not have joined the majority in *Roe v. Wade.* Stewart was part of that majority.

The two abortion cases argued during the October 1985 term gave the *Roe* majority the opportunity to restructure the constitutional underpinnings of *Roe v. Wade.* At the same time they provided the dissenting justices with the chance to win two more votes to overturn that ruling.

During the 1970s Stewart voted against mandatory quotas but for voluntary affirmative action programs. O'Connor's only vote on affirmative action came in 1984 when she joined the Court majority that found a federal judge had exceeded his authority when he ordered a city to disregard its usual seniority-based procedure for lay-offs in order to preserve the jobs of blacks recently hired under a court-ordered affirmative action plan.

The case of *Wygant v. Jackson Board of Education,* involving a voluntarily adopted school board plan to lay off more senior white teachers to preserve the jobs of recently hired black teachers, argued during the October 1985 term, was expected to reveal more fully O'Connor's views on that issue.

First Amendment

With the single exception of school prayer, Stewart compiled a liberal record on First Amendment issues, generally supporting the individual right of free speech, the right of a free press, and the Court's rulings maintaining a wall of separation between church and state.

When the Burger Court moved in the early 1970s to permit more restrictions on offensive material by revising its definition of obscenity, Stewart dissented along with

Sandra Day O'Connor

Brennan, Marshall and Douglas. He also dissented in 1976, when the Court, 5-4, held that a city could use its zoning powers to prevent the concentration of "adult" movie theaters and bookstores in one neighborhood.

O'Connor takes a far more conservative stance on First Amendment questions. She espouses the current Court's emphasis on accommodation, rather than separation, of church and state, forming part of the narrow majorities that have upheld state income tax deductions for tuition payments to parochial schools, the practice of opening legislative sessions with a prayer by a state-employed chaplain, and the inclusion of a crèche in a city's holiday display.

On the central issue of school prayer, however, O'Connor seems willing to adhere to the Warren Court's 1962 decision forbidding state-sponsored school prayer. In June 1985 she joined the Court majority striking down Alabama's law that permitted a "moment of silence" for voluntary silent prayer or meditation in public school classrooms each day. She indicated, however, that state laws providing for a neutral moment of silence — during which prayer was not clearly indicated as the approved activity — would be permissible in her view.

O'Connor generally has supported the press in its First Amendment claims — with the important exception of libel. In 1984 she dissented when the Court, 6-3, reaffirmed the "actual malice" standard erected by the Warren Court in *New York Times v. Sullivan* to protect the press against libel damage suits by public officials. But the same term, she joined the Court's liberals to strike down, 5-4, a congressional ban on editorializing by publicly funded radio and television stations.

As her rulings on questions of church and state demonstrate, O'Connor is reluctant to apply the First Amendment to constrain government action. She dissented in 1982 when the Court applied the First Amendment to censorship cases involving public school libraries.

She voted to permit Los Angeles to curtail the posting of signs on public property, to permit the Reagan administration to ban overnight sleeping in Lafayette Park and to permit government employers to limit the First Amendment rights of their employees.

During the October 1985 term the Court was expected to consider whether or not a city can use its zoning power to confine all "adult" bookstores and movie theatres to one particular area in the city. In 1976 Stewart dissented when the Court approved such restrictions in a similar case. O'Connor's vote in the case of *Renton v. Playtime Theaters* will further illuminate her views on this aspect of First Amendment freedoms.

A Fresh Approach

O'Connor brought a fresh approach and abundant energy to a Court that had little of either. Age and the inevitable repe-

tition of issues over 10 or more Supreme Court terms had taken its toll on the enthusiasm and vigor that the sitting justices brought to their task. On a number of issues, some of the justices preferred simply to cite their previous opinions rather than once again rehash their views.

The classic example is the way Justices Brennan and Marshall express themselves on capital punishment. In 1972 when the Court struck down existing death penalty laws as unconstitutional, Brennan and Marshall declared that in their view death was always an unconstitutional punishment. In 1976, over Brennan's and Marshall's dissenting votes, the Court approved some of the newly drafted state death penalty laws. Since then, death sentences meted out under these new laws have been challenged again and again before the Court. The two justices dissent every time the Court upholds a death sentence — often simply citing their 1972 opinions.

Even when a justice does restate his views on an issue, he rarely exhibits the passion — or plumbs the depths of an issue — as he did in his first opinions on the subject.

Clarity

As a state judge responsible for applying Supreme Court rulings in her courtroom, O'Connor became aware of the difficulty that an ambiguous or confusing opinion created for lower court judges, and she does not hesitate to express dissatisfaction with the quality of a majority opinion.

Gifted with the ability to analyze clearly and focus precisely on the point at issue, she often adds concurring opinions when she feels that the majority does not properly explain its reasoning — or does not adopt the proper reasoning.

In her first term O'Connor politely rebuked Chief Justice Burger for writing an opinion which, she said, contributed to "an uncertain jurisprudence." Her own concurring opinion, she explained, reached "the same destination as the Court, but along a course that more precisely identifies the evils of the challenged statute."

A year later O'Connor refused to join a dissenting opinion written by Rehnquist and joined in by Burger and Powell, although she shared their views. Sounding rather like a schoolmarm, O'Connor criticized both the majority opinion and that written by Rehnquist:

"Both opinions engage in exhaustive, but ultimately unilluminating, exegesis of the common law of the availability of punitive damages in 1871. Although both the Court and Justice Rehnquist display admirable skills in legal research and analysis of great numbers of musty cases, the results do not significantly further the goal of the inquiry: to establish the intent of the 42nd Congress.... The battle of the string citations can have no winner."

O'Connor rejects superficial or automatic responses to legal questions. In 1983 she wrote the Court's opinion analyzing what the Constitution required a judge to do in the case of an indigent probationer facing prison for failure to pay a fine that was a condition of his probation.

"Whether analyzed in terms of equal protection or due process, the issue cannot be resolved by resort to easy slogans or pigeonhole analysis, but rather requires a careful inquiry," O'Connor wrote. "A defendant's poverty in no way immunizes him from punishment." But on the other hand, the Court had held that when a crime is punishable by a fine only, a court cannot send a defendant to jail just because he is too poor to pay the fine.

It is of critical importance, O'Connor wrote, that the judge look to the reasons for non-payment. "If the probationer has willfully refused to pay the fine or restitution when he has the means to pay, the State is perfectly justified in using imprisonment as a sanction to enforce collection."

"But if the probationer has made all reasonable efforts to pay the fine ... and yet cannot do so through no fault of his own, it is fundamentally unfair to revoke probation automatically without considering whether adequate alternative methods of punishing the defendant are available," she concluded.

Accustomed to addressing citizens more often than lawyers, O'Connor often summarizes the meaning of a decision in succinct and ordinary language. Two of her first opinions for the Court clarified the rules that prisoners must follow in seeking release from custody — not through a direct challenge to their conviction but through a petition for a federal *writ of habeas corpus.* When a judge issues a *writ of habeas corpus,* he or she is ordering state officials to justify their detention of a particular person. In effect, the issuance of a writ usually requires the state to release that person.

The subject can quickly become murky — as "exhaustion requirements" and "waivers" and "timely objections" are discussed. After some of that discussion, O'Connor cut to the heart of the Court's ruling. State prisoners hoping to win release through such a writ must simply remember that "before you take any claims to federal court, be sure you have first taken each one to state court."

Energy

The most emphatic early demonstration of O'Connor's energy and incisive analytical approach is her 1983 abortion dissent. The Court, 6-3, struck down an Akron, Ohio, ordinance imposing a variety of requirements and restrictions upon women seeking and doctors performing abortions in that city.

The Court majority reaffirmed its commitment to the 1973 decision, *Roe v. Wade,* in which it had first extended constitutional protection to a woman's right of privacy in making a decision about an abortion.

The vote in *Roe* was 7-2. Dissenting then and 10 years later were Rehnquist and White, who had disagreed with all intervening decisions in which the Court had upheld a woman's freedom in this area. But in 1983 O'Connor joined them, spoke for them and for the first time pointed out a basic logical flaw in *Roe*. Scientific advances, she noted, had put the rationale underlying *Roe* "on a collision course with itself."

Simply stated, *Roe* held that a state could ban abortions only after the point in pregnancy at which a fetus was "viable" — that is, it could survive outside the mother's body. In 1973 that point was considered to be no earlier than 24 weeks, six months, into a pregnancy. Thus, *Roe* held that a state could ban only third-trimester abortions.

But in the intervening decade, advances in medical science and technology had enabled doctors to keep alive, at least for hours or days, children born even earlier in pregnancy. Such advances raised the distinct possibility that the point at which a state could ban abortion would also move back earlier and earlier in pregnancy, curtailing the freedom initially set out in *Roe*.

Neither White nor Rehnquist had pointed out this development, despite ample opportunity in their dissenting opinions on abortion in 1976 and 1979. But O'Connor, who obviously had studied *Roe v. Wade* closely, made this point in 1983, challenging the Court majority to rebuild the logical underpinnings of this landmark — or watch it transformed into an anachronism by advances in medical science.

The New Conservative Alliance

The Supreme Court in 1981 was divided into three parts. On one side stood the liberals, Brennan, Marshall and Stevens, and on the other side, the conservatives, Burger, Powell and Rehnquist. In the middle were White, Stewart and Blackmun.

White often joined the conservatives, Blackmun the liberals, leaving Stewart the deciding vote.

O'Connor's arrival to succeed Stewart changed all that. From the first, she allied herself consistently with the two justices she already knew: Rehnquist, her law school colleague, and Burger — and with Powell.

The 3-3-3 division suddenly became a 3-2-4 split and the conservatives found it much easier to prevail in close votes. With four certain votes, they only had to convince one of the remaining swing men, White or Blackmun, to join them. The liberals, on the other hand, had to win both swing votes to prevail.

O'Connor's alliances within the Court can be traced through voting statistics compiled each year by the *Harvard Law Review*. These statistics highlight further the contrast between Stewart's moderate stance within the Court and O'Connor's conservative posture.

—Stewart never voted with any other justice as consistently as O'Connor voted with Burger and Rehnquist during her first three terms.

—For the period from 1973-1977, Stewart voted most frequently with Powell (75 percent of the time) and least often with Douglas (42.9 percent).

—In his last three terms, 1978-1980, that range narrowed further. Stewart still voted most often with Powell (72.3 percent), but he agreed in 50.4 percent of all decisions with Marshall, the justice with whom he voted the least consistently.

—In her first three terms, O'Connor voted most often with Rehnquist (83.6 percent) and least often with Marshall (43.6 percent). This 40-point gap is almost twice the 22 points that separated Stewart's most frequent ally, Powell, from his least frequent voting companion, Marshall.

The year-by-year figures show how O'Connor's alliance with Rehnquist, Burger and Powell tightened over her first three terms on the Court.

In her first term, O'Connor voted with Rehnquist 81.7 percent of the time; two years later, she and Rehnquist agreed in 91.9 percent of the decisions issued during the October 1983 term. O'Connor voted with Burger in 77.2 percent of the cases decided in the October 1981 term. They agreed in 91.9 percent of the decisions issued in the October 1983 term. O'Connor voted with Powell in 72 percent of the cases decided in the October 1981 term (right where Stewart left off!). The Powell-O'Connor agreement rate had risen to 84.9 percent by the October 1983 term.

The crucial shift of White and Blackmun toward the conservative side of many issues in the October 1983 term is reflected in these same figures. White's agreement rate with O'Connor jumped 15 points between the 1982 and 1983 terms, to 84.5 percent.

White and O'Connor agreed almost as often in that term as O'Connor and Powell, one of her original allies. Blackmun moved away from his liberal allies of the late 1970s to agree with O'Connor in the 1983 term in three out of four cases, 75.2 percent of the time.

This was a dramatic increase of 17 points over the 1982 term. O'Connor and Blackmun agreed almost as often in her third term as she and Burger had agreed in her first.

To place these figures in perspective, O'Connor agreed least often with the most liberal justices — with Brennan 56.6 percent of the time in 1983 and with Marshall, 51.3 percent of the time.

Who Wins the Close Ones?

The increasing power of the conservative alliance was also reflected in a sharp increase in the number of times it won when the Court divided closely on a case. About 30 cases were decided by 5-4 votes in each of O'Connor's first three terms.

October 1981 Term. In O'Connor's first term the liberals won decisively, prevailing in 17 of the close decisions, while the conservatives won 12. O'Connor was on the winning side in 13, less than half of these cases. She joined the conservatives, Burger, Rehnquist, Powell and White or Stevens, in the majority 11 times on 5-4 votes. She joined the liberals — Brennan, Marshall, Blackmun and often Stevens — twice in the majority.

Among the 5-4 splits in which O'Connor joined the majority were those in which the Court:

—Declared presidents immune from civil damage suits for official actions during their term in the White House (*Nixon v. Fitzgerald*);

—Dismissed a First Amendment challenge by a citizens' group to the transfer of surplus government property to church-related schools, reasoning that the group was unable to demonstrate that it had suffered any injury as a result of this transfer and thus had no standing to challenge it in federal court (*Valley Forge Christian College v. Americans United for Separation of Church and State*);

—Required workers challenging a seniority system as discriminatory to prove both that it was designed to discriminate and that it had that effect (*American Tobacco Co. v. Patterson*);

—Emphasized to sentencing judges that they must consider all possible mitigating circumstances when deciding whether or not to impose a sentence of death (*Eddings v. Oklahoma*);

—Declared it unconstitutional for a state university to exclude men from a nursing program just because of their sex (*Mississippi University for Women v. Hogan*).

During her first term O'Connor disagreed when the Court, 5-4:

—Denied prosecutors the use of a confession from a suspect who had been illegally arrested (*Taylor v. Alabama*);

—Held it unconstitutional to impose a death sentence on a man who drove the getaway car used by killers, but who did not himself kill anyone (*Enmund v. Florida*);

—Invalidated a state law prohibiting busing as a means of desegregating public schools (*Washington v. Seattle School District No. 1*);

—Ruled that a state may not deny illegal alien children a free public education (*Plyler v. Doe*);

—Applied the First Amendment to a school board's decision to remove certain books from public school libraries (*Board of Education, Island Trees Union Free School District #26 v. Pico*).

October 1982 Term. The conservative victories of the 1983 term were foreshadowed the previous year by a decisive shift from liberal to conservative predominance in the Court's 5-4 decisions. In the October 1982 term there were 33 votes of 5 to 4; the conservatives prevailed in 21, twice as many as the liberals.

O'Connor voted with the conservatives on all but two of their 21 victories. She joined the liberals in two of their 10 victories. She was in the majority as the Court:

—Upheld a state law permitting parents to take a state income tax deduction for tuition, textbook and transportation expenses for their children attending elementary or secondary schools (*Mueller v. Allen*);

—Refused to use the First Amendment to protect public employees from dismissal because of their loud complaints about working conditions (*Connick v. Myers*);

—Voided a court order banning the use of certain choke holds by Los Angeles police (*City of Los Angeles v. Lyons*);

—Upheld a state law directing judges in capital sentencing proceedings to tell juries that a life sentence without possibility of parole could be commuted to a sentence

permitting parole (*California v. Ramos*);

—Found it permissible to confine in a mental institution a person who had been found not guilty by reason of insanity for a longer period than he would have been incarcerated, had he been found guilty (*Jones v. United States*);

—Upheld Wyoming's law that every county have at least one representative in the state government's lower chamber — even though the law resulted in an 89 percent population variance between the most populous and least populous districts (*Brown v. Thomson*);

—Struck down New Jersey's congressional redistricting plan, because the variation (less than 1 percent) between the most populous and the least populous districts was not justified by the state (*Karcher v. Daggett*);

—Held it illegal for employers to offer retirement plans under which women workers receive smaller monthly payments than men just because women, as a group, live longer (*Arizona Governing Committee for Tax Deferred Annuity and Deferred Compensation Plans v. Norris*).

Although she disagreed less often with the Court's 5-4 decisions, O'Connor dissented when the Court:

—Held that police must have more reason to arrest someone than simply the fact that his or her characteristics match a certain "profile" of characteristics (*Florida v. Royer*);

—Held it unconstitutional for a state to sentence a man to life in prison without the possibility of parole after he has been convicted seven separate times of non-violent crimes (*Solem v. Helm*);

—Cleared the way for a prison inmate beaten and raped by his cellmates to sue and recover punitive damages from the guard on duty at the time of the assault (*Smith v. Wade*);

—Upheld as not infringing too far into

state affairs the federal law forbidding states to force certain employees to retire at age 55 (*EEOC v. Wyoming*).

October 1983 Term. The conservatives remained dominant in close cases in the October 1983 term, winning 16 of the 5-4 votes, while the liberals won only 8.

Only once did the conservatives win without O'Connor's vote. When the Court carved out a "public safety exception" to the *Miranda* requirement that a suspect in custody be warned of his rights before he is questioned, O'Connor dissented (*New York v. Quarles*). She complained that the Court should have adhered to *Miranda* more strictly and barred the use by a prosecutor of the suspect's unwarned answer to a policeman's question about the whereabouts of his gun.

"Were the Court writing from a clean slate, I could agree," she said. "But *Miranda* is now the law . . . and the Court has not provided sufficient justification for . . . blurring its now clear strictures." O'Connor agreed with the majority, however, that the gun itself, located as a result of the suspect's reply, could be used as evidence.

During this term O'Connor joined the liberals in the majority only once on a 5-4 split. That liberal leap came when the Court held unconstitutional the act of Congress forbidding public broadcasting stations that accepted federal funds to editorialize (*FCC v. LWV*).

O'Connor was part of the majority when the Court by the margin of a single vote:

—Upheld the Reagan administration's tightened curbs on travel to Cuba (*Regan v. Wald*);

—Permitted the inclusion of a crèche in a city's holiday display (*Lynch v. Donnelly*);

—Sanctioned the unilateral rejection of a collective bargaining agreement by a failing company filing for bankruptcy (*NLRB v. Bildisco & Bildisco*);

—Permitted states to use punitive damage awards to penalize companies that violated federal nuclear safety regulations (*Silkwood v. Kerr-McGee Corp.*);

—Denied states a veto over federal offshore lease sales (*Secretary of the Interior v. California*);

—Held that federal judges could not set deadlines for the government to meet in dealing with contested Social Security claims (*Heckler v. Day*);

—Held that the Constitution denies federal judges the power to order state officials to comply with state law when that order is sought by the state's own citizens charging state officials with failing to carry out the state's law (*Pennhurst State School and Hospital v. Haldeman*).

But O'Connor was not always on the winning side. She dissented when the Court:

—Required a warrant before law enforcement officers could enter and search a burned residence after the fire was out (*Michigan v. Clifford*);

—Declared that federal labor law protected a worker from being fired for refusing to drive a vehicle he believed to be unsafe (*National Labor Relations Board v. City Disposal Systems Inc.*);

—Held that judges could be ordered to stop infringing on the civil rights of individuals and to pay the attorneys' fees of individuals who successfully sue them for such unconstitutional actions (*Pulliam v. Allen*).

October 1984 Term. Because Powell was absent from the Court following surgery in January 1985 and did not participate in more than 50 cases, there were fewer 5-4 votes during the October 1984 term. Only 19 cases were decided by this vote, although eight others were affirmed without opinion, 4-4.

The gap between liberals and conservatives closed a bit this term; conservatives won 11 of the 19 and liberals seven. O'Connor was in the majority in 10 of the 19, nine times with the conservatives and once with the liberals.

She was part of the conservative majority that ruled that:

—Congress could not constitutionally limit independent spending on behalf of a presidential candidate by a political action committee (*Federal Election Committee v. National Conservative Political Action Committee*);

—The National Labor Relations Board acted properly in denying unions the power to discipline members who resigned in the face of a strike to return to work (*Pattern Makers' League v. NLRB*);

—The First Amendment does not extend to cover libel suits that involve issues essentially of private, not public, interest (*Dun & Bradstreet v. Greenmoss Builders*);

—The Racketeer Influenced and Corrupt Organizations Act may be used by private individuals and companies to sue respected businesses, even in the absence of any showing of a "racketeering" injury (*Sedima S.P.R.L. v. Imrex Co. Inc.*);

—Congress, in banning discrimination against handicapped persons by federally funded programs, did not override the constitutional immunity of a state from being sued in federal court without its consent (*Atascadero State Hospital v. Scanlon*);

—The Environmental Protection Agency is within its authority when it grants individual plants exceptions from the law governing discharge of toxic wastes (*Chemical Manufacturers Association v. National Resources Defense Council*).

O'Connor's one-time participation in a liberal 5-4 majority came when the Court permitted the Oneida Indians to sue two New York counties for reimbursement for the use of land that the Indians contend was illegally taken from them by the state in 1795 (*County of Oneida, N.Y. v. Oneida Indian Nation*).

O'Connor's most vigorous dissenting votes in 5-4 cases came when the Court:

—Reversed its 1976 decision in *National League of Cities v. Usery* and held that the Constitution places no specific limits on the power of Congress to interfere in state affairs (*Garcia v. San Antonio Metropolitan Area Transit Authority*);

—Held unconstitutional programs of aid to non-public, primarily parochial schools, run by New York City and Grand Rapids, Mich. (*Aguilar v. Felton; School District of the City of Grand Rapids v. Ball*).

A New Conservative Voice

Every Supreme Court justice creates a judicial self-portrait by his or her votes and opinions. The votes provide the outline, the skeleton. The words, whether in majority opinions, in concurrences or in dissents, fill in the characteristic features, colors, shades and textures that infuse the justice's votes with life and meaning. O'Connor's votes have made a difference in the Court's work; her words are likely to prove of equal or even greater significance.

Junior justices rarely speak for the Court on major cases. By and large, the senior justices reserve for themselves such opportunities. O'Connor has written her share of majority opinions, and they are of interest for the themes they sound and the agreement they reflect.

But it is in dissenting opinions that O'Connor speaks her mind most clearly, free of any need to tailor her language to win votes. These dissents could shape the judicial landscape of the future. O'Connor is the youngest justice and is expected to serve well into the next century.

And if President Reagan has the opportunity to fill more seats on the Court, he has made plain that he would like to find some additional justices just like O'Connor, who has to a surprising degree been just the sort of different justice Reagan wanted.

Recurring Themes

Two themes are predominant in O'Connor's opinions: the importance of recognizing the states as full partners with the national government within the federal system and the belief that judges and courts have a limited function in a democracy.

Federalism. Federalism, the balance of power between the national government and the states, is reflected in and affected by almost every Supreme Court decision. When the Court orders state officials to act, or directs a federal judge to free a state prisoner or strikes down a city ordinance or invalidates a redistricting plan, state prerogatives suffer. When the Court permits states to halt nuclear power plant construction, or to experiment with new ways of taxing interstate business, or to accommodate rather than separate religion and politics, federal concerns are implicated.

As the first justice since Brennan in the 1950s to come to the Court from state government, O'Connor is an outspoken advocate for the states. Her belief in the importance of strong and independent state governments and her hope of curtailing federal encroachment on the state's domain pervade her judicial writings. Time and again, she argues that state judges and legislators and other officials govern well without being told what to do by Congress, the national bureaucracy or federal judges, Supreme Court justices included.

One way to measure a justice's philosophy is to note who is given the benefit of the doubt on close questions. O'Connor gives state officials the benefit of the doubt. She has faith in the political decisions of state officials and in the judicial decisions of state trial judges and consistently urges the Court to defer to them.

Judicial Restraint. Closely related to her belief in federalism is O'Connor's view of the limited role of federal courts in the American system. In a democracy, O'Connor believes, priority should be given to the decisions of officials and representatives who have been directly elected by the voters and who therefore are more in touch with public opinion than judges.

Judges, particularly federal judges, have only a limited — reactionary, not innovative — role to play, keeping the political branches within constitutional limits, but exercising little initiative.

She agrees with Chief Justice Burger and several times has quoted his declaration that "the Constitution does not constitute us as 'Platonic Guardians' nor does it vest in this Court the authority to strike down laws because they do not meet our standards of desirable social policy, 'wisdom,' or 'common sense.'"

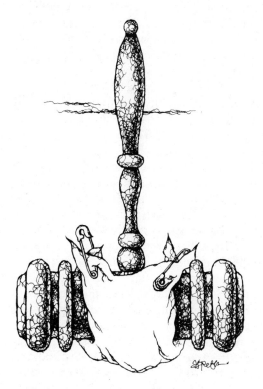

State Powers

The intensity of O'Connor's concern about state prerogatives can be measured by her persistent efforts to resuscitate the 10th Amendment, the last provision of the Bill of Rights which declares: "The powers not delegated to the United States by the Constitution, nor prohibited by it to the States, are reserved to the States respectively, or to the people."

Until the mid-1930s, states wielded this amendment with considerable effect to curtail federal power, particularly over the economy in areas ranging from child labor to farm production. The "Court-packing" fight of the 1930s was in large measure brought on by the Court's vigorous use of this amendment to strike down portions of Roosevelt's New Deal program.

After the turnabout on such questions in 1937, the Court discarded this amendment as a limit on federal power, acknowledging that changing economic and political conditions required the national government to take over functions and to exercise powers that were once considered the exclusive prerogative of the states.

In 1941 Justice Harlan Fiske Stone wrote that the 10th Amendment "states but a truism that all is retained which has not been surrendered. There is nothing in the history of its adoption to suggest that it was more than declaratory of the relationship between national and state governments as it had been established by the Constitution." For 35 years this provision of the Constitution was virtually a dead letter.

Then in 1976 the Court, 5-4, used the 10th Amendment to deny Congress the power to require state and local governments to pay the federal minimum wage and overtime compensation to their employees. This, wrote Rehnquist in *National League of Cities v. Usery,* reached too far into the internal affairs of states and violated the 10th Amendment. Joining Rehnquist in the majority were Burger, Blackmun, Powell and Stewart.

The states made valiant efforts to convince the Court to expand on this 10th Amendment pronouncement, but with no success. In 1985 the Court — Blackmun having changed sides — overruled *National League of Cities,* 5-4.

This self-reversal had been foreshadowed by several earlier rulings. In 1982 the Court, 5-4, upheld against 10th Amendment challenge two titles of the Public Utility Regulatory Policies Act of 1978, which directed state utility regulatory commissions to consider certain standards and factors in making rate decisions.

O'Connor dissented from the Court's decision in *Federal Energy Regulatory Commission v. Mississippi.* The challenged titles, she wrote, "conscript state utility commissions into the national bureaucratic army. This result is contrary to the principles of *National League of Cities v. Usery* . . . antithetical to the values of federalism, and inconsistent with our constitutional history. . . . The Court's conclusion . . . rests upon a fundamental misunderstanding of the role that state governments play in our federalist system.

"State legislative and administrative bodies are not field offices of the national bureaucracy. Nor are they think tanks to which Congress may assign problems for extended study. Instead, each state is sovereign within its own domain, governing its citizens and providing for their general welfare. While the Constitution and federal statutes define the boundaries of that domain, they do not harness state power for national purposes."

Furthermore, wrote O'Connor, the federal system was devised to prevent the evil of an all-powerful central government. Power was allocated between state and national authority and national power was allocated among the three branches of government.

"Unless we zealously protect these distinctions, we risk upsetting the balance of power that buttresses our basic liberties," she continued. "In analyzing this brake on governmental power, Justice Harlan noted that '[t]he diffusion of power between federal and state authority . . . takes on added significance as the size of the federal bureaucracy continues to grow.' Today, the Court disregards this warning and permits Congress to kidnap state utility commissions into the national regulatory family."

In 1983 the Court, 5-4, refused to use the 10th Amendment to shield states from the federal law against mandatory retirement. O'Connor again dissented.

When in 1985 the Court overruled *National League of Cities,* O'Connor's dissent in *Garcia v. San Antonio Metropolitan Transit Authority* was vehement. "The Court today surveys the battle scene of federalism and sounds a retreat," she wrote. "Like Justice Powell, I would prefer to hold the field and, at the very least, render a little aid to the wounded.

"The central issue of federalism is whether any realm *is* left open to the States by the Constitution — whether any area remains in which a State may act free of federal interference.

"Just as surely as the Framers of our Constitution envisioned a National Government capable of solving national problems, they also envisioned a republic whose vitality was assured by the diffusion of power not only among the branches of the Federal Government, but also between the Federal Government and the States," O'Connor wrote.

With O'Connor's vote, states have won some important victories, among them the power to halt nuclear power plant construction within the state, pending development of an adequate national plan for disposing of nuclear waste and the power to penalize manufacturers of nuclear materials who violate federal safety rules.

In 1984 the Court upheld Hawaii's land reform law under which the government used its power of eminent domain to take land from a few large landowners and transfer it to many smaller landowners. A federal court of appeals had held the law unconstitutional. It found that Hawaii was using government power to benefit some private individuals at the expense of other individuals. Government power should be used for public benefit, not for the benefit of certain private persons, it reasoned.

With O'Connor as its spokesman, the Supreme Court reversed the appeals court and upheld the law. In *Hawaii Housing Authority v. Midkiff* the Court gave states wide leeway to use the power of eminent domain for the public's benefit. "There is . . . a role for courts to play in reviewing a legislature's judgment of what constitutes a public use," wrote O'Connor, but that role is a narrow one.

"The people of Hawaii have attempted, much as the settlers of the original 13 colonies did, to reduce the perceived social and economic evils of a land oligopoly traceable to their monarchs," O'Connor continued. "Regulating oligopoly and the evils associated within it is a classic exercise of a state's police powers.

"Judicial deference is required because, in our system of government, legislatures are better able to assess what public purposes should be advanced by an exercise of the taking power. State legislatures are as capable as Congress of making such determinations within their respective spheres of authority. . . . Thus if a legislature, state or federal, determines there are substantial reasons for an exercise of the taking power, courts must defer to its determination that the taking will serve a public use," she concluded.

State Courts

The revolution in police procedures set off by the Supreme Court in the 1960s made federal judges the "supervisors" of state trials. As a state judge, O'Connor wrote that state trial judges were sensitive to the fact that federal judges reviewed and reversed so many of their rulings in criminal cases, finding that they had insufficiently protected the defendant's rights.

"The states possess primary authority for defining and enforcing the criminal law," O'Connor wrote in her first term. "In criminal trials they also hold the initial responsibility for vindicating constitutional rights. Federal intrusions into state criminal trials frustrate both the states' sovereign power to punish offenders and their good faith attempts to honor constitutional rights."

Soon after O'Connor's debut, the Court held that state prisoners may not ask a federal judge to order their release until they have presented all their complaints about their state trial to state judges. O'Connor spoke for the Court in *Rose v. Lundy,* putting state prisoners and federal judges on notice that all claims raised by a state prisoner in a petition for a writ of habeas corpus must first be presented to the state courts. If they have not been, she wrote, the federal judge must dismiss the petition.

This "total exhaustion" rule "will encourage state prisoners to seek full relief first from the state courts, thus giving those courts the first opportunity to review all claims of constitutional error," O'Connor wrote.

A month later O'Connor again wrote for the Court as it held that a state defendant who fails to object to some aspect of his trial at the time of the trial, as state law requires, can later use that objection as a basis for a petition for habeas corpus only if he can show good reason for failing to make the objection at trial and actual prejudice to his case as a result of the constitutional flaw that he now points out.

The writ of habeas corpus "imposes special costs on our federal system," wrote O'Connor in *Engle v. Isaac.* "These costs are particularly high" when a defendant's failure to object to a constitutional violation — at his trial — denies the trial court the opportunity to correct the problem.

"The defendant's counsel, for whatever reasons, has detracted from the trial's significance by neglecting to raise a claim in that forum. The state appellate courts have not had a chance to mend their own fences and avoid federal intrusion."

While O'Connor urges federal judges to defer more often to the decisions of state and local judges, she holds the latter to high standards. In May 1983 she spoke for the Court as it ruled it fundamentally unfair for a state court automatically to revoke a man's probation simply because he had not paid the fine that was a condition of his probation.

O'Connor directed the state judge to focus on the reasons behind the probationer's failure to pay his fine. "Whether analyzed in terms of equal protection or due process, the issue cannot be resolved by resort to easy slogans or pigeonhole analysis, she said."

"The State, of course, has a fundamental interest in appropriately punishing persons — rich and poor — who violate its criminal laws," O'Connor continued. "A defendant's poverty in no way immunizes him from punishment."

"We hold, therefore, that in revocation proceedings for failure to pay a fine or restitution, a sentencing court must inquire into the reasons for the failure to pay. If the probationer willfully refused to pay or failed to make sufficient bona fide efforts legally to acquire the resources to pay, the court may revoke probation and sentence the defendant to imprisonment.... If the probationer could not pay despite sufficient bona fide efforts to acquire the resources to do so, the court must consider alternate measures of punishment other than imprisonment."

The Suspect's Rights

While adhering to the criminal law landmarks of the Warren era, O'Connor is inclined to give police and prosecutors the benefit of the doubt on close questions. Toward the end of her first term, in June 1982, the Court told Alabama courts that they must suppress the confession of Omar Taylor to a grocery store robbery, because Taylor was illegally arrested by police who had neither warrant nor probable cause for his arrest.

O'Connor, joined by Burger, Powell and Rehnquist, dissented, arguing that the events intervening between the arrest and the confession furnished a sufficient "break" in any connection between the arrest and confession that the confession could be used as evidence. "The petitioner [Taylor] was warned of his rights to remain silent and to have a lawyer present," she wrote, "and there is no dispute that he understood those rights or that he waived them voluntarily and without coercion. After receiving three sets of such warnings, he met with his girlfriend and neighbor, at his request. Following that meeting, at which no police officers were present, the petitioner decided to confess to his participation in the robbery. The petitioner's confession was not proximately caused by his illegal arrest, but was the product of a decision based both on the knowledge of his constitutional rights and on the discussion with his friends."

O'Connor reads certain provisions of the Bill of Rights literally, an approach that generally produces a narrow interpretation of the guarantee at issue. When a man charged with drunk driving in South Dakota came to the Supreme Court in 1982 arguing that it was unconstitutional for the prosecutor to tell the court that he had refused to take a blood-alcohol test, O'Connor quickly disposed of that argument.

The Fifth Amendment, the provision upon which the driver based his claim, provides that no person "shall be compelled in any criminal case to be a witness against himself," O'Connor pointed out. The Court had repeatedly held that this limited physical or moral compulsion on a suspect or defendant. Here, there was no compulsion, O'Connor explained. The driver was given the choice of taking the test or refusing and having the refusal used against him.

"We recognize . . . that the choice to submit or refuse to take a blood-alcohol test will not be an easy or pleasant one for a suspect to make. But the criminal process often requires suspects and defendants to make difficult choices. . . . We hold . . . that a refusal to take a blood-alcohol test, after a police officer has lawfully requested it, is not an act coerced by the officer, and thus is not protected by the privilege against self-incrimination." (*South Dakota v. Neville.*)

In general, she reads this Fifth Amendment guarantee narrowly, declaring in a concurring opinion early in 1984 "the Fifth Amendment provides absolutely no protection for the contents of private papers of any kind." In a subsequent opinion, she elaborated, "Only the introduction of a defendant's own *testimony* is proscribed by the Fifth Amendment's mandate that no person 'shall be compelled in any criminal case to be a witness against himself.'. . . That mandate does not protect an accused from being compelled to surrender *nontestimonial* evidence against himself."

O'Connor dissented in 1984 when the Court created a "public safety exception" permitting the use of a suspect's reply when he was asked by police "Where's your gun?" before being warned of his rights.

But she wrote the opinion in 1985 when the Court held that the initial failure of police to warn a suspect of his constitutional rights, as the Court's ruling in *Miranda* requires, did not so taint all subsequent confessions by that suspect — given after he was warned of his rights — to bar their use as evidence.

Again, O'Connor emphasized that *Miranda* was intended to protect the suspect against being coerced — physically or psychologically — into confessing. "There is a vast difference between the direct consequences flowing from coercion of a confession by physical violence or other deliberate means calculated to break the suspect's will and the uncertain consequences of disclosure of a 'guilty secret' freely given in response to an unwarned but noncoercive question, as in this case," she wrote.

O'Connor also has displayed a sensitivity to the problems that can arise if police are given too much leeway in dealing with individual citizens. In May 1983 the Court struck down a California law that required people who seemed to be loitering or wandering the streets to provide "credible and reliable" identification to any policeman who asks to see it. O'Connor wrote the Court's opinion in *Kolender v. Lawson,* explaining that the law was so vague that it gave police too much discretion in deciding whether or not the person questioned provided sufficiently authentic evidence of his identity.

A month later, O'Connor demonstrated her skill in satisfying opposing interests, as she wrote that federal drug agents had acted unconstitutionally in seizing a man's luggage at New York's La Guardia Airport and holding it for 90 minutes until a specially trained dog could "sniff" the luggage to detect whether it contained narcotics. A brief detention of the luggage might be reasonable, O'Connor wrote, but this was not brief.

Even while ruling for the defendant in *United States v. Place,* O'Connor handed the government a victory as she stated that the Court did not consider such a "sniff test" a search. With that statement, the Court cleared the way for drug agents to routinely use such tests without first obtaining search warrants.

Searches and Arrests

Just as O'Connor gives state officials the benefit of the doubt when their decisions are challenged, so she tends to lend a sympathetic ear to police officers and prosecutors when on-the-spot decisions are attacked as unconstitutional. In July 1981 the Court ruled that police must obtain a search warrant before searching a closed container found in a car. The Court's decision in *Robbins v. California* was one of the last announced by Potter Stewart. Eleven months later, the dissenters in that case, joined by O'Connor and two concurring justices, reversed *Robbins,* giving police complete authority to search a car they have legitimately stopped just as thoroughly as if they had a warrant. They are free to search any container within the car.

Since then, O'Connor has sided with police in almost two dozen search and seizure cases decided by Court. In July 1984 the Court adopted the "good faith" exception, which permits use at trial of evidence taken by police who had a warrant and thought they were acted legally only to find out later that the warrant they obtained was defective.

In 1985 O'Connor argued the police officer's case forcefully in dissent when the Court held in *Tennessee v. Garner* that the constitutional guarantee against unreasonable seizures — in other words, arrests — contained in the Fourth Amendment, prohibited an officer from shooting to kill a suspect fleeing from the scene of a crime, unless the suspect threatened the officer with a weapon or the crime involved serious physical harm.

Joined by Rehnquist and Burger, O'Connor refused to join the Court in "creat[ing] a Fourth Amendment right allowing a burglary suspect to flee unimpeded from a police officer who has probable cause to arrest, who has ordered the suspect to halt, and who has no means short of firing his weapon to prevent escape."

"The clarity of hindsight cannot provide the standard for judging the reasonableness of police decisions made in uncertain and often dangerous circumstances," O'Connor continued. "I am far more reluctant than is the Court to conclude that the Fourth Amendment proscribes a police practice that was accepted at the time of the adoption of the Bill of Rights and has continued to receive the support of many state legislatures.

"Although the Court has recognized that the requirements of the Fourth Amendment must respond to the reality of social and technological change, fidelity to the notion of *constitutional* — as opposed to purely judicial — limits on governmental action requires us to impose a heavy burden on those who claim that practices accepted when the Fourth Amendment was adopted are now constitutionally impermissible," she wrote.

The majority's emphasis upon the suspect's interest in his own life fails to acknowledge "the distinctive manner in which the suspect's interest in his life is even exposed to risk," O'Connor continued. "Without questioning the importance of . . . [that] interest . . . I do not think this interest encompasses a right to flee unimpeded from the scene of a burglary."

O'Connor found the law under challenge to provide a proper accommodation of interests. "To avoid the use of deadly force and the consequent risk to his life, the suspect need merely obey the valid order to halt," she wrote.

"Whatever the constitutional limits on police use of deadly force in order to apprehend a fleeing felon, I do not believe they are exceeded in a case in which a police officer has probable cause to arrest a suspect at the scene of a residential burglary, orders the suspect to halt, and then fires his weapon as a last resort to prevent the suspect's escape into the night," O'Connor concluded.

Criminal Trials

O'Connor does not view the Constitution as guaranteeing perfect criminal trials. In *Engle v. Isaac* she wrote: "We have long recognized . . . that the Constitution guarantees criminal defendants only a fair trial and a competent attorney. It does not insure that defense counsel will recognize and raise every conceivable constitutional claim."

O'Connor wrote two opinions in 1984 concerning the right to the effective aid of counsel and showing how she balanced the factors involved in deciding whether or not a trial has been fair and legal representation appropriate. In *McKaskle v. Wiggins* the Court backed the action of a trial judge in appointing an attorney to assist a defendant who claimed his right to represent himself. Writing for the Court, O'Connor explained that the judge might have done this "to relieve the judge of the need to explain and enforce basic rules of courtroom protocol."

"We recognize that a . . . defendant may wish to dance a solo, not a *pas de deux*," O'Connor concluded. In this case the standby counsel did not deny the defendant the opportunity to make his own appearances as he saw fit and thus did not infringe upon his right to represent himself.

Several months later, O'Connor wrote the Court's opinion in *Strickland v. Washington,* setting out for the first time a standard for lower courts to use in reviewing a defendant's claim that he had been denied the effective aid of an attorney.

"The benchmark for judging any claim of ineffectiveness must be whether counsel's conduct so undermined the proper functioning of the adversarial process that the trial cannot be relied on as having produced a just result," she wrote.

To win reversal of a conviction or sentence, a defendant must show that his attorney's performance was seriously deficient and that the deficient representation deprived the defendant of a fair trial.

The proper standard is "reasonably effective assistance," she continued, and the lawyer deserves the benefit of the doubt. "Judicial scrutiny of counsel's performance must be highly deferential.... Because of the difficulties inherent in making the evaluation, a Court must indulge a strong presumption that counsel's conduct falls within the wide range of reasonable professional assistance."

O'Connor displays impatience with the seemingly endless round of litigation that can follow a criminal conviction. Writing in 1982, she held that federal prisoners, like state ones, can only bring a tardy constitutional objection to their trial if they can show reason for their belated challenge and actual prejudice as a result of the problem they cite.

"Once the defendant's chance to appeal has been waived or exhausted," she wrote in *United States v. Frady,* "we are entitled to presume he stands fairly and finally convicted, especially when . . . he already has had a fair opportunity to present his federal claims to a federal forum.

"Our trial and appellate procedures are not so unreliable that we may not afford their completed operation any binding effect beyond the next in a series of endless post-conviction collateral attacks. To the contrary, a final judgment commands respect," she concluded.

Capital Punishment

Although O'Connor has, with only two exceptions, voted to uphold death sentences reviewed by the Supreme Court, those exceptions bear examination — as does the general tenor of her opinions in support of such sentences.

Less than two months after O'Connor was sworn in, the Court on Nov. 2, 1981, heard the case of *Eddings v. Oklahoma,* in which Monty Lee Eddings challenged his death sentence, imposed upon him for the shotgun killing of an Oklahoma highway patrolman who stopped the auto Eddings was driving. Eddings, then 16, was with several younger companions, all of whom were running away from home.

Eddings was tried and convicted as an adult. At the sentencing hearing, the state presented evidence of the aggravating conditions that must be present for a death sentence to be imposed. The defense presented, as evidence of mitigating conditions, testimony concerning Eddings' troubled childhood, his broken and unhappy home, abuse by his father and his emotionally disturbed condition at the time of the crime.

The judge considered Eddings' youth at the time of the crime, but refused to consider the circumstances of his violent background or evidence of his emotional disturbance. He sentenced Eddings to death. After the state court affirmed that sentence, Eddings appealed to the Supreme Court, arguing that the Constitution required the judge to consider the mitigating factors in his background before imposing sentence.

The Supreme Court, 5-4, agreed with Eddings and reversed the state court's action. O'Connor was in the majority, with Powell, Brennan, Marshall and Stevens. In a concurring opinion, she explained her vote: "Because sentences of death are 'qualitatively different' from prison sentences . . . this Court has gone to extraordinary measures to ensure that the prisoner sentenced to be executed is afforded process that will guarantee as much as is humanly possible, that the sentence was not imposed out of whim, passion, prejudice or mistake."

In 1978 the Court, in *Lockett v. Ohio,* had declared that the Constitution required that a sentencing judge be permitted to consider, as a mitigating factor, "any aspect of a defendant's character or record and any of the circumstances of the offense that the defendant proffers as a basis for a sentence less than death." That ruling, O'Connor reasoned, required resentencing in Eddings' case "because the trial court's failure to consider all of the mitigating evidence risks erroneous imposition of the death sentence."

Just a few months later, however, O'Connor disagreed strongly with the Court's decision to overturn a death sentence imposed on a man who drove the getaway car in a robbery in which an elderly couple was killed. By a 5-4 vote the Court held in *Enmund v. Florida* that it was unconstitutional to sentence a man to death for a murder he himself did not actually commit.

O'Connor wrote for herself and the other dissenting justices, Burger, Rehnquist and Powell, that nearly half the states permit a sentence of death for a defendant who neither killed the victim himself nor intended that the victim die. These legislative judgments indicate that contemporary standards of decency permit capital punishment for this sort of crime.

The Constitution also requires that a sentence in a capital case be proportional to the harm caused by the crime and the defendant's blameworthiness, O'Connor continued. "Although the Court disingenuously seeks to characterize Enmund as only a 'robber,' . . . it cannot be disputed that he is responsible . . . along with . . . [the actual killers] for the murders. . . . There is no dispute that their lives were unjustifiably taken, and that . . . [Enmund] as one who aided and abetted the armed robbery, is legally liable for their deaths."

A year later, in *California v. Ramos,* O'Connor displayed a similar unwillingness to place additional limits on the use of capital punishment. California law requires a trial judge to inform a jury that is considering a sentence in a capital case that a sentence of life in prison without possibility of parole may be commuted by the governor to a sentence that includes the possibility of parole.

The Court, 5-4, upheld that requirement against constitutional challenge. O'Connor wrote the opinion, explaining that the Court deferred to the state's decision to require these instructions. She found them similar to other state laws that required the jury to consider a defendant's future dangerousness to society as one element in deciding whether or not to impose a death sentence.

O'Connor emphasized that the Court's decision left state legislatures free to decide that capital sentencing juries in their states should not be permitted to consider the governor's power to commute a sentence. "It is elementary that states are free to provide greater protections in their criminal justice system than the federal constitution requires," she wrote.

"We sit as judges, not as legislators, and the wisdom of the decision to permit juror consideration of possible commutation is best left to the states," she concluded.

But while O'Connor would leave it to states to decide what sort of information a jury might be given, she made clear in a 1985 case that it was not permissible for inaccurate information to be given to a jury regarding the importance of their role in a capital case.

She joined the Court's liberals in the case of *Caldwell v. Mississippi,* setting aside a death penalty that was imposed upon a convicted murderer by a jury whose members had heard the prosecutor minimize their responsibility in imposing sentence by emphasizing that a death sentence would automatically be reviewed by the state Supreme Court.

The Court's Role

O'Connor sees the line dividing judges from legislators as a bright one, drawn by the Constitution and underscored by political reality. She views the Court's role in interpreting acts of Congress as narrow. When the Court chooses to rule on a highly charged issue, such as abortion, she feels that it should take into account the actions of legislatures.

Dissenting in 1981 when the Court permitted the FBI to withhold information sought under the Freedom of Information Act, O'Connor criticized the majority for engaging in "judicial alteration" of the law. "It is not the function of this Court ... to apply the finishing touches needed to perfect legislation. Our job does not extend beyond attempting to fathom what it is that Congress produced, blemished as the Court may perceive that creation to be," she wrote.

"Reform of legislation is a task constitutionally allocated to Congress, not this Court," she declared. Quoting Justice Felix Frankfurter's 1947 *Columbia Law Review* article, she said, " 'The Courts are not at large. . . . They are under the constraints imposed by the judicial function in our democratic society. . . . [That] function in construing a statute is to ascertain the meaning of words used by the legislature. To go beyond it is to usurp a power which our democracy has lodged in its elected legislature. . . . A judge must not rewrite a statute, neither to enlarge it nor to contract it. . . . He must not read in by way of creation. He must not read out except to avoid patent nonsense or internal contradiction.' "

And dissenting when the Court struck down an Akron, Ohio, city ordinance as infringing too far on the rights of privacy in making the decision to have an abortion, she wrote: "In determining whether the state imposes an 'undue burden' [upon a constitutional right], we must keep in mind that when we are concerned with extremely sensitive issues ... 'the appropriate forum for their resolution in a democracy is the legislature.' We should not forget that 'legislatures are ultimate guardians of the liberties and welfare of the people in quite as great a degree as the courts.' " She was quoting

Justice Oliver Wendell Holmes Jr., who wrote those words in 1904.

But O'Connor does not see this precept as dictating absolute deference to legislative decisions. In the Akron case she continued: "This does not mean that ... we defer to the judgments made by state legislatures," but rather that in dealing with complex questions that have no easy answers " 'we do well to pay careful attention to how the other branches of Government have addressed the same problem.' "

When the Court in 1985 took the unusual step of using the equal protection guarantee to invalidate an Alabama tax that imposed higher taxes on out-of-state insurance companies than on in-state companies, O'Connor wrote a vigorous dissent. (This case, *Metropolitan Life Insurance Co. v. Ward,* produced one of the most unusual voting alignments in recent terms. Powell wrote the opinion, joined by Burger, White, Blackmun and Stevens; in dissent were O'Connor, Rehnquist, Brennan and Marshall.)

"Today's opinion charts an ominous course," wrote O'Connor. "I can only hope this unfortunate adventure away from the safety of our precedents will be an isolated episode. I had thought the Court had finally accepted that 'the judiciary may not sit as a superlegislature to judge the wisdom or desirability of legislative policy determinations made in areas that neither affect fundamental rights nor proceed along suspect lines.' "

As in the "deadly force" case, decided the next day, O'Connor argued the losing side's case with persuasive vigor. "It is obviously legitimate for a State to seek to promote local business and attract capital investment," as Alabama hoped to do through the tax differential, O'Connor wrote. "Currently at least 28 of the 50 states employ a combination of investment incentives and differential premium taxes favoring domestic insurers to encourage local investment of policy-holders' premiums and to partially shelter smaller domestic insurers from competition with the large multistate companies.

"Apparently, the majority views any favoritism of domestic commercial entities as inherently suspect. The majority ignores a long line of our decisions," wrote O'Connor, pointing out that the Court had generally upheld such differential treatment so long as it had a rational basis.

Because Alabama's distinction between domestic and foreign insurance companies "bears a rational relationship to a legitimate purpose, our precedents demand that it be sustained," she continued, criticizing the majority for avoiding "the deferential inquiry we have adopted as a brake on judicial impeachment of legislative policy choices."

The result, she said, was an "astonishing" holding that "subtly distorts the constitutional balance, threatening the freedom of both state and federal legislative bodies to fashion appropriate classifications in economic legislation.

"Nothing in the Constitution or our past decisions supports forcing such an economic straight-jacket on the federal system," she concluded.

Access to the Courts

Federal courts have limited jurisdiction; most lawsuits are filed and litigated in state or local courts. Only certain types of cases can be heard in federal court.

Early in the 1970s, just after Nixon had appointed his quartet of justices to the Court — and before Blackmun moved away from the Burger-Rehnquist-Powell wing — the Court began curtailing the role of federal judges in social change simply by strictly enforcing the rules governing federal court jurisdiction over cases.

Russell W. Galloway Jr., professor of law at the University of Santa Clara and author of several studies on the modern

Court, wrote, "The early Burger Court's primary strategy for dealing with the myriad Warren Court doctrines that were no longer congenial but could not easily be overruled *en masse* . . . [was simply to] erect threshold barriers preventing lower courts from reaching the merits [of a given case] so they would not have many chances to use the old liberal-activist rules."

In 1971, Galloway notes, the Court in the case of *Younger v. Harris* retreated to the classic position of denying federal judges the power to intervene in state court proceedings except in the most extraordinary circumstances. This "non-intervention doctrine provided a perfect threshold barrier that could negate Warren era . . . law without overruling it explicitly," Galloway explained.

O'Connor found this a congenial position, dovetailing neatly with her concern to leave state courts free to operate without undue federal interference and with her belief that many controversial matters were better dealt with by the political branches of government.

Within two months of taking her seat on the Court, O'Connor joined the five-person majority that shut the doors of federal courts to Americans United for Separation of Church and State, a citizens' group that had filed a First Amendment lawsuit in federal court challenging the government's transfer of 77 acres of surplus property to Valley Forge Christian College, a sectarian college.

Americans United argued that the transfer of this property was unconstitutional government action supporting and "establishing" religion. After Americans United lost the first round, a federal court of appeals gave their suit the go-ahead, finding that these citizens had legal standing to bring such a case.

But the Supreme Court reversed and found that Americans United had not suffered sufficient injury from this transfer of property to justify their coming into federal court to challenge it. Writing for the Court, Rehnquist rejected the idea that federal "judicial power requires nothing more for its invocation than important issues and able litigants." O'Connor agreed.

Two and a half years later, O'Connor spoke for the Court as it rebuffed the effort of black parents of public school children to challenge as inadequate the government's enforcement of its policy of denying tax-exempt status to discriminatory private schools. The parents, whose children were attending schools in seven states where school desegregation was under way, argued that lax enforcement of this policy resulted in aid to discriminatory private schools and thus interfered with the effort to desegregate the area's public schools.

Although a federal district court had dismissed the case, declaring that "the judicial task proposed by respondents is inappropriately intrusive for a federal court," the court of appeals had reversed that ruling, permitting the case to proceed. When the Supreme Court considered *Allen v. Wright, Regan v. Wright*, it found that these parents had no legal standing to bring such a federal suit. The vote was 5-3.

O'Connor explained: "Article III of the Constitution confines the federal courts to adjudicating actual 'cases' and 'controversies.'. . . The case-or-controversy doctrines state fundamental limits on federal judicial power in our system of government." She cited the *Valley Forge* decision as an example of such limits.

The requirement that a person have "standing" to come into federal court with a complaint is perhaps the most significant of these case-or-controversy doctrines, O'Connor went on. To invoke the power of a federal court, a person must charge that he has suffered "personal injury fairly traceable to the defendant's allegedly unlawful conduct and likely to be redressed by the requested relief."

This requirement "is built on a single basic idea," O'Connor continued, "the idea of separation of powers . . . the Art. III notion that federal courts may exercise power only 'in the last resort, and as a necessity.' "

Neither of the parents' claims in this case sufficed as a basis for standing, O'Connor explained. The claim that the government's policy resulted in aid to discriminatory private schools was too abstract; the parents did not allege that they or their children had personally been denied equal treatment as a result of this policy.

To consider this sort of claim a proper basis for bringing a federal case would "transform the federal courts into 'no more than a vehicle for the vindication of the value interests of concerned bystanders,' " O'Connor wrote. "Constitutional limits on the role of the federal courts preclude such a transformation."

The parents' other claim, that this policy impeded efforts to desegregate public schools and therefore diminished their ability to receive an education in a racially integrated setting, was certainly "one of the most serious injuries recognized in our legal system," O'Connor acknowledged.

"Despite the constitutional importance of curing the injury alleged . . . the federal judiciary may not redress it unless standing requirements are met. In this case, respondents' second claim of injury cannot support standing because the injury alleged is not fairly traceable to the Government conduct respondents challenge as unlawful," she wrote.

"The diminished ability of respondents' children to receive a desegregated education would be fairly traceable to unlawful IRS grants of tax exemptions only if there were enough racially discriminatory private schools receiving tax exemptions in respondents' communities for withdrawal of those exemptions to make an appreciable difference in public-school integration. Re-

spondents have made no such allegation. . . .
The links in the chain of causation between
the challenged Government conduct and
the asserted injury are far too weak for the
chain as a whole to sustain respondent's
standing," O'Connor concluded.

Brennan, in dissent, criticized O'Connor's reasoning as displaying "a startling
insensitivity to the historical role played by
the federal courts in eradicating race
discrimination from our nation's schools."
Once again, he complained, the Court was
using the concept of legal standing " 'to
slam the courthouse door' " against plaintiffs with a legitimate complaint.

First Amendment Freedoms

O'Connor is reluctant to use the First
Amendment to limit the freedom of state or
local governments. At the end of her first
term in June 1982, she dissented when the
Court, 5-4, ruled that the First Amendment
applied to a school board's decision to remove certain books from the shelves of high
school libraries.

"If the school board can set the curriculum, select teachers, and determine initially what books to purchase for the school
library," she wrote, "it surely can decide
which books to discontinue or remove from
the school library so long as it does not also
interfere with the right of students to read
the material and to discuss it."

Once again emphasizing the narrow
role of the courts to interfere in such matters, she noted, "I do not personally agree
with the board's action . . . but it is not the
function of the courts to make the decisions
that have been properly relegated to the
elected members of school boards."

On the other hand, O'Connor can be
equally emphatic when she sees government
action that violates these constitutional
guarantees of freedom. She spoke for the
Court in 1983 when it invalidated a state
law that taxed paper and ink purchased in
large quantities to produce a newspaper.

"Whatever the motive of the legislature in this case, we think that recognizing a
power in the State not only to single out the
press but also to tailor the tax so that it
singles out a few members of the press
presents such a potential for abuse that no
interest suggested by Minnesota can justify
the scheme," she wrote in *Minneapolis Star
& Tribune Co. v. Minnesota Commissioner
of Revenue.*

In 1984 she joined the Court's more
liberal members to strike down, as a violation of the free speech guarantee, the act of
Congress denying public broadcasters the
right to editorialize.

In general, however, O'Connor votes
against First Amendment claims. In 1984
she joined the majority in upholding Los
Angeles' ban on the posting of signs on
public property and the Reagan administra-

tion's regulation prohibiting overnight sleeping in Lafayette Park across from the White House. She dissented, with White and Rehnquist, when the majority reaffirmed the "actual malice" standard protecting the press from libel suits brought by public figures.

Also in that term, she spoke for the Court to uphold a Minnesota law that required that state college instructors communicate with their employers on certain subjects only through the individuals chosen to speak for the collective bargaining unit. The instructors argued that this limitation curtailed their First Amendment rights.

Not so, held the Supreme Court in *Minnesota State Board for Community Colleges v. Knight*. The teachers "have no constitutional right to force the government to listen to their views. They have no such right as members of the public, as government employees, or as instructors in an institution of higher education," wrote O'Connor.

"Public officials at all levels of government daily make policy decisions based only on the advice they decide they need and choose to hear. To recognize a constitutional right to participate directly in government policymaking would work a revolution in existing government practices," she continued.

"It is inherent in a republican form of government that direct public participation in government policymaking is limited," O'Connor wrote. "Faculty involvement in academic governance has much to recommend it as a matter of academic policy, but it finds no basis in the Constitution."

As the Court in the early 1980s moved to permit government to accommodate the interests of religious groups more and to separate church and state less strictly, O'Connor was right in step.

She agreed with the Court as it required state university officials to permit religious student groups equal access to use

of buildings and grounds, as it upheld a state income-tax deduction for tuition and related school expenses paid for parochial or public school students and as it affirmed the historic practice of opening legislative sessions with prayer.

When the Court, 5-4, ruled that nothing in the First Amendment precluded Pawtucket, R.I., city officials from including a crèche in a holiday display, O'Connor added a concurring opinion to suggest that the Court clarify its test for laws and practices challenged as "establishing religion."

"The Establishment Clause prohibits government from making adherence to a religion relevant in any way to a person's standing in the political community," she wrote. "Government can run afoul of that prohibition in two principal ways. One is excessive entanglement with religious institutions.... The second and more direct infringement is government endorsement or disapproval of religion....

"Pawtucket did not intend to convey any message of endorsement of Christianity or disapproval of non-Christian religions" by including the crèche in its holiday display, wrote O'Connor. "The evident purpose ... was not promotion of the religious content of the crèche but celebration of the public holiday through its traditional symbols. Celebration of public holidays, which have cultural significance even if they also have religious aspects, is a legitimate secular purpose.

"What is crucial is that a government practice not have the effect of communicating a message of government endorsement or disapproval of religion. It is only practices having that effect, whether intentionally or unintentionally, that make religion relevant, in reality or public perception, to status in the political community," O'Connor explained.

Applying that test, O'Connor agreed with a liberal majority in June 1985 that Alabama's moment-of-silence law was unconstitutional because the legislature approving it had plainly intended it to encourage prayer in the public schools. "Alabama has intentionally crossed the line between creating a quiet moment during which those so inclined may pray, and affirmatively endorsing the particular religion's practice of prayer," she wrote.

Mindful of the storm that followed the Court's 1962 and 1963 school prayer rulings, however, O'Connor emphasized in her concurring opinion what the Court's 1985 decision in *Wallace v. Jaffree* did *not* say: "Nothing in the United States Constitution as interpreted by this Court or in the laws of the State of Alabama prohibits public school students from voluntarily praying at any time before, during or after the school day."

Indeed, O'Connor continued, "by mandating a moment of silence, a state does not necessarily endorse any activity that might occur" during that moment. "The crucial question is whether the state has conveyed or attempted to convey the message that children should use the moment of silence for prayer." If that message is conveyed or intended, the law is invalid.

Aware of the difficulties encountered by judges attempting to apply Supreme Court decisions, O'Connor added a word to her brethren: "We must strive to do more than erect a constitutional 'signpost.' . . . Instead our goal should be 'to frame a principle for constitutional adjudication that is not only grounded in the history and language of the first amendment, but one that is also capable of consistent application to the relevant problems.' "

A month later, however, O'Connor rejoined her conservative colleagues in dissent from the Court's decisions striking down — as "establishing" religion — programs run by New York City and Grand Rapids under which publicly paid teachers were sent into parochial schools to teach secular subjects.

In the New York case, *Aguilar v.*

Felton, the subjects taught were primarily remedial, funded under the federal Title I program designed to aid culturally deprived children. O'Connor described the ruling as "tragic" for children who are entitled to these programs but who live in cities where it would not be feasible to provide public facilities for these classes near their parochial schools.

O'Connor said she could not deny these children "a program that offers a meaningful chance at success in life . . . on the untenable theory that public schoolteachers . . . are likely to start teaching religion merely because they have walked across the threshold of a parochial school."

The majority based its decision primarily on its view that the supervision necessary to ensure that these teachers did not bring religion into their classes resulted in excessive "entanglement" of church and state. O'Connor scoffed at the idea that such supervision was necessary, saying that the majority's "reasoning would require us to close our public schools, for there is always some chance that a public schoolteacher will bring religion into the classroom, regardless of its location."

Entanglement was insufficient reason to invalidate New York's program, wrote O'Connor. "If a statute lacks a purpose or effect of advancing or endorsing religion, I would not invalidate it merely because it requires some ongoing cooperation between church and state or some state supervision to ensure that state funds do not advance religion."

Sex Discrimination

As the only member of the Court known to have suffered discrimination because of her sex, O'Connor's opinions on issues involving such bias have drawn particular attention. Although she generally supports those who challenge sex bias, she displays a down-to-earth practicality in her approach to such cases that sometimes limits the sweep of her opinion.

In June 1982 she spoke for the Court when it ruled that when an employer charged with refusing to hire women offers a job to the woman bringing that charge, his offer terminates the period for which he may be held liable to the plaintiff for back pay.

"The question has considerable practical significance," O'Connor began, "because of the lengthy delays that too often attend Title VII litigation. . . . Court delays, of course, affect all litigants. But for the victim of job discrimination delay is especially unfortunate. The claimant cannot afford to stand aside while the wheels of justice grind slowly toward the ultimate resolution of the lawsuit. The claimant needs work that will feed a family and restore self-respect. A job is needed — now.

"The victims of job discrimination want jobs, not lawsuits," summarized O'Connor, expressing the hope that this ruling, in *Ford Motor Co. v. Equal Employment Opportunity Commission,* would encourage employers to make such job offers.

A month later O'Connor again spoke for the Court when it told Mississippi University for Women that it violated the Constitution by refusing to admit men to its nursing program. The Court rejected the state's argument that it maintained the women-only program as educational affirmative action, compensating for discrimination against women in other areas of life. To the contrary, wrote O'Connor, the challenged policy "of excluding males from admission to the school of nursing tends to perpetuate the stereotyped view of nursing as an exclusively woman's job."

O'Connor was the key swing vote in July 1983 when the Court held that an employer could not legally offer a retirement plan to its employees under which women retirees received smaller monthly payments than men because women as a group live longer after retirement than men.

She joined Marshall, Brennan, White and Stevens to hold such a differential payment plan illegal under the 1964 Civil Rights Act.

But in a swing that substantially undercut the usefulness of the decision to women retirees and older women workers, she joined Burger, Blackmun, Powell and Rehnquist to hold that the ruling in *Arizona Governing Committee for Tax Deferred Annuity and Deferred Compensation Plans v. Norris* would not be retroactive, but would apply only to benefits derived from contributions to retirement plans made after this decision.

O'Connor joined the majority the following year in rejecting the claim of the U.S. Jaycees that their First Amendment right of association was violated when Minnesota applied its civil rights laws to require it to accept women as full voting members.

But in a concurring opinion, she disagreed with the majority's analysis and suggested that there were in fact two types of First Amendment rights of association. There was a right of "expressive association," she wrote, entitled to full First Amendment protection of the content of its message and the choice of its members. Among associations of this type were the Girl Scouts, the NAACP and most political parties.

"Protection of the association's right to define its membership derives from the recognition that the formation of an expressive association is the creation of a voice, and the selection of members is the definition of that voice," she explained.

"On the other hand, there is only minimal constitutional protection of the freedom of commercial association," O'Connor continued. "The state is free to impose any rational regulation on the commercial transaction itself. The Constitution does not guarantee a right to choose employees, customers, suppliers or those with whom one engages in simple commercial transactions without restraint from the state. A shop-keeper has no constitutional right to deal only with persons of one sex."

The state and federal courts reviewing the case of *Roberts v. U.S. Jaycees* had characterized the Jaycees as engaged in commercial activities, the promotion of the art of management and solicitation and the sale of Jaycee memberships. When an association "enters the marketplace of commerce in any substantial degree, it loses the complete control over its membership that it would otherwise enjoy if it confined its affairs to the marketplace of ideas."

"The First Amendment is offended by direct state control of the membership of a private organization engaged exclusively in protected expressive activity," she summarized, "but no First Amendment interest stands in the way of a State's rational regulation of economic transactions by or within a commercial association."

Through her written words, Sandra Day O'Connor has begun to draw her judicial self-portrait. Her conservative views draw criticism. Many disagree with her belief that state and local officials should be permitted to exercise more power, and federal officials — particularly federal judges — less. Many mistrust her inclination to favor the police or the prosecutor, rather than the defendant, in a dispute over a point of criminal law or procedure.

But few can find fault with the manner of her judging. She approaches an issue aggressively, familiarizing herself thoroughly with the facts and the law and probing the limits of the matter through penetrating questions. She considers the practical consequences of her vote, as well as the legal doctrines it reflects.

Her path to her conclusion is clearly set out in her opinions. Although she is not the Court's most original member, she does occasionally shed new light on an old issue, pointing out an unseen flaw in an old precedent or proposing a new solution to a recurring problem.

Whatever one thinks of O'Connor's conservative views, it is quite possible that over the span of time she will likely serve on the Court, the way she reaches a decision may be of more importance than the substance of the decisions she has made in her first years on that bench.

5

The Brethren

Change seems to come slowly to the Supreme Court. Indeed, to the casual observer, there appeared to be virtually no change at all between 1975 — when Justice Douglas was succeeded by Justice Stevens — and 1981, when O'Connor arrived.

Amid the regular transitions in power at the White House and in Congress, every two, four or six years, the life tenure of Supreme Court justices cloaks the Court in an aura of permanence and immutability.

That perception is a mistaken one. Change is continous at the Court. The nine justices, historian Charles Warren wrote decades ago, "are not abstract and impersonal oracles," but living, breathing, growing persons who learn and change with time and experience. And when a decision depends on just nine people, any change of mind or heart in any one of them can have a far-reaching effect.

Sandra Day O'Connor's presence was the most obvious difference at the Supreme Court during Ronald Reagan's first term, but it was not the only reason for the changes that took place there. O'Connor acted as a catalyst for the actions and interactions of all nine justices — O'Connor and "the brethren," the eight veterans she joined on the bench. To understand the events of these years it is necessary to know more about each of the justices.

The Court in 1985 was composed of:

—Chief Justice Warren E. Burger, appointed 1969;

—Justice William J. Brennan Jr., appointed 1956;

—Justice Byron R. White, appointed 1962;

—Justice Thurgood Marshall, appointed 1967;

—Justice Harry A. Blackmun, appointed 1970;

—Justice Lewis F. Powell Jr., appointed 1971;

—Justice William H. Rehnquist, appointed 1971;

—Justice John Paul Stevens, appointed 1975; and

—Justice Sandra Day O'Connor, appointed 1981.

Some alliances among these justices are virtually fixed, like that of liberals Brennan and Marshall, but the alignment among the nine shifts to some degree every term. The career of Potter Stewart provides one example of that shift. During the liberal era of the Warren Court, he often found himself allied with the more conservative members of the Court. Then, in the more

The Swing Vote

When nine people vote on a case, each one is potentially "a swing vote." What does that label mean?

If four of the justices are known to hold strong feelings on one side of an issue, and four others clearly are on the other side, the one whose views are not known becomes the swing vote.

In 1985 the Court divided 4-4 on a labor case argued and decided without Justice Lewis F. Powell Jr., who was absent from the Court while recuperating from surgery. The case was re-argued after Powell returned, and it was resolved, 5-4. Powell was the swing vote that made the difference between a deadlocked Court and a decisive one.

A justice also becomes a swing vote when he or she undergoes a change of heart. In 1976 Justice Harry A. Blackmun was part of the five-man majority that told Congress it could not tell states and cities how to compensate their employees for overtime. By 1985, however, Blackmun had changed his mind, voting with four other justices to overturn the 1976 decision, clearly swinging the Court on that issue.

conservative context of the Burger Court, Stewart found himself frequently allied with the Warren Court's liberal veterans.

Harry Blackmun's career provides another example. After spending his first several years in tight alliance with the more conservative members of the Court, Blackmun, by 1980, had moved into a clear alliance with the liberals — Brennan, Marshall and Stevens. That alliance remained strong during O'Connor's first two terms,

but showed signs of dissolving during the October 1983 term.

Most of the justices shield their private lives and characters from public view. But with every opinion and dissent, each gradually sketches a judicial self-portrait. Their public pronouncements and appearances — primarily during oral arguments at the Court — add to the picture.

This chapter provides, not completed portraits, but sketches of the other eight justices' judicial personalities: first, O'Connor's usual allies — Burger, Rehnquist and Powell; next, the liberals — Brennan and Marshall; and then the less predictable justices — Stevens, White and Blackmun.

Burger: Conservative Chief

Warren E. Burger's most famous opinion ended the political career of the man who named him to the nation's highest judicial post. With his announcement in July 1974 that President Richard Nixon must surrender certain White House tapes to the Watergate special prosecutor, Burger made Nixon's resignation from the presidency inevitable.

Burger's opinion siding with the special prosecutor and against the president reflected the very characteristics that had commended him to Nixon as a potential chief justice: an abiding sympathy for law enforcement officials and a firm belief that the public interest demanded a swift and effective system of criminal justice.

But if Nixon lost his argument to withhold the tapes, he won on the larger principle of executive privilege. For in *United States v. Nixon,* the Court for the first time acknowledged a constitutional right of executive privilege, a privilege to preserve the confidentiality of communications between a president and his advisers.

Burger, a handsome white-haired man who is the very image of a chief justice, had served 16 years on the Court by the end of the October 1984 term, the same length of time that his predecessor Earl Warren served. He marked his 78th birthday in September 1985.

Burger is a native of Minnesota and a graduate of St. Paul College of Law. He came to the Supreme Court from the U.S. Court of Appeals for the District of Columbia Circuit, to which he had been appointed by President Eisenhower in 1956.

He presides graciously over the Court's public proceedings and clearly enjoys the public aspects of his role as chief justice, which includes swearing in the president, and serving as head of the judicial conference, the policy-making body of the federal judiciary.

Burger remains quiet during most oral arguments, although when questions of criminal law are before the Court — particularly search and seizure issues — he takes a more active role.

Burger often delivers the Court's opinion in major cases, but he is not considered an intellectual leader. Some of his opinions have announced a "liberal" ruling — such as that upholding the Internal Revenue Service policy of denying tax exempt status to discriminatory schools and colleges — but his most memorable statements are invariably on the conservative side of a case.

Burger's conservative views are most in evidence in his opinions on criminal law issues. He argues for limiting the reach of many of the Warren Court landmarks and for cutting back on the rule excluding illegally obtained evidence from criminal trials. He would limit such exclusion to situations in which it is essential to safeguard the "integrity of the truth-seeking process."

The importance of maintaining the Constitution's system of separated powers is a frequent theme in Burger's opinions. In 1982 he dissented — along with Rehnquist, White and O'Connor — when the Court told states they could not refuse to educate the children of illegal aliens.

Warren E. Burger

"Were it our business to set the Nation's social policy," Burger wrote, "I would agree without hesitation that it is senseless for an enlightened society to deprive any children — including illegal aliens — of an elementary education. . . .

"However, the Constitution does not constitute us as 'Platonic Guardians' nor does it vest in this Court the authority to strike down laws because they do not meet our standards of desirable social policy, 'wisdom,' or 'common sense.'. . . We trespass on the assigned function of the political branches under our structure of limited and separate powers when we assume a policy-making role, as the Court does today," he said.

In a succinct statement of the core of his belief in judicial restraint, Burger concluded: "The Constitution does not provide a cure for every social ill, nor does it vest judges with a mandate to try to remedy every social problem."

Earlier, the chief justice sounded a

similar theme in dissenting when the Court struck down state death penalty laws as unconstitutional: "Our constitutional inquiry . . . must be divorced from personal feelings as to the morality and efficacy of the death penalty. . . . It is essential to our role as a Court that we not seize upon the enigmatic character of the guarantee as an invitation to enact our personal predilections into law."

There are some matters that are not for Courts to resolve, Burger believes. As early as 1974, he wrote to reject a taxpayer's challenge to the secrecy shrouding the budget of the Central Intelligence Agency: "It can be argued that if [the plaintiff] . . . is not permitted to litigate this issue, no one can do so. In a very real sense the absence of any particular individual or class to litigate these claims gives support to the argument that the subject matter is committed to the surveillance of Congress, and, ultimately, to the political process. Any other conclusion would mean that the Founding Fathers intended to set up something in the nature of an Athenian democracy or a New England town meeting to oversee the conduct of the national government by means of lawsuits in the federal Courts."

The need to remain faithful to the constitutional scheme of government, including the separation of powers, was central to Burger's 1983 opinion explaining the Court's decision to declare the legislative veto unconstitutional.

"The hydraulic pressure inherent within each of the separate Branches to exceed the outer limits of its power, even to accomplish desirable objectives, must be resisted," he wrote.

"The veto . . . doubtless has been . . . a convenient shortcut; the 'sharing' with the Executive by Congress of its authority . . . in this manner is, on its face, an appealing compromise. In purely practical terms, it is obviously easier for action to be taken by one House without submission to the President; but it is crystal clear from the records of the Convention, contemporaneous writings and debates, that the Framers ranked other values higher than efficiency. . . .

"The choices we discern as having been made in the Constitutional Convention impose burdens on governmental processes that often seem clumsy, inefficient, even unworkable, but those hard choices were consciously made by men who had lived under a form of government that permitted arbitrary governmental acts to go unchecked. . . . With all the obvious flaws of delay, untidiness, and potential for abuse, we have not yet found a better way to preserve freedom than by making the exercise of power subject to the carefully crafted restraints spelled out in the Constitution."

On matters of church and state, Burger agrees that the First Amendment's religion clauses require government to "take pains not to compel people to act in the name of any religion," but he feels that the Court is too eager to read that amendment to require the "separation" of church and state when the interests of both could be constitutionally "accommodated" instead.

In 1984 Burger wrote the Court's opinion permitting inclusion of a crèche in a city's holiday display and endorsing accommodation in place of separation. "No significant segment of our society and no institution within it can exist in a vacuum or in total or absolute isolation from all the other parts, much less from government," Burger wrote. "Nor does the Constitution require complete separation of church and state; it affirmatively mandates accommodation, not merely tolerance, of all religions and forbids hostility toward any."

When the Court majority in 1985 seemed to return to the "separation" concept in striking down Alabama's "moment-of-silence" statute, Burger dissented. The idea that this law was "a step toward creating an established church borders on, if it does not trespass into, the ridiculous," he wrote.

This law "does not remotely threaten religious liberty," Burger continued. "It accommodates the purely private, voluntary religious choices of the individual pupils who wish to pray while at the same time creating a time for nonreligious reflection for those who do not choose to pray. . . . The statute 'endorses' only the view that the religious observance of others should be tolerated and, where possible, accommodated."

The Court in July 1985 held unconstitutional New York City's method of providing remedial courses to parochial school students. The city had been sending publicly paid instructors to teach the secular courses at parochial schools during the school day. Burger's dissent was vehement: "The notion that denying these services to students in religious schools is a neutral act to protect us from an Established Church has no support in logic, experience, or history. Rather than showing the neutrality the Court boasts of, it exhibits nothing less than hostility toward religion and the children who attend church-sponsored schools."

Burger resists the idea that other First Amendment guarantees — freedom of speech, petition and the press — can be used as shields against persons injured by their exercise. In June 1985 he wrote the Court's opinion rejecting the claim that a person who wrote a letter to the president criticizing a potential appointee could invoke the right of petition as a complete defense against a libel suit based on the letter and brought by the disappointed office seeker. "The right to petition is guaranteed," was Burger's terse comment, "the right to commit libel with impunity is not."

In similar fashion, Burger not only agreed when the Court refused to extend First Amendment protection to libel defendants in cases involving private disputes

rather than matters of public interest, but also he urged the Court to reconsider its earlier libel rulings and narrow the First Amendment's protection against libel suits.

The press should be held liable to individuals whose reputations were damaged by its reports, wrote Burger, if the press is "shown to have published defamatory material which, in the exercise of reasonable care, would have been revealed as untrue. . . . The great rights guaranteed by the First Amendment carry with them certain responsibilities as well."

Rehnquist: Radical Conservative

William H. Rehnquist is the Court's doctrinaire conservative. Next to O'Connor, he is the youngest justice, turning 61 just before the Court began its October 1985 term, and he is its most ardent advocate of judicial restraint.

Rehnquist sees the Court as the brakes on the engine of government, not the accelerator. In his view the Court should call a halt to unconstitutional actions or policies

William H. Rehnquist

— and then leave it to the popularly elected branches of the government to decide what action to take or policy to adopt in their place. Rehnquist feels innovation should come from elected officials, not appointed judges.

Rehnquist came to the Court from the post of assistant attorney general, head of the office of the legal counsel, in the Justice Department run by John Mitchell. Before coming to Washington, he had practiced law in Phoenix, Ariz., where he continued a friendship with his law school classmate, Sandra Day O'Connor, and her husband John, also a Stanford law graduate.

Rehnquist takes a literal approach to questions of individual rights, an approach reinforced by his unwavering belief that the Court should exercise its powers with deference to its partners in the federal system — Congress, the president and the states.

Rehnquist often speaks for the conservative majority advocating such deference. When the Court in 1981 upheld the decision of Congress to exclude women from the requirement to register for the military draft, he emphasized that "the scope of Congress' constitutional power in this area [is] broad" and "the lack of competence on the part of the Courts [in this area] is marked."

Three years later, when the Court upheld the Reagan administration's power to tighten restrictions on travel to Cuba, Rehnquist explained that "given the traditional deference to executive judgment" in matters of foreign policy, the majority found such restrictions justified to limit the flow to Cuba of hard currency that could be used to support "Cuban adventurism," armed violence and terrorism in the Western Hemisphere.

When the Court, 5-4, in 1976 declared in *National League of Cities v. Usery* that Congress could not tell states and cities how to compensate their employees, Rehnquist wrote the opinion. Nine years later, when

the Court, 5-4, reversed that ruling, Rehnquist in dissent predicted yet another reversal.

Throughout his tenure on the Court, Rehnquist has displayed strong support for law enforcement officers and a notable lack of concern for the arguments of suspects and prisoners. In oral arguments, Rehnquist bluntly challenges attorneys arguing before the Court, often using his questions to guide the arguments for the prosecution — as Justice Brennan sometimes does for the defense.

Pointing out that neither police efforts nor trials are required by the Constitution to be perfect, but only fair, Rehnquist has steadily backed the arguments of police and prosecutors in criminal cases and emphasized that federal judges should not second-guess state trial judges' actions. It was important, he wrote in 1977, that a state trial be "the 'main event' so to speak ... rather than a tryout on the road for what will later be the determinative federal hearing."

Sharing the view of the chief justice that many of the Warren Court landmarks in criminal law protected the rights of criminal suspects at too great a cost to the public, Rehnquist was an apt spokesman when the Court in 1984 recognized the "public safety exception" to *Miranda.* In upholding the right of police to ask an armed rape suspect, "Where's the gun?" before advising him of his rights and then to use the suspect's answer and the gun as evidence against him, Rehnquist summarized the effect of the Court's ruling as simply freeing police officers "to follow their legitimate instincts when confronting situations presenting a danger to the public safety."

When the Court in 1985 upheld the decision of customs officials to detain incommunicado and without a warrant for almost 24 hours a woman suspected of smuggling cocaine in her alimentary canal

— until "natural processes" forced her to expel the drugs — Rehnquist wrote the opinion.

Customs officials, he wrote, are responsible for "protecting this Nation from entrants who may bring anything harmful into this country, whether that be communicable diseases, narcotics, or explosives. In this regard, the detention of a suspected alimentary canal smuggler at the border is analogous to the detention of a suspected tuberculosis carrier." The detention in this case was "long, uncomfortable, indeed humiliating," Rehnquist acknowledged, "but both its length and its discomfort resulted solely from the method by which she chose to smuggle illicit drugs into this country."

Rehnquist has disagreed when the Court has struck down death penalty laws. He urges the Court to pay "rigorous attention" to the limits of its own authority so that the justices might avoid "the natural desire that beguiles judges along with other human beings into imposing their own views of goodness, truth and justice upon others." He criticizes his liberal colleagues for "turning every perceived departure from ... optimum procedure in a capital case into a ground for constitutional reversal" of a death sentence.

Rehnquist, more than any other justice, is in tune with the Reagan administration's argument that the original intentions of the men who drafted the Constitution and the Bill of Rights are the only proper standard for use in applying the language of those documents today.

When the Court in June 1985 reaffirmed its commitment to the view that the First Amendment ban on establishment of religion left no room for states to require or encourage prayer in public schools, Rehnquist used his dissenting opinion to set out an entirely different view of that ban. He urged the Court to discard entirely the idea that the First Amendment required a "wall of separation between church and state." That, he said, was "a metaphor based on bad history, a metaphor which has proved useless as a guide to judging. It should be frankly and explicitly abandoned."

"The true meaning of the Establishment Clause can only be seen in its history," Rehnquist continued. "The Framers intended the Establishment Clause to prohibit the designation of any church as a 'national' one ... to stop the Federal Government from asserting a preference for one religious denomination or sect over others."

That constitutional provision does "not require government neutrality between religion and irreligion nor did it prohibit the federal government from providing nondiscriminatory aid to religion," Rehnquist concluded. "There is simply no historical foundation for the proposition that the Framers intended to build ... [a] 'wall of separation' " between these areas of American life.

In like fashion, Rehnquist can locate no specific right of privacy guaranteed in the Constitution and so has steadily dissented from the Court's opinions, based on that right, permitting abortions.

On other questions of civil and individual rights, Rehnquist has dissented from the Court's rulings expanding remedies for victims of job bias; striking down laws discriminating against women, illegitimate children and aliens; granting First Amendment protection to commercial speech and striking down state aid to church schools.

Only Rehnquist dissented when the Court in 1983 rejected a challenge to the Internal Revenue Service's authority to deny tax-exempt status to Bob Jones University, a religiously affiliated school that discriminated against blacks. Rehnquist endorsed the administration's view that Congress must first specifically authorize the IRS to adopt this policy.

Once again, he predicated his position on his view of the Court's role vis-à-vis

Congress: "I have no disagreement with the Court's finding that there is a strong national policy in this country opposed to racial discrimination. I agree with the Court that Congress has the power to further this policy by denying . . . [tax-exempt status] to organizations that practice racial discrimination. But as of yet Congress has failed to do so. Whatever the reasons for the failure, this Court should not legislate for Congress."

Rehnquist has steadily disagreed with the modern trend of extending First Amendment protection to commercial speech and to corporate speech. The First Amendment, in his view, protects primarily political speech. So it was no surprise that in 1985, he spoke for the majority to hold invalid the $1,000 limit that Congress had placed on independent spending by political action committees (PACs) in behalf of a presidential candidate.

In his view, the limit clearly restricted the sort of speech that the First Amendment was designed to protect. He wrote: "The PACs in this case, of course, are not lone pamphleteers or street corner orators in the Tom Paine mold; they spend substantial amounts of money in order to communicate their political ideas through sophisticated media advertisements. . . .

"But for purposes of presenting political views in connection with a nationwide presidential election, allowing the presentation of views while forbidding the expenditure of more than $1,000 to present them is much like allowing a speaker in a public hall to express his views while denying him the use of an amplifying system."

Powell: Right In Step

The justice most in step with the zigs and zags of the Burger Court is Lewis F. Powell Jr., who turned 78 in September 1985. Powell came to the Court in 1971 at the age of 64, capping a distinguished career in law and community service. He is the only member of the current Court who came from the private practice of law.

During his years on the Court, Powell consistently has been on the prevailing side — more than any other justice — in most major cases. No justice has dissented less.

Although he generally agrees with Burger, Rehnquist and now O'Connor, Powell diverges from their conservative line just often enough to win himself the reputation as the most moderate of the four conservatives. It was just that sort of independence from his conservative colleagues during the October 1984 term that swung the Court back toward its earlier moderation and away from the strongly conservative stance of the previous term.

Powell's commitment to judicial restraint — although strong and well articulated — does not outweigh a clear concern for individual rights. That concern caused Powell to vote with the Court's more liberal members in the 1985 school prayer and parochiaid rulings, both bitter disappointments to the Reagan administration.

As a junior justice, Powell was careful to restrain judicial interference in matters of policy. Early in his tenure, he justified the Court's refusal to hold school financing systems based on property taxes unconstitutional because they were inherently unequal. "The ultimate solutions [to such problems] must come from the lawmakers and from the democratic pressures of those who select them," he wrote.

A year later, he emphasized the importance — for the Court — of avoiding "repeated and essentially head-on confrontations between the life-tenured branch and the representative branches of the government." Although both would suffer, Powell emphasized that "the public confidence essential" to the judiciary's influence "may well erode if we do not exercise self-restraint in the utilization of our power to negate the action of other branches."

By the time Powell completed his first decade on the Court, however, his concern for the individual had intensified and he was less reluctant to step in where the political branches did not act. This attitude is particularly evident when education is involved. Powell, a civic leader in Richmond, Va., before his appointment to the Court, is a firm believer in the importance of public schools. He served as a member of both the city and state school boards during some of the difficult years during which those boards were working to desegregate the state's public schools.

When the Court in 1982 told states that they could not deny a free public education to the children of illegal aliens, Powell made clear that he felt the Court must act because "Congress — vested by the Constitution with the responsibility of protecting our borders and legislating with respect to aliens — has not provided effective leadership in dealing with this problem. It therefore is certain that illegal aliens will continue to enter the United States.... I agree with the Court that their children should not be left on the streets uneducated."

In general, however, Powell agrees with Burger, Rehnquist and O'Connor that judges should leave policy decisions to others. Writing in 1977 to declare that neither the Constitution nor the Social Security Act required states to fund Medicaid abortions, he made clear that the Court's decision left Congress and the states "entirely free ... through the normal processes of democracy, to provide the desired funding. The issues [involved in that decision] present policy decisions of the widest concern. They should be resolved by representatives of the people, not by this Court."

On the other hand, when the Court reaffirmed the basic abortion decision, *Roe v. Wade,* in 1983, Powell was the majority's spokesman. His wording was careful, however, and seemed to reflect the majority's

Lewis F. Powell Jr.

commitment to doctrine of *stare decisis,* following settled precedent, rather than to the substance of *Roe* itself. He wrote: "These cases come to us a decade after we held in *Roe v. Wade* ... that the right of privacy, grounded in the concept of personal liberty guaranteed by the Constitution, encompasses a woman's right to decide whether to terminate her pregnancy.... Arguments continue to be made ... that we erred in interpreting the Constitution. Nonetheless, the doctrine of *stare decisis* while perhaps never entirely persuasive on a constitutional question, is a doctrine that demands respect in a society governed by the rule of law. We respect it today, and reaffirm *Roe v. Wade.*"

Powell in mid-1985 is considered a key vote on abortion, and his continued presence on the Court through the Reagan years is of vital interest to those who wish to preserve *Roe.* With O'Connor's arrival, the majority supporting that landmark eroded from the original seven to six votes. Chief Justice

Burger is thought to be wavering in his commitment to that precedent. Without Burger, there are only five votes — including Powell's — in favor of *Roe*.

Powell is the only member of the current Court who did not come to his seat from a government post. Like O'Connor, however, he places his basic faith in the strength and capability of state and local, rather than federal, government; he criticizes the Court when it permits Congress to intrude too far into the domain of the state.

When the Court in 1985 overruled its 1976 decision in *National League of Cities v. Usery* and permitted Congress to dictate pay scales for employees of state and local governments, Powell wrote for the dissenting quartet to protest both this breach of stare decisis and the permissive attitude of the majority toward federal power.

"The stability of judicial decision, and with it respect for the authority of this Court, are not served by the precipitous overruling of multiple precedents that we witness in this case," Powell wrote in dissenting from *Garcia v. San Antonio Metropolitan Transit Authority.*

"Whatever effect the Court's decision may have in weakening the application of *stare decisis,* it is likely to be less important that what the Court has done to the Constitution itself. A unique feature of the United States is the *federal* system of government guaranteed by the Constitution and implicit in the very name of our country. Despite some genuflecting in the Court's opinion to the concept of federalism, today's decision effectively reduces the 10th Amendment to meaningless rhetoric when Congress acts pursuant to the Commerce Clause."

The ruling, Powell continued, "reflects the Court's unprecedented view that Congress is free under the Commerce Clause to assume a State's traditional sovereign power, and to do so without judicial review of its action. Indeed the Court's view of federalism appears to relegate the States to precisely the trivial role that opponents of the Constitution feared they would occupy.

"Members of the immense federal bureaucracy are not elected, know less about the services traditionally rendered by States and localities, and are inevitably less responsive to recipients of such services, than are state legislatures, city councils, boards of supervisors, and state and local commissions, boards and agencies," Powell concluded. "It is at these state and local levels — not in Washington as the Court so mistakenly thinks — that 'democratic self-government' is best exemplified."

Powell is gracious and diplomatic as he questions attorneys during oral arguments, evidence of the skills that place him in a central position on some of the Court's most difficult cases. The pivotal role he holds in the dynamic relationships of the Court was illustrated in 1978 when the Court addressed the controversial issue of affirmative action for the first time.

In the landmark case, *Regents of the University of California v. Bakke,* the other eight justices divided evenly over whether a school could set aside a quota of places in an entering class for members of a minority group. Powell cast the crucial vote holding such quotas illegal.

The constitutional guarantee of equal protection, he explained, "cannot mean one thing when applied to one person and something else when applied to a person of another color. . . . Preferring members of any one group for no reason other than race or ethnic origin is discrimination for its own sake. This the Constitution forbids."

Bakke also presented the question of whether race could be considered at all by admissions committees as a factor favoring a minority student over a non-minority student. Again, the other eight justices were evenly divided. Powell cast the deciding vote permitting consideration of race in this benign manner.

The frequency with which Powell casts the deciding vote was highlighted in 1985 when surgery for prostate cancer kept him off the bench for two and a half months, during which the Court heard argument in 56 cases. Of those 56, the Court divided evenly in eight, simply affirming the lower court. Four others were set for reargument, probably because the Court was again evenly divided.

When the Court finally decided a major labor case, *Pattern Makers' League of North America v. National Labor Relations Board,* re-argued after Powell's return, it was clear that Powell held the deciding vote. He cast it in favor of the Reagan-dominated NLRB, upholding its decision — loudly protested by organized labor — that labor unions could not enforce rules that denied union members the right to resign in the face of a strike.

Once again, Powell sounded the theme of deference in his opinion for the Court. The NLRB, he wrote, "has the primary responsibility for applying 'the general provisions ... [of federal labor law] to the complexities of industrial life." Because the NLRB decision denying unions this power is reasonable, that decision, Powell concluded, "merits our deference."

On at least two other issues, libel and parochiaid, Powell holds the key to the Court's position. He spoke for the majority in 1985 when it declined to permit use of the First Amendment to limit damage awards in libel cases involving private issues, rather than matters of general public concern. The decision was reached by a 5-4 vote. Powell explained that in such cases the state's interest in protecting an individual's reputation outweighed First Amendment considerations of free speech.

Powell's vote was also decisive in striking down programs of publicly funded aid to parochial school students in New York City and Grand Rapids, Mich. Powell explained that he had joined the more liberal members of the Court to place these programs outside constitutional limits primarily because of his concern that such aid was politically divisive.

"There ... is small chance that these programs would result in significant religious or denominational control over our democratic processes.... Nonetheless, there remains a considerable risk of continuing political strife over the propriety of direct aid to religious schools and the proper allocation of limited governmental resources.... In short, aid to parochial schools of the sort at issue here potentially leads to 'that kind and degree of government involvement in religious life that, as history teaches us, is apt to lead to strife and frequently strain a political system to the breaking point.' "

Brennan: Liberal Spokesman

"From its founding, the nation's basic commitment has been to foster the dignity and well-being of all persons within its borders," wrote Justice William J. Brennan Jr. in 1970. This concern for individual dignity and the affirmative view of federal power have been the hallmarks of Brennan's judicial writings on a variety of issues that have come before the Court in his almost three decades there.

When the Court in 1982 told Texas that it could not deny a free public education to children who were illegal aliens, Brennan spoke for the majority. The Court has not held there to be a constitutional right to a public education, but Brennan's opinion left no doubt that the Constitution denies states the power to decide they will educate some children and not others.

"The inability to read and write will handicap the individual deprived of a basic education each and every day of his life," he wrote. "The inestimable toll of that deprivation on the social, economic, intellectual and psychological well-being of the individual, and the obstacles it poses to individual achievement, makes it most difficult to reconcile . . . a status-based denial of basic education with the frame-work of equality embodied in the Equal Protection Clause."

During the first half of his career on the Court, Brennan, who will turn 80 in early 1986, often spoke for the liberal majority of the Warren Court. It was Brennan who wrote in 1962 to assert federal court jurisdiction over the "political" question of electoral district populations, clearing the way for the "one person, one vote" ruling that required nationwide redistricting. Four years later he wrote the Court's opinion upholding the Voting Rights Act of 1965, enacted to end the disenfranchisement of thousands of black Americans.

In the second half of his career, the post-Warren era, Brennan found himself in a shrinking minority. One by one his liberal colleagues had departed, leaving Brennan and Thurgood Marshall the only certain liberal votes. Together they have dissented time and again, particularly vehement in their criticism when the Court curtails the rights of individuals or restricts access to the federal courts.

Brennan sees the federal courts as the individual's protectors against mistreatment by the other branches of the government. Those courts were intended "to provide a hospitable forum" for those whose constitutional rights have been violated.

When the Court in 1984 denied access to black parents of school children who sought to force the federal government to toughen its enforcement of the policy denying tax-exempt status to discriminatory schools, Brennan dissented: "Once again, the Court 'uses "standing" to slam the courthouse door against plaintiffs who are entitled to full consideration of their claims. . . .

"The Court displays a startling insensitivity to the historical role played by the

William J. Brennan Jr.

federal courts in eradicating race discrimination from our nation's schools. . . . What is most disturbing about today's decision therefore, is . . . the indifference evidenced by the Court to the detrimental effects that racially segregated schools supported by tax-exempt status from the federal government, have on the respondents' attempt to obtain an education in a racially integrated school system. I cannot join such indifference."

A year later, the Court held that states could not be sued, without their consent, by a handicapped person who argued that he had been denied a job by a state agency because of his handicap. In protest, Brennan wrote one of the longest dissenting opinions of his career.

"The Court has put the federal judiciary in the unseemly position of exempting the states from compliance with laws that bind every other legal actor in our nation," Brennan warned. "Despite the presence of the most clearly lawless behavior by the State government, the Court's doctrine holds that the judicial authority of the United States does not extend to suits by an individual against a state in federal court.

"If this doctrine were required to enhance the liberty of our people in accordance with the Constitution's protections, I could accept it. If the doctrine were required by the structure of the federal system created by the Framers, I could accept it. Yet the current doctrine intrudes on the ideal of liberty under law by protecting the States from the consequences of their illegal conduct."

In keeping with his affirmative view of federal judicial power, Brennan wrote the Court's pioneer rulings striking down laws and regulations treating men and women differently. In 1976 Brennan formulated the standard used today to test such laws. "To withstand constitutional challenge," he wrote, "classifications by gender must serve important government objectives and must be substantially related to achievement of those objectives." Not surprisingly, it was Brennan who wrote the Court's opinion in 1984 telling the U.S. Jaycees that states could require them to accept women as full members.

Brennan also champions the individual's right of privacy, basically defined as freedom from government interference. The Court's only Catholic member, Brennan quietly but staunchly sides with the prochoice forces on the issue of abortion. He has also written the Court's opinions denying states the freedom to restrict access to contraceptives.

"If the right of privacy means anything," he has written, "it is the right of the individual, married or single, to be free from unwarranted governmental intrusion into matters so fundamentally affecting a person as the decision whether to bear or beget a child."

On questions of criminal law Brennan is as concerned about the impact of improper law enforcement methods on society as about its effect on the individual suspect or defendant. To him the Fourth Amendment is not simply a protection that criminals may invoke to block unreasonable searches, but one that every citizen may claim.

The Court in 1984 approved the "good faith" exception to the exclusionary rule. This ruling permitted the use of evidence taken by police in a search authorized by a warrant that they, in good faith, thought to be valid, although it was later found defective. Brennan dissented vehemently. "What the Framers understood ... remains true today — that the task of combatting crime and convicting the guilty will in every era seem of such critical and pressing concern that we may be lured by the temptations of expediency into forsaking our commitment to protecting individual liberty and privacy. It was for that very reason that the Framers ... insisted that law enforcement efforts be permanently and unambiguously restricted in order to preserve personal freedoms.

"In the constitutional scheme they ordained, the sometimes unpopular task of ensuring that the government's enforcement efforts remain within the strict boundaries fixed by the Fourth Amendment was entrusted to the courts. . . . If those independent tribunals lose their resolve, however, as the Court has done today, and give way to the seductive call of expediency, the vital guarantees of the Fourth Amendment are reduced to nothing more than a 'form of words.' "

When the Court in 1985 upheld customs officials' long, warrantless, incommunicado detention of a suspected drug smuggler, Brennan railed at the majority for permitting "such a ring of unbridled authoritarianism surrounding freedom's soil."

"Many people from around the world travel to our borders precisely to escape such unchecked executive investigatory discretion. What a curious first lesson in

American liberty awaits them on their arrival," he added.

Brennan is a steadfast opponent of the death penalty, viewing it as invariably cruel, unusual and unconstitutional. "The calculated killing of a human being by the state," he wrote in 1972, "involves, by its very nature, a denial of the executed person's humanity." The Constitution, he believes, requires courts to determine "whether a punishment comports with human dignity: Death, quite simply, does not," Brennan declared.

Brennan is the Court's strongest advocate of the separation of church and state. He has agreed with the Court's decisions denying states the right to prescribe prayer or Bible reading in public schools, or to provide any sort of direct aid to parochial schools.

When the Court in 1984 approved the inclusion of a crèche in Pawtucket's holiday display, Brennan dissented, describing the city's action as "a coercive, though perhaps small, step toward establishing the sectarian preferences of the majority at the expense of the minority, accomplished by placing public facilities and funds in support of the religious symbolism and theological tidings that the crèche conveys.

"That the Constitution sets this realm of thought and feeling apart from the pressures and antagonisms of government is one of its supreme achievements. Regrettably, the Court today, tarnishes that achievement."

As the Court ended its October 1984 term, Brennan wrote a pair of opinions vigorously reaffirming the principle that the First Amendment does require a careful separation of church and state. Striking down programs in Grand Rapids and New York City through which publicly funded teachers were sent to parochial schools to teach secular subjects, Brennan emphasized that the First Amendment was intended to "guard the right of every individual to worship according to the dictates of conscience while requiring the government to maintain a course of neutrality among religions, and between religion and non-religion."

In these cases, Brennan found that "the symbolic union of church and state inherent in the provision of secular, state-provided instruction in the religious school buildings threatens to convey a message of state support for religion to students and to the general public," precisely the type of message the First Amendment was intended to prevent.

Marshall: Social Conscience

In announcing his nomination of the first black man to the Supreme Court, President Lyndon B. Johnson said that Thurgood Marshall had "already earned his place in history." Marshall, the nation's first black solicitor general when he was selected for the Court, was unlikely to issue any opinion from the bench equal in importance to *Brown v. Board of Education,* which he had won in 1954. Marshall, director and counsel of the NAACP Legal Defense and Educational Fund for 20 years, was one of the founders and chief legal strategists of the civil rights movement.

The *Brown* decision began the Warren Court era; Marshall came to the Court at its end. As the Court's membership changed in the 1970s, Marshall found himself more and more often in dissent — and rarely the Court's spokesman on any major issue. Along with Brennan, with whom he agreed on all but a few issues each term, Marshall wrote often in dissent.

An advocate of a strong role for the courts and, secondarily, the executive, Marshall distrusts the more political branches of government. His distrust is rooted in the long history of political neglect of blacks and other minority groups. "When elected leaders cower before public pressure," Marshall wrote in 1977, in dissent, "this Court, more than ever, must not shirk its duty to enforce the Constitution for the benefit of the poor and powerless."

When the Court in 1981 upheld the decision of Congress to exclude women from registering for the military draft, Marshall dissented, criticizing his colleagues for overdoing their deference to Congress. "It is as if the majority has lost sight of the fact that 'it is the responsibility of this Court to, act as the ultimate interpreter of the Constitution,' " he wrote. "Congressional enactments in the area of military affairs must, like all other laws be judged by the standards of the Constitution. For the Constitution is the supreme law of the land and all legislation must conform to . . . [its] principles."

When the Court in 1982 voted 8-1 to uphold California's Proposition 1 limiting the power of state courts to order busing, Marshall dissented. "Proposition 1 has placed an enormous barrier between minority children and the effective enjoyment of their constitutional rights, a barrier that is not placed in the path of those who seek to vindicate other rights granted by state law," he wrote.

By coincidence or design, Marshall has written few major opinions in the area he knows best — civil rights. He was the author, however, of the Court's first opinion interpreting the Equal Pay Act and requiring a company to equalize the salaries of men and women doing the same work. He also wrote the opinion giving white victims of job bias the same rights as black victims to sue under federal law. And it was Marshall who wrote the Court's 1985 opinion putting teeth into the federal law forbidding employers to discriminate against older workers.

Of all the present justices, Marshall is most sympathetic to the plight of the nation's poor. His concern for them sounds in many of his opinions, but in none more

Thurgood Marshall

poignantly than in 1977 when he disagreed with the Court's decision to back state power to refuse to provide Medicaid abortions: "The enactments challenged here brutally coerce poor women to bear children whom society will scorn for every day of their lives.

"Many thousands of unwanted minority and mixed race children now spend blighted lives in foster homes, orphanages and 'reform' schools. . . . Many children of the poor will sadly attend second-rate segregated schools. . . . And opposition remains strong against increasing AFDC [Aid to Families with Dependent Children] benefits for impoverished mothers and children so that there is little chance for the children to grow up in a decent environment. . . .

"I am appalled at the ethical bankruptcy of those who preach a 'right to life' that means, under present social policies, a bare existence in utter misery for so many poor women and their children."

Marshall finds capital punishment

"morally unacceptable" and hence unconstitutional. Because only Brennan agrees with this point of view, Marshall insists that the majority enforce strictly the procedural safeguards it set out in 1976 to guide judges and juries in imposing a sentence of death. It is essential, he wrote in 1985, that "capital sentencers ... view their task as the serious one of determining whether a specific human being should die at the hands of the state."

Marshall spoke for the Court when it set aside a death sentence imposed by a jury that had been misled by a prosecutor as to its responsibility in determining sentence. Marshall insisted: "It is constitutionally impermissible to rest a death sentence on a determination made by a sentencer who has been led to believe that the responsibility for determining the appropriateness of the defendant's death rests elsewhere."

Marshall frequently dissents from decisions relaxing procedural protections for criminal suspects, warning that absolute fidelity to the constitutional guarantees is required. "Good police work," he wrote in 1977, "is something far different from catching the criminal at any price."

In 1985 the Court held that the Constitution requires a state to provide an indigent defendant seeking to use insanity as a defense with the aid of a psychiatrist in making that defense. Marshall wrote the opinion. He emphasized the long line of rulings, stretching back to Warren Court landmarks like *Gideon v. Wainwright* requiring states to appoint attorneys to represent indigents charged with misdemeanors.

"Meaningful access to justice has been the consistent theme of these cases. We recognized long ago that mere access to the courthouse doors does not by itself assure a proper functioning of the adversary process, and that a criminal trial is fundamentally unfair if the State proceeds against an indigent defendant without making certain that he has access to the raw materials integral to the building of an effective defense."

In clear contrast to Rehnquist's views that the original intent of the Framers is the only proper guide for the justices' decisions, Marshall argues that constitutional values evolve.

Writing in partial dissent from the 1985 ruling that a law treating mentally retarded people differently from other citizens is valid if it is found to be a rational means to a legitimate end, Marshall observed: "Courts ... do not sit or act in a social vacuum. Moral philosophers may debate whether certain inequalities are absolute wrongs, but history makes clear that constitutional principles of equality, like constitutional principles of liberty, property and due process, evolve over time; what once was a 'natural' and 'self-evident' ordering later comes to be seen as an artificial and invidious constraint on human potential and freedom.

"Shifting cultural, political, and social patterns at times come to make past practices appear inconsistent with fundamental principles upon which American society rests, an inconsistency legally cognizable under the Equal Protection Clause. It is natural that evolving standards of equality come to be embodied in legislation. When that occurs, courts should look to the fact of such change as a source of guidance on evolving principles of equality."

Marshall argued that the Court should approve a tougher test for laws discriminating against the retarded. "Prejudice, once let loose, is not easily cabined," he wrote. "For the retarded, just as for Negroes and women, much has changed in recent years, but much remains the same; outdated statutes are still on the books, and irrational fears or ignorance, traceable to the prolonged social and cultural isolation of the retarded, continue to stymie recognition of the dignity and individuality of retarded people."

Stevens: Independent Thinker

Least political and most independent of the current justices is John Paul Stevens, who completed a decade on the Court in December 1985. Stevens couples an active intellect with an open judicial mind, characteristics that make him the least predictable member of the Court.

Stevens began his career on the Court as a swing vote. A master at drawing and justifying constitutional lines, the very junior justice in 1976 wrote one of three opinions explaining to the nation why mandatory death penalty laws were unconstitutional while less inflexible capital punishment laws could stand.

In his first terms, Stevens most often agreed with Stewart, the "man in the middle" between liberals and conservatives. But with Stewart's departure, O'Connor's arrival and the resulting strengthening of the conservative wing of the Court, Stevens moved into a firm alliance with the liberals, Brennan and Marshall. In the October 1983 term, he voted with Brennan on three of every four cases.

Stevens shares Brennan's view of the Court's most important function — the protection of the individual. He reminded his colleagues in 1984 that "the Court must be ever mindful of its primary role as the protector of the citizen and not the warden or the prosecutor. The Framers surely feared the latter more than the former."

Stevens is an easy, skillful writer, and he consistently writes more opinions than any other justice. In the October 1983 term, he wrote 68 opinions — of which 34 were dissents.

Stevens is praised for his intelligence and for his ability to crystallize an issue in a single question and to illustrate complex concepts in blunt, down-to-earth language. Dissenting from the majority's 1976 holding that it was not sex discrimination for employers to treat pregnancy differently from

John Paul Stevens

other temporary disabilities, Stevens gave his colleagues a succinct biology lesson: "By definition, such a rule discriminates on account of sex; for it is the capacity to become pregnant which primarily differentiates the female from the male."

Among the most active questioners during oral arguments, Stevens views the argument period as an opportunity to clarify his thinking — and perhaps that of his colleagues — on an issue.

When the Court wishes to state its position with precision, it often chooses Stevens as its spokesman. Few areas of constitutional law are as unclear as the law governing police searches. The Court traditionally has permitted police to stop and search an automobile without a warrant, if they suspect it is involved in illegal activity. But what about a closed or wrapped container inside the car? Can police search it without obtaining a warrant?

In 1981 the Court said *no* — a warrant was required — but in 1982, the Court reversed itself and clarified its position.

Stevens explained that the only fair or practical solution was to permit police to conduct a thorough search of such packages: "When a legitimate search is under way, and when its purpose and its limits have been precisely defined, nice distinctions between closets, drawers, and containers, in the case of a home, or between glove compartments, upholstered seats, trunks and wrapped packages, in the case of a vehicle, must give way to the interest in the prompt and efficient completion of the task at hand.

"The rule applies equally to all containers. . . . A constitutional distinction between 'worthy' and 'unworthy' containers would be improper. . . .

"For just as the most frail cottage in the kingdom is absolutely entitled to the same guarantees of privacy as the most majestic. mansion, so also may a traveler who carries a toothbrush and a few articles of clothing in a paper bag or knotted scarf claim an equal right to conceal his possessions from official inspection as the sophisticated executive with the locked attaché case."

Three years later, when the Court for the first time in 22 years fully addressed the politically explosive issue of school prayer, Stevens wrote for the majority to reaffirm its controversial view that the First Amendment forbids any state sponsored religious activity in the nation's public schools.

The touchstone for this ruling, Stevens explained, was the view that the First Amendment was drafted to protect the individual's freedom of conscience — his freedom to voice his views or remain silent, to attend church or not attend church, to write what he wished or refrain from writing.

Applied to the issue of school prayer, Stevens wrote, this individual freedom "embraces the right to select any religious faith or none at all." The government cannot intrude on that freedom by encouraging or endorsing prayer in the schools, even when

it is done through a supposedly neutral "moment-of-silence" statute. "The Government must pursue a course of complete neutrality toward religion."

Steven's school prayer opinion was a "liberal" opinion, but he is not the kind of liberal who believes citizens should be coddled. On the same day he announced the school prayer decision, he also announced the Court's decision that Massachusetts had given food stamp recipients adequate notice of a change in the law that would reduce, or even terminate, their benefits. Stevens made plain that food stamp recipients, like other citizens, were expected to act on their own behalf. "All citizens are presumptively charged with knowledge of the law," he wrote.

"Surely Congress can presume that such a notice relative to a matter as important as a change in a household's food-stamp allotment would prompt an appropriate inquiry if it is not fully understood. The entire structure of our democratic government rests on the premise that the individual citizen is capable of informing himself about the particular policies that affect his destiny."

The same justice who understands how confusing it must be for policemen to try to conduct constitutional searches — when the Supreme Court cannot seem to agree on what is constitutional — can poignantly capture the pain of a prison inmate's loss of personal papers. Stevens was the dissenters' voice in 1983 when the Court ruled against a prisoner who charged that a guard's intentional destruction of his personal property violated the constitutional guarantee of due process. He reminded his colleagues that "the courts . . . have a special obligation to protect the rights of prisoners. Prisoners are truly the outcasts of society" who have nowhere but the courts to look for their protection.

"Personal letters, snapshots of family members, a souvenir, a deck of cards, a hobby kit, perhaps a diary or a training manual for an apprentice in a new trade, or even a Bible — a variety of inexpensive items may enable a prisoner to maintain contact with some part of his past and an eye to the possibility of a better future. Are all of these items subject to unrestrained perusal, confiscation or mutilation at the hands of a possibly hostile guard?"

Stevens' open-mindedness and his mastery of the fine points of constitutional law are demonstrated by his major opinions on First Amendment issues other than church and state. He wrote the Court's 1976 opinion upholding a city's right to use its zoning power to disperse adult bookstores and adult theaters throughout the city — and in 1984 he spoke for the Court when it sanctioned Los Angeles' ban on posted signs on public property. Both these measures were challenged as First Amendment violations.

But in 1982 he wrote the landmark opinion forbidding a state to ban a nonviolent civil rights boycott or to assess its participants damages for economic losses they cause. And in 1984 he was the majority's voice as it reaffirmed the "actual malice" standard protecting the nation's press in libel suits by public officials.

Increasingly in the 1980s Stevens has criticized the Court's conservative stance. When the justices in 1985 upheld an antique statute limiting to $10 the amount veterans can pay attorneys for pressing their benefit claims with the government, Stevens dissented with characteristic vigor. "The Court does not appreciate the value of individual liberty," he began. "If the Government, in the guise of a paternalistic interest in protecting the citizen from his own improvidence, can deny him access to independent counsel of his choice, it can change the character of our free society. . . .

"Regardless of the nature of the dispute between the sovereign and the citizen — whether it be a criminal trial, a proceeding to terminate parental rights, a claim for social security benefits, a dispute over welfare benefits, or a pension claim asserted by the widow of a soldier who was killed on the battlefield — the citizen's right to consult an independent lawyer and to retain that lawyer to speak on his or her behalf is an aspect of liberty that is priceless. It should not be bargained away."

White: Mystery Man

When the Supreme Court handed the Reagan administration major victories in civil rights and criminal law, it was usually Byron R. White, at 68 the second most senior justice, who delivered the majority's opinion.

It may seem odd that the one justice named to the Court by John F. Kennedy would endorse the Reagan administration's conservative views on civil rights and criminal law. But that is only the beginning of the enigma of Byron White, according to those who have watched him closely. He is the Court's most mysterious justice, actively questioning the attorneys arguing a

Byron R. White

case, pressing them to give "yes" or "no" answers to his questions, and then holding his judicial cards close to his chest until a decision is announced.

White demonstrates a consistently literal approach to the law, which often lands him on the conservative side of an issue. But not always. White would have permitted Congress to retain the legislative veto; he dissented from the decision striking it down. He did not approve of allowing police to shoot to kill fleeing suspects and wrote the majority opinion saying so.

White's literalism was evidenced in his opinion for the Court in *Grove City College v. Bell,* in which he agreed with the Reagan administration that when Congress in 1972 banned sex discrimination in any "program or activity" receiving federal aid, it meant "program or activity," not "school or institution."

For a decade the executive branch had enforced the ban against all programs at any recipient school. The Reagan administration wished to change that policy and enforce the ban only against the particular programs receiving aid. The Supreme Court agreed. Only by ignoring the language of the law, White wrote, could one conclude that aid to a particular part of an institution was aid to the entire college. "We have found no persuasive evidence suggesting that Congress intended that the Department's regulatory authority follow federally aided students from classroom to classroom, building to building, or activity to activity," he added.

White has steadfastly dissented from the Court's rulings curtailing state power to regulate abortions, perhaps because those rulings are founded upon an elusive right of privacy that the literal White does not find in the Constitution.

White's literalism is leavened with a pragmatic assessment of reality, which yields a voting record that cannot be neatly labeled conservative or liberal. That prag-

matism spurred him to dissent from the Court's 1982 decision invalidating the legislative veto as violating the Constitution's separation of powers.

White warned that without the legislative veto, Congress would have to choose "either to refrain from delegating the necessary authority, leaving itself with a hopeless task of writing laws with the requisite specificity to cover endless special circumstances across the entire policy landscape, or in the alternative to abdicate its lawmaking function to the executive branch and independent agencies.

"To choose the former leaves major national problems unresolved," he wrote. "To opt for the latter risks unaccountable policymaking by those not elected to fill that role."

Such pragmatism also pervades White's opinions on official immunity. In 1978 he wrote for the Court when it held that Cabinet officials did not have absolute immunity from damage suits brought by persons who felt they had been injured by the official's actions. Five years later, when the Court held that presidents did enjoy such absolute immunity, White was the voice for the four justices in dissent. "Attaching absolute immunity to the office of the President, rather than to particular activities that the President might perform, places the President above the law. It is a reversion to the old notion that the King can do no wrong."

In 1985, when the Court ruled that the attorney general enjoyed only a limited immunity from civil suits for his actions to protect the nation's security, White wrote: "This standard will not allow the Attorney General to carry out his national security functions wholly free from concern for his personal liability; he may on occasion have to pause to consider whether a proposed course of action can be squared with the Constitution and laws of the United States.

"But this is precisely the point . . .

'[w]here an official could be expected to know that his conduct would violate statutory or constitutional rights, he *should* be made to hesitate.'... We do not believe that the security of the Republic will be threatened if its Attorney General is given incentives to abide by clearly established law."

When the Court approved the good faith exception to the exclusionary rule, White wrote the opinion, explaining that in that situation the costs of excluding evidence far outweighed the benefits and "offend[ed] basic concepts of the criminal justice system."

Aware that the decision was likely to be interpreted, both by advocates and critics, as a sweeping one, White was careful to confine its breadth. "We do not suggest ... that exclusion is always inappropriate in cases where an officer has obtained a warrant and abided by its terms," he wrote, outlining various situations in which the evidence so obtained should still be excluded. "The good-faith exception," White concluded, "is not intended to signal our unwillingness strictly to enforce the requirements of the Fourth Amendment."

But there are limits on how far White will go to approve law enforcement policies. When the Court in 1985 struck down part of a Tennessee law that authorized police to shoot to kill a suspect fleeing from the scene of a crime — even if the suspect was unarmed and seemed to pose no danger to police or bystanders — White's blunt majority opinion reflected his indignant rejection of such unrestrained power. "A police officer may not seize an unarmed nondangerous suspect by shooting him dead," White wrote. "It is not better that all felony suspects die than that they escape."

White has long been concerned that judicial remedies for victims of discrimination be closely tailored to the scope of the actual wrong. He has emphasized in several opinions that discriminatory effect is not enough to prove a law impermissible; there must be intent to discriminate as well.

It was no surprise that White spoke for the Court when in 1984 it held that federal courts should not disregard the "last hired, first fired" rules of valid seniority systems as a way of protecting recently hired minority employees from layoffs. As is characteristic, White tied his opinion closely to the particular facts of the case before him, seeming to limit its sweep. But the Reagan administration, which claimed the ruling as a major victory, emphasized his statement that federal civil rights laws in general "provide make-whole relief only to those who have been actual victims of illegal discrimination."

It was not enough in seniority situations like this, White wrote, just to be a member of a class that had suffered discrimination. To win special treatment, "each individual must prove that the discriminatory practice had an impact on him."

Since the early 1970s White has voted consistently with Burger, Rehnquist, Powell and Blackmun. In the 1980s his agreement rate with Burger, Rehnquist, Powell — and now O'Connor — is even higher. In the October 1983 term, he agreed with each of those four more than 80 percent of the time.

Like them, White has a strong belief that federal judges should defer to the decisions of the other branches of the government on many matters. Refusing to narrow the reach of a 1970 law enacted for use against organized crime but invoked more in the 1980s in business disputes against legitimate enterprises, White was definite: "This defect — if defect it is — is inherent in the statute as written, and its correction must lie with Congress," not the courts.

And when the Court in 1985 deferred to the expertise of the National Labor Relations Board and upheld the board's ruling denying unions the power to forbid members from resigning during a strike, White — in concurrence — declared he would have supported the board's position either way. When statutory language is ambiguous, "deference to the board is not only appropriate but necessary," he wrote.

White is out of step with the current majority on several key First Amendment questions, including libel, school prayer and parochiaid. Dissenting from the 1985 rulings in each area, he urged the Court to reconsider its precedents and to adopt new positions less restrictive of state power in each area.

Blackmun: Practical Pioneer

"Continuity with change are words that might well be inscribed in our marble panels along with 'Equal Justice Under Law,' " said Justice Harry A. Blackmun in 1972. "Continuity with change" aptly describes Blackmun's career on the Court. More than any other sitting justice, he has changed and grown in his years as a justice.

The seeds of growth and the willingness to accept change were evident early. In one of Blackmun's first terms, he asked rhetorically, "Must our law be so rigid and our procedural concepts so inflexible that we render ourselves helpless when the existing methods and the traditional concepts do not quite fit and do not prove to be entirely adequate for new issues?"

In Blackmun's first years on the Court, he aligned himself closely with Burger, a longtime friend also from Minnesota, and too quickly, observers labelled them the Minnesota Twins. But in 1973 Blackmun was chosen by Burger to explain the most controversial Supreme Court ruling of the 1970s — that curtailing state power to ban abortions.

His opinion in *Roe v. Wade* clearly displayed his willingness to stretch traditional legal concepts to cover new situations and to meet new concerns. "Our law should not be that rigid," he said, dismissing the argument that the challenge to laws ban-

Harry A. Blackmun

ning abortion was moot because in the period of time that it took the case to reach the Supreme Court, the women bringing the case would either have delivered or obtained abortions.

Blackmun has commented that writing the opinion in *Roe v. Wade* changed his life. It also marked the beginning of a change in his judicial career. Not only did it set him apart in the public mind from Burger, Rehnquist and Powell — often considered as a block of Nixon nominees — but also it set him on a course toward the Court liberals on a number of important issues.

By the late 1970s Blackmun was voting with Brennan as often as he was voting with Burger. In the October 1981 and 1982 terms he voted with Brennan in three out of four cases and with Marshall almost as often. The striking conservative shift of the October 1983 term in part reflected the loosening of Blackmun's alliance with the liberals, and his willingness to vote with Powell, Burger, O'Connor and White, particularly on questions of criminal law, but also on the issues of affirmative action and sex discrimination.

Early in his career on the Court, Blackmun espoused a position of restraint for justices. Explaining his dissent from the Court's holding that existing capital punishment laws were unconstitutional, he wrote: "Cases such as these provide for me an excruciating agony of the spirit. I yield to no one in the depth of my distaste, antipathy and indeed, abhorrence, for the death penalty . . . buttressed by a belief that capital punishment serves no useful purpose.

"Were I a legislator I would vote against the death penalty. . . . There — on the legislative branch . . . and, secondarily, on the executive branch — is where the authority and responsibility for this kind of action lies. The authority should not be taken over by the judiciary. . . . We should not allow our personal preferences . . . to guide our judicial decisions," he warned.

In time, however, Blackmun, a reticent, hard-working justice who rarely speaks during oral arguments, has become more willing to exercise judicial power. In 1982 he explained why the Court found unconstitutional Washington State's anti-busing initiative: "[W]hen the state's allocation of power places unusual burdens on the ability of racial groups to enact legislation specifically designed to overcome the 'special condition' of prejudice, the governmental action seriously 'curtail[s] the operation of those political processes ordinarily to be relied upon to protect minorities.' "

At that point, Blackmun wrote, the Court must assume "the judiciary's special role in safeguarding the interest of those groups that are 'relegated to such a position of political powerlessness as to command extraordinary protection from the majoritarian political process.' "

Blackmun's concern for those he views as less powerful erupted in a vigorous dissent late in the October 1984 term in *Pattern Maker's League of North America*

v. NLRB. Criticizing the majority for "supinely" deferring to the NLRB, he wrote that the Court's ruling was "an affront to the autonomy of the American worker."

To permit one dissatisfied worker to go back to work in violation of his promise not to resign during a strike, wrote Blackmun, "is to allow the breaching individual to become a free rider, enjoying the benefits of his bargain without having to live with the risks that all who sought those benefits agreed to share."

In the decade from 1976 to 1985, Blackmun's views on the proper balance of state and federal power changed notably. That change of mind brought about an important reversal in constitutional law. In 1976 the Court, for the first time since the New Deal era, struck down an act of Congress by invoking the 10th Amendment, which reserves to the states and the people powers not delegated to the federal government nor prohibited to the states by the Constitution.

In *National League of Cities v. Usery*, a five-man majority — Blackmun, Burger, Rehnquist, Powell and Stewart — held that Congress violated that amendment and intruded too far on state sovereignty when it applied federal minimum wage law to employees of state and local governments. In 1985 the Court overruled *National League of Cities*. The vote was again 5-4. Blackmun joined the dissenters from the 1976 decision to form the new majority, which declared that the 10th Amendment did not limit Congress' power to pass laws regulating commerce, a broad category that covers all manner of concerns, including public accommodations and the wages paid to government employees. Burger, Rehnquist, Powell and O'Connor dissented.

Not only did Blackmun's shift create the new majority on this issue, but also he wrote the majority opinion explaining that "due respect for the reach of congressional power within the federal system mandates" reversal of the 1976 decision.

The Constitution set up a political structure that protected states from overreaching federal power by giving states the power to participate in the selection of the president and the members of Congress, Blackmun wrote. "The Framers chose to rely on a federal system in which special restraints on federal power over the States inhered principally in the workings of the National Government itself, rather than in discrete limitations on the objects of federal authority," he said. "State sovereign interests, then, are more properly protected by procedural safeguards inherent in the structure of the federal system than by judicially created limitations on federal power."

In summary, he explained: "The principal and basic limit on the federal commerce power is that inherent in all congressional action — the built-in restraints that our system provides through state participation in federal governmental action. The political process ensures that laws that unduly burden the states will not be promulgated."

Blackmun's view of the need for innovation in the law has sparked a line of rulings in which the Court has extended First Amendment protection to commercial speech. In 1975 Blackmun wrote the Court's opinion holding that a state could not prosecute a newspaper editor for printing an advertisement about legal abortion services in another state.

The next year, he wrote the opinion striking down a state law forbidding the advertisement of drug prices: "Advertising

... is nonetheless dissemination of information as to who is producing and selling what product, for what reason and at what price. "So long as we preserve a predominantly free enterprise economy, the allocation of our resources in large measure will be made through numerous private economic decisions. It is a matter of public interest that those decisions ... be intelligent and well informed. To this end, the free flow of commercial information is indispensable."

In their own words, the eight brethren have sketched their judicial self-portraits. Like O'Connor's, each reflects a distinct judicial personality, but the portraits are dynamic, not static. Justices change their minds — and their votes, sometimes with dramatic consequences. The dynamics of a decision made by nine people can be radically altered by a change in a single participant.

The Supreme Court is not a legal vending machine into which cases are inserted and from which decisions emerge. Nor is it a bureaucracy of diffused responsibility and confused procedures. It is nine human beings who repeatedly put themselves on record on some of the most controversial issues of any given day, setting out their reasons and signing their work.

Each justice has a particular set of values and ideals, concerns and cares, virtues and flaws, all of which take on added significance as they are reflected in his or her work, and so affect the course of American life and law for years to come.

6

Reagan's Other Campaign: 1981-1982

As soon as Ronald Reagan's campaign for the presidency ended with his election, another campaign began. Reagan had been blunt about the interference of the national government in the affairs of citizens and promised to curtail it.

"It is my intention," Reagan said in his first inaugural address, "to curb the size and influence of the federal establishment and to demand recognition of the distinction between the powers granted to the Federal Government and those reserved to the states or the people.

"It is no coincidence that our present troubles parallel and are proportionate [to] the intervention and intrusion in our lives that have resulted from unnecessary and excessive growth of government."

Reagan could trace a number of those "troubles" right to the mahogany bench of the U.S. Supreme Court. From its decisions sprang national controversies over abortion, affirmative action, busing, school prayer and parochiaid. To succeed in his plans for changing the shape of American life, Reagan had to persuade the Court to go along.

Politics and the Court

The Supreme Court is not a political institution; it is not an elected body respond-ing directly to the wishes of the polity, the people. It is a judicial institution bracketed by politics: political decisions determine its personnel; political decisions determine the shape of its docket and the tone of the arguments before it.

The Court is a lens through which a myriad of political, legal, social and economic pressures focus upon a particular issue to produce a single decision. That decision is made by people who sit where they do because a president found it politically appropriate to place them there.

But the justices are only part of the equation. The Court cannot reach out for issues; it must react to those that come before it. In considering those issues, the parameters of the Court's inquiry are once again limited by the arguments made by the opposing sides.

Here again, politics play a role. No one comes before the Court as often as the solicitor general or one of his staff, representing the federal government — sometimes as a party, sometimes as simply a "friend of the court." The solicitor general is selected by the president to argue the president's policies to the Court.

The Court, therefore, is populated with politically chosen individuals, and it is concerned with cases of immense political import. The Court itself is not political, but the environment in which it operates is — and properly so.

The Solicitor General

Every president has two means to persuade the Supreme Court to adopt his vision of America: the power to appoint new members as vacancies occur and the power to argue cases before the Court.

Early on, Reagan had the chance to use the appointment power, and he used it effectively with his selection of Justice Sandra Day O'Connor. But Reagan and those around him knew that it would take more than one justice to convince the Court to endorse many of the changes Reagan planned in the nation's course. Having set the stage by naming O'Connor, he chose Rex E. Lee as his solicitor general, the man who would argue his proposals for change before the Court.

The solicitor general and his staff of 22 attorneys are the most successful of all advocates before the Court, both in winning Supreme Court review of the cases they appeal and in winning Supreme Court endorsement of their position after oral argument. *(Box, p. 102)*

There is, Lee observed after his years in the office, a special relationship of trust and credibility between the Court and the solicitor general's office, a relationship that some have described as making the solicitor general the Court's "10th" justice.

Lee, born 1935, was dean of Brigham Young University Law School in Provo, Utah, when he was appointed solicitor general in 1981. But Washington was familiar territory to him. He had served as a clerk to Justice Byron R. White after graduating from law school and had spent two years, 1975-1977, as head of the Justice Department's Civil Division during the Ford administration.

More important in the White House

view, Lee was a committed advocate of judicial restraint, of keeping judges out of matters that were properly left to legislators and executives. In his book *A Lawyer Looks At the Constitution* (1981), Lee urged judges to "weight the judicial balance scales in favor of government" as a general rule, upsetting legislative decisions "only . . . where the error is quite clear and where the balance scales quite clearly disfavor the policymakers' judgment."

In his four years as solicitor general, Lee presented to the Court Reagan's arguments in areas of national policy as diverse as antitrust, abortion and affirmative action. Through Lee and the skilled advocates of his office, Reagan encouraged the justices to leave key decisions about controversial matters to legislators and prosecutors.

Reagan's Agenda

Ronald Reagan came into office convinced that, by electing him, the American people had endorsed his call for a dramatic change in the nation's direction on key points of economic and social policy. Among the changes Reagan proposed were:

—a constitutional amendment to ban abortion;

—restoration of voluntary prayer in public schools;

—an end to the use of mandatory busing for racial balance in schools;

—abandonment of quotas and ratios as a remedy for racial injustice;

—relaxation of certain judicial rules that ensure the constitutional rights of the accused by denying police and prosecutors the use of illegally obtained evidence;

—rechanneling power from the federal government to state and local governments.

Reagan saw litigation as an effective means of bringing about some of those changes. "There is no question," said one attorney who has observed this process close up, "that the Reagan administration is more willing than some to use litigation as an instrument of policy." Lee was right in step with this inclination, setting out his own agenda — a list of Supreme Court cases that could be used to implement the administration's policies.

The administration urged Lee to select as his new deputy and counselor a person whose political views were also in line with those of the Reagan White House. This position was held first by Paul Bator and then by Charles Fried, both from Harvard Law School. The two were viewed as emissaries of the administration's views in a way that Lee's other deputies, all career attorneys, were not.

Bator and Fried were involved in the most sensitive of the issues before the Court on which the administration took a position. Bator, for example, successfully argued the *Grove City* case, in which the justices narrowed the reach of the federal ban on sex discrimination in federally aided schools and colleges. Bator also put forth the administration's position urging accommodation, not separation, of church and state, in the Pawtucket, R.I., crèche case.

A Court Marking Time

The Supreme Court is insulated in many ways from the ebb and flow of political tides. Its term, which begins in October and ends in July, bridges the political calendar. Presidents are elected just after a new Court term begins; they take office midway through the term. It is traditional for the outgoing solicitor general to complete the Court term during which the new president is inaugurated. Reagan was inaugurated halfway through the October 1980 term, and, for all practical purposes, his administration had no impact on the Court during that time.

When Reagan moved into the White House, the Court seemed ripe for firm policy suggestions from the new president.

Rex E. Lee

The decisions of the term appeared to come from a Court marking time; they generally preserved the status quo. The justices seemed quite willing to wait for signals on new policy directions from Congress or the White House.

Some of the term's decisions were conservative in result, like that upholding the male-only military draft. Others were liberal, like those endorsing stringent federal health and safety standards for the workplace, and others extending and expanding some of the key criminal law rulings of the 1960s. But liberal or conservative, the hallmark of most of this term's rulings was a willingness to preserve existing precedents, structures, policies and systems.

In the framework of its liberal past, the Court in 1980 was able to use a conservative approach — adherence to precedent — to achieve a liberal result. By taking a narrow view of its own role, the Court produced a string of decisions upholding liberal precedents and existing regulation. This version

The Solicitor General's Office . . .

Until Solicitor General Robert H. Bork catapulted into the public eye in 1973 as the man who carried out Richard Nixon's order to fire Watergate Special Prosecutor Archibald Cox, few Americans even knew there was a solicitor general. But since 1870 the solicitor general, appointed by the president, has argued the government's case before the Supreme Court. Before Congress established the post as part of the creation of the Department of Justice, the attorney general usually represented the government.

A number of prominent men have held the position. William Howard Taft served as solicitor general under President Benjamin Harrison (1890-1892). Taft was later president and chief justice (1920-1929).

Stanley Reed and Robert H. Jackson were rewarded for their service as solicitors general under President Franklin Roosevelt by being appointed to the Supreme Court. Reed had argued a number of the critical New Deal cases before the Court between 1935 and 1938. Jackson succeeded Reed as solicitor general.

Cox also had served as solicitor general during the Kennedy-Johnson years, 1961-1965. He was succeeded by Thurgood Marshall, who served for two years before President Lyndon Johnson named him to the Supreme Court.

'A Specialized Law Firm'

The solicitor general's office is not involved in a case until it works its way through the lower courts — state or federal — and is ready for appeal to the Supreme Court. "We are a specialized law firm representing only one client in only one court, the Supreme Court," Rex E. Lee explained. Lee served as solicitor general for the Reagan administration from 1981 until June 1985.

Indeed, the solicitor general has been described as the highest government official who actually functions as a practicing attorney. He counsels with his client, studies the legal issues and argues the case. In 1985 the "firm" consisted of 22 lawyers, five of whom are deputy solicitors general. They generally oversee various areas of the law, analyzing lower court decisions to determine whether to ask the Supreme Court to review them.

As of mid-1985, these deputies were:

—Lawrence G. Wallace, born 1931, the office veteran who had, since 1969, served five presidents and four solicitors general. He has argued 87 cases before the Court, more than all but two other men in the 20th century. Until 1985 Wallace oversaw most of the government's civil rights and individual rights arguments, although he had argued almost every type of case during his tenure.

—Andrew L. Frey, born 1938, a deputy solicitor general since 1972, who oversees the government's arguments on criminal law issues. Frey is, in the view of many observers, one of the most effective attorneys to argue before the Court.

—Kenneth S. Geller, born 1947, who has served in the office since 1975, when he came there after serving as assistant special prosecutor for the Watergate affair. Since 1979 he has been the deputy in charge of civil, administrative and regulatory cases.

...A Very Special Law Firm

—Louis Claiborne, born 1927, who has served two stints as a deputy solicitor general. Claiborne held the post from 1964 until 1970, when he moved to England for eight years to practice law and teach. Upon his return in 1978 he resumed the post, overseeing cases involving land and natural resources. Claiborne resigned October 1985.

—Charles Fried, born in Prague, 1935, the second occupant of the "political" deputy post created in 1982 and first held by Paul Bator, born 1929. In October 1985 Fried was named Lee's successor as solicitor general.

Requesting Review/Filing a Brief

Once the decision to request Supreme Court review of a case is made, the solicitor general's office then drafts the formal petition to the Court. That document is called a petition for certiorari in most cases or in others, a jurisdictional statement. In it the solicitor general's office tells the Supreme Court why it should review the lower court's decision. More often than not, the Court agrees with the government and accepts the cases it recommends.

Once the case is granted review, an attorney in the solicitor general's office either drafts the government's argument, filed in what is misnamed a "brief," or reviews the brief written by the branch of the Justice Department or the independent agency that had argued the case in the lower courts. One of the deputies usually signs the brief, along with another attorney in the office and the original attorneys on the case.

The solicitor general signs the brief in cases of particular significance — sometimes joined by the assistant attorney general in charge of the division that argued the case in the lower courts. Assistant Attorney General William Bradford Reynolds, head of the Civil Rights Division of the Justice Department, signed on to several key briefs during the early 1980s — including the 1985 school prayer and parochiaid cases.

Arguing the Case

If the government is a party to the case and it is a particularly important case, the solicitor general or one of his deputies argues it. Otherwise, it is assigned for argument to one of the other attorneys on the staff.

During Reagan's first term, the most important policy cases were argued by Lee and Bator. Lee argued, among others, the 1983 legislative veto case, the 1983 air bag deregulation case, the 1984 exclusionary rule case and the 1985 parochiaid case. Bator argued the *Grove City* sex bias case, the Cuban travel restriction case and the clean air "bubble concept" case.

If the government acts as a friend of the court, it must request and receive permission from the justices to present its argument orally as well as in its brief. Generally, that request is granted. Lee argued as a friend of the court in the 1983 abortion cases, the 1984 Pawtucket crèche case and the 1984 affirmative action case. Bator argued as a friend of the court in the 1985 school prayer case.

of judicial restraint worked in direct opposition to the new administration's push to curtail judicial activism and lighten the burden of federal regulation in American life.

This was the challenge facing Lee: could he persuade the justices that they could at the same time stand on the principle of judicial restraint and hop on the bandwagon of Reagan's plan to change American law and American life?

Prelude: October 1981

When the curtain went up Oct. 5, 1981, on the new Supreme Court term, Reagan's actors were in place. His appointee had taken the oath of office in time to participate in the marathon conference sessions that precede opening day. During these conferences the justices dispose of hundreds of cases that have arrived at the Court since the last public session in early July.

On opening day, O'Connor sat next to her old friend William Rehnquist, at the far right of the Court's curved bench. Facing the justices was the new solicitor general.

Lee had inherited quite an agenda. As the Court began its term, it had already agreed to hear arguments in 102 cases, two-thirds the total it would hear that term.

The government's position in these cases still reflected the moderately liberal policies of the administration of President Jimmy Carter. Many of them concerned institutional matters on which Lee and Reagan agreed with the earlier administration, including a pair of cases urging the Court to reaffirm the confidentiality of census data and a case defending a 1978 energy law against the challenge that it interfered too far into state affairs.

The ABCs of Change

In two cases — one concerning the education of illegal alien children and the other, voluntary busing — the Reagan administration refused to follow the Carter administration's lead. In a third case, in which a citizens' group challenged the transfer of government property to a church-related school, the Reagan administration abandoned the Carter administration's neutral stance to argue that the group could not bring the case in federal court.

Aliens. In *Plyler v. Doe,* the Carter administration had sided with the children of illegal aliens who challenged a Texas law denying them a free public education. They had won a ruling that the law was unconstitutional, a violation of the 14th Amendment promise that no state shall "deny to any person within its jurisdiction the equal protection of the laws."

Texas asked the Court to reverse this decision, and the Reagan administration — changing the government's position — did not oppose that request. There was no conflict between the Texas law and federal laws, Lee told the Court. Therefore, the administration wished to "leave to the parties directly affected the arguments concerning whether the equal protection clause requires Texas to educate alien children who were not lawfully admitted to the United States."

Busing. The case of *Washington v. Seattle School District* tested the validity of a state law forbidding the voluntary use of busing by school districts for the purpose of desegregating schools.

In one of the Reagan administration's earliest policy pronouncements, Attorney General William French Smith declared that the Justice Department would no longer endorse mandatory busing as a means of desegregating schools. Over-reliance on that remedy, he told the American Law Institute in May 1981, had "compromised the principle of color-blindness." Smith emphasized that the Justice Department would continue to combat vigorously any efforts to foster segregation, but that it would use other remedies, preferably remedies that "actually improve the quality of public education."

The Washington State law, however, denied school districts the authority to adopt voluntary busing as a means of desegregating their schools. This law had been declared unconstitutional, like the Texas law, as a violation of the equal protection guarantee.

The Carter administration had urged the Supreme Court to agree that the law was invalid. The Reagan administration abandoned the Carter position, asking the justices to uphold the law as a proper exercise of the state's authority to adopt a neighborhood school policy. Signing this brief, in addition to Lee, was William Bradford Reynolds, the new assistant attorney general for civil rights, one of the administration's most outspoken advocates of a new conservative stance on civil rights issues.

In October 1981 the Court agreed to hear another busing case, *Crawford v. Board of Education of the City of Los Angeles.* Lee and Reynolds filed a similar brief supporting an amendment to the California Constitution that limited busing to that required under the Equal Protection Clause.

Coming into Court. The last case in Lee's inherited agenda, *Valley Forge Christian College v. Americans United for Separation of Church and State Inc.,* began as a First Amendment challenge to the government's policy of transferring surplus property to church-related colleges. By the time the case came to the Supreme Court, however, the justices were not asked to rule on the government's policy, but instead on the "legal standing" of the citizens group, Americans United, to bring the case into federal court.

Federal courts have limited jurisdiction; they can only hear certain kinds of cases. Most legal disputes are resolved in state and local courts. To bring a federal case, the person or group bringing it must meet certain qualifications to invoke the jurisdiction — the power to decide — of the federal court.

This case was brought in federal court because Americans United, a group of taxpayers, argued that they were injured because this policy was in conflict with the U.S. Constitution's ban on the establishment of religion. A lower court had found that Americans United had standing to bring the case and that it could proceed.

The Carter administration had taken no position in the case. The Reagan administration, however, intent upon limiting federal litigation of this kind, joined the case. In November 1981 Lee argued, along with the college's attorneys, that Americans United lacked the legal standing to bring the case.

An Apt Prelude. These cases provided an apt prelude to the full-scale campaign that was to unfold in succeeding terms. Often the solicitor general chose cases in which the government was not directly involved as the vehicles to promote the Reagan administration's desire for change. When the government volunteers its views to the Court in cases to which it is not a party, it files *amicus curiae* briefs, also known as "friend of the court" briefs.

Again and again, as in these first cases, the administration would sound the theme of deference to state policy decisions — of letting local sentiment prevail. Institutional interests would come into conflict here, and so this particular theme would never be sounded as firmly or as effectively in the administration's briefs as some states' rights advocates had hoped. *(Box, p. 120)*

Another theme would resound more successfully, however. The *Valley Forge* brief's emphasis on limiting federal judicial power and narrowing citizen access

---

'Friend of the Court'

The solicitor general's office files briefs in at least half the cases heard by the Supreme Court in a given term. In most of these, the government is directly involved as a party to a case. In some, however, the government files a "friend of the court" brief — either because the Court has requested its views on a case or because the administration wants to make clear to the Court its interest in a particular case.

The Reagan administration has made particularly vigorous use of this kind of brief. Most of its major proposals that the Court change its ways have come in friend of the court briefs the adminstration volunteered to file. This was true in both the 1983 and the 1985 abortion cases and in the 1983 and 1985 affirmative action cases. In none was the federal government directly involved. The administration chose to file these briefs to tell the Court the Reagan position on the issues.

---

to federal courts would recur throughout the Reagan years.

An Initial Victory

Indeed, it was on that very point that the Court early in 1982 handed the new solicitor general his first big victory. On Jan. 12 the Court ruled, 5-4, that Americans United for Separation of Church and State lacked the standing to challenge the transfer of federal property to Valley Forge Christian College.

O'Connor cast the deciding vote, joining Chief Justice Warren E. Burger and Justices Lewis F. Powell Jr., William H.

Rehnquist and Byron White in the majority. Writing for the Court, Rehnquist emphasized again and again the limited role of federal courts in American society. "The federal courts were simply not constituted as ombudsmen of the general welfare," he declared. Citizen groups, no matter how intense or sincere their constitutional concerns, do not have "a special license to roam the country in search of governmental wrongdoing and to reveal their discoveries in federal court."

To bring a federal case, a person or group must show that they have suffered or been threatened with an actual injury from the practice or statute they challenge, Rehnquist continued. To wander from this standard would be to endorse "the idea that the judicial power requires nothing more for its invocation than important issues and able litigants."

The majority, Rehnquist concluded, "was unwilling to countenance such a departure from the limits on judicial power" set out in the constitutional language that limits federal courts to hearing real "cases" and "controversies."

Justice William J. Brennan Jr. wrote in dissent, "The Court disregards its constitutional responsibility when, by failing to acknowledge the protections afforded by the Constitution, it uses 'standing to slam the courthouse door against plaintiffs who are entitled to full consideration of their claims on the merits.' "

Lee was pleased, describing the decision as "a really significant victory," a ruling that could serve as the "linchpin" of the administration's campaign against judicial activism. "It will substantially affect the extent to which citizens can raise public-interest issues in court," he told the *Washington Post*.

A Political Mess

But the *Valley Forge* victory was quickly overshadowed by an embarrassing chapter in the Reagan administration's relationship with the Court. It all started with Bob Jones University and the Internal Revenue Service. In 1970 the IRS began refusing to grant tax-exempt status to private schools that discriminated against or refused to accept black students. This policy change was spurred by a federal court order barring the IRS from granting such status to several schools in Mississippi. Despite criticism of this shift from members of Congress whose constituents included such schools and their patrons, the policy remained in force into the 1980s.

Tax-exempt status is of dual importance to schools. Not only does it exempt the institution from paying federal taxes, but also it permits individuals and groups who contribute money to the school to deduct the amount from their income taxes.

Bob Jones University in Greenville, S.C., and the Goldsboro Christian Schools of Goldsboro, N.C., discriminate against blacks because of a religious belief that God intended the black and white races to remain separate. Bob Jones admits black students but bans interracial dating and expels persons who engage in such dating. Goldsboro does not admit black students.

In 1971 the IRS moved to revoke Bob Jones University's tax-exempt status. The university challenged the revocation and in 1978 won a favorable ruling from a federal district court in South Carolina. That court held that the IRS had exceeded its authority by revoking the tax exemption and had violated the institution's First Amendment rights of religious freedom.

The Carter administration appealed that ruling and in 1980 won reversal from the U.S. Court of Appeals for the 4th Circuit. The appeals court held the IRS action proper and constitutional. Bob Jones appealed to the Supreme Court. Goldsboro, which was denied tax-exempt status, brought a similar court challenge, but lost. It also appealed.

The Government's Case. Just as it would defend any other government agency, the solicitor general's office defended the IRS before the Supreme Court. Lee disqualified himself from participating in the case, citing a possible conflict of interest. Before becoming solicitor general, he had represented some other religious schools challenging the IRS policy.

In September 1981 the solicitor general's office filed a brief urging the Court to uphold the IRS policy as applied to Bob Jones and Goldsboro. Federal tax laws, said the brief signed by Deputy Solicitor General Lawrence G. Wallace, the senior career attorney in the office, "do not countenance Federal tax benefits to organizations operated for educational purposes that discriminate against students or applicants on the basis of race."

In October the Court agreed to hear arguments in the cases, consolidating them for consideration. Wallace began drafting a brief presenting the government's defense of the IRS more fully. It was to be filed in January 1982. In that draft he argued that the IRS policy was consistent with the "strong national commitment to the eradication of racial discrimination, and in particular, racial discrimination by educational institutes, public and private."

Reversal No. 1. On Jan. 8, 1982, just days before this brief was to be filed, the administration changed course, moving to withdraw from the Bob Jones and the Goldsboro cases and asking the Court to dismiss them. The administration further announced that it was reversing the challenged IRS policy and revoking the applicable IRS regulations.

Officials from the Treasury and Justice departments said that Bob Jones University's tax-exempt status would be reinstated and Goldsboro Christian Schools would be granted that status. Administration officials explained that their policy shift was based on the belief that Congress, not the IRS, should decide to adopt such a policy and had never formally done so.

The announcement was hailed by fundamentalist religious schools and denounced by the civil rights community. Sen. Daniel P. Moynihan, D-N.Y., criticized the move as "surely immoral, and in my view, illegal as well," a sign that the administration would "give in to the forces ... that want to undo the civil rights movement." The Council for American Private Education, which represents schools that enroll the majority of private school students in the country, described the administration move as "a highly regressive step."

The intensity of the criticism caught Reagan and his advisers off guard. On Jan. 12, the day of the *Valley Forge* decision, Reagan sought to defuse the storm by saying that he would formally ask Congress to pass a law barring tax exemptions for racially discriminatory organizations.

Reagan said he was "unalterably opposed to racial discrimination in any form," but that he also objected to "administrative agencies exercising powers that the Constitution assigns to Congress. Such agencies, no matter how well intentioned, cannot be allowed to govern by administrative fiat."

Until Congress acted, however, the new policy of granting tax-exempt status to discriminatory schools was in effect. On Feb. 18 a three-judge federal court temporarily forbade the administration to grant such exemptions.

Reversal No. 2. A week after the court order, the administration again changed its mind and urged the Supreme Court to proceed with the *Bob Jones* and *Goldsboro* cases. But, the administration said, it would not defend the IRS action. It would argue — on the side of the schools — that the IRS was required to grant such exemptions until Congress changed the law to require denial. The September brief arguing the other side, the government now told the Court, was based on an "erroneous interpretation" of the tax laws.

The new brief was signed by Wallace and Reynolds. The denial of tax exemptions challenged here, the brief told the Court, was "unauthorized agency action that should not, in the absence of congressional action, be countenanced." In an extraordinary footnote, Wallace told the Court that, although he signed the new brief, he still held the contrary views set out in the September brief. (According to the *New York Times,* it was essential that someone in the solicitor general's office sign the brief. Lee had disqualified himself and none of the other lawyers who had worked on the case would sign it, so Wallace added his signature — and the footnote.)

New Lawyer. Lee suggested that the Court might select someone else to argue the IRS side of the case, defending denial of the exemptions. On April 19 the justices appointed William T. Coleman Jr., a prominent black attorney who had served as secretary of transportation in the Ford administration, to present the IRS' case as a friend of the court. The cases of *Bob Jones University v. United States* and *Goldsboro Christian Schools v. United States* would be argued and decided — but not until the October 1982 term.

Sex Discrimination

As Lee's tenure lengthened, he became the target of criticism from radically conservative groups who complained that he did not push the administration's agenda as forcefully as possible at the Court. And indeed, his moderating influence was evident as early as this first term. In two cases involving sex bias, Lee's refusal to shift the government's position proved wise.

In *North Haven Board of Education v. Bell,* a Connecticut school board argued that the sex discrimination ban in Title IX of the 1972 Education Amendments prohibited only discrimination among students — not discriminatory treatment of school employees.

The Carter administration successfully defended the broad sweep of this law, winning an appeals court ruling in its favor. The board appealed, and the Supreme Court early in 1981 agreed to review the case.

In late summer 1981, Secretary of Education T. H. Bell tried to persuade Lee to change course — to argue with the school board against the broad interpretation of the law. Such a shift would have paralleled the administration's reversal in the *Bob Jones* case, leaving the appeals court ruling without a defender.

Lee refused, arguing the case himself in December 1981, and winning it, 6-3, in May 1982. Justice Harry A. Blackmun wrote the opinion; Burger, Powell and Rehnquist dissented.

In the second case, *Mississippi University for Women v. Hogan,* the state nursing school challenged a finding that it was guilty of sex discrimination for refusing to admit men. Lee's office resisted urgings from other administration officials that it intervene to defend such single-sex programs.

In July 1982 the Court ruled, 5-4, against the school. In one of her few disagreements with her more conservative brethren, O'Connor voted with Brennan, Thurgood Marshall, John Paul Stevens and White to hold the school guilty of sex discrimination — and she wrote the Court's opinion. Burger, Blackmun, Powell and Rehnquist dissented.

Aliens and Busing

Lee's hesitance to shift the government's gears too quickly seemed a prudent policy after the Court rebuffed the administration on the alien education case and the busing cases.

In June 1982 the Court, 5-4, ruled that Texas could not refuse to educate the children of illegal aliens. Obviously outraged by the shortsightedness of the state's stance, Justice Brennan wrote vividly of the "enduring disability" imposed on children who are deprived of an education and the "significant social costs" that such deprivation imposes on a nation.

Justice Powell joined the liberals to make up the majority. Whatever wrong illegal aliens have done, he wrote, "their children should not be left on the streets uneducated."

The dissenters, Burger, White, Rehnquist and O'Connor, criticized this "unabashedly result-oriented approach." Burger wrote: "Were it our business to set the nation's social policy, I would agree without hesitation that it is senseless for an enlightened society to deprive any children — including illegal aliens — of an elementary education." But, he said, that is not the Court's function and in assuming such a policy-making function "we trespass on the assigned function of the political branches under our structure of limited and separated power."

Late in the month, the Court ruled in the two busing cases. It upheld the California constitutional amendment, 8-1, reasoning that it was racially neutral, did not deny federal courts the power to order busing nor school boards the freedom to adopt busing plans. Justice Powell wrote the Court's opinion; only Marshall dissented.

But the justices found the Washington State law both discriminatory and unduly restrictive because it prohibited busing for racial purposes while permitting it for other reasons. Justice Blackmun wrote the Court's opinion.

Powell, Burger, Rehnquist and O'Connor dissented — agreeing with the administration and criticizing the majority for an "unprecedented intrusion into the structure of state government."

Disappointment: October 1982

Over the summer of 1982, Lee intensified the administration's campaign at the Court. The issue he chose was abortion. In May the Court had accepted five abortion cases from Virginia, Ohio and Missouri. In each the Court was asked to review state or local efforts to regulate abortion. The federal government was not a party to any of the cases.

Just before the October 1982 term began, the administration filed an unexpected friend of the court brief in these cases, urging the justices to bow out of the abortion controversy altogether. "The time has come to call a halt" to the long line of abortion cases coming to the Court since 1973, wrote Lee. The Court should stop "constitutionalizing" this matter and defer to the political process, leaving "further refinements" of abortion law to legislative wisdom.

Lee later explained to the *Washington Post* his decision to file this brief. The president and his administration felt that the Supreme Court had moved directly and unfortunately into the legislative arena with its 1973 decision in *Roe v. Wade.* This seemed like a good time to officially inform the Court of the administration's views on that matter.

"I thought, what's the point in having the engine at your disposal if you don't take it out and drive it in the direction you really want when the chance comes?" Lee told the *Post* in the August 1983 interview. "That's one of the reasons you elect a president and one of the reasons a president appoints a solicitor general."

In the brief Lee acknowledged that the federal government had no interest in the particular regulations at issue in these cases. He explained that he was filing the government's brief to defend its "substantial interest in preserving the proper sphere of legislative action."

Although President Reagan backed the efforts of pro-life groups to win reversal of *Roe v. Wade,* Lee did not ask the Court to overrule that decision. Just in case the justices wondered, however, he added a cryptic footnote stating that "the government's position in these cases . . . does not indicate agreement with *Roe v. Wade.*"

The Administration's Agenda

There were already 120 other cases on the Supreme Court argument schedule when the term began on Oct. 4. As is traditional, the solicitor general was involved in many of them.

In some, such as the legislative veto case — already argued once during the previous term and then set for re-argument — Lee as solicitor general represented the institutional interest of the executive branch. He argued its traditional position in opposition to the veto as a violation of the separation of powers, an intrusion in the executive's duty to carry out the laws.

In similar fashion, Lee was representing the federal position, rather than the administration position, when he defended the power of Congress to override state rules requiring certain employees to retire early. Reagan had promised to curtail federal interference in state affairs, but the solicitor general was responsible for defending federal laws before the Supreme Court even when they were challenged as just that kind of meddling.

For some years the Court had been increasingly inclined to rule in favor of police and prosecutors on questions of criminal law, while maintaining a more liberal position on questions of individual rights. In a number of the pending criminal cases, Lee urged the Court to continue its support for law enforcement officials. At the same time, on individual rights matters, Lee suggested that it was time for the justices to adopt a more conservative posture leaving decisions on such issues to legislators.

Enlarging the Agenda

The Court in late 1982 added to its docket a number of other issues from the Reagan administration's agenda for change: parochiaid, affirmative action, deregulation and the much-debated exclusionary rule.

Tuition and Taxes. On Oct. 4, the first day of the term, the justices agreed to decide whether a Minnesota law that gave parents a state tax deduction for tuition and other educational expenditures was within the bounds of the First Amendment's ban on state action "establishing" religion.

President Reagan was asking Congress to approve a similar plan for tuition tax credits to taxpayers whose children attend non-public schools. The Court's decision in the Minnesota case — *Mueller v. Allen* — was expected to boost or doom chances for congressional approval of the Reagan plan.

Lee filed an amicus curiae brief urging the Court to uphold the law. It provided only an indirect benefit to parochial schools, he argued, and should be upheld as the state's judgment "that income devoted to an educational expense . . . should not be subjected to the burden of taxation."

Deregulation. In November the Court set the stage for a major test of Reagan's push to deregulate American industry. The Court agreed to review a lower court's ruling that blocked the administration's rescission of a rule requiring air bags or automatic seat belts in all cars by September 1983.

This rule, first adopted in 1977, was bitterly opposed by the auto industry and had been rescinded by the Reagan administration in 1981. Insurance and consumer groups went to court protesting this deregulation move. They won an appeals court decision that the rescission in this case was "arbitrary and capricious."

The administration appealed, arguing that the court should have deferred to the administrative decision in this case, upholding it unless it was irrational or completely unreasonable.

Affirmative Action. The same day the justices added the air bag case to the argument schedule, they also took on the hotly debated question of affirmative action. Eighteen months earlier Attorney General Smith had made clear that the Reagan administration firmly opposed the use of any sort of racial quota in the workplace.

Speaking to the American Law Institute in May 1981, Smith said, "We have come perilously close in recent years to fostering discrimination by establishing racial quotas" in certain areas. The use of quotas and affirmative action plans, he said, often results in unfair discrimination against a "previously advantaged" group. The administration's goal "must always be genuinely color-blind state action."

To implement that policy, Lee filed a friend of the court brief supporting white police officers and firefighters from Boston. The Boston employees had asked the Supreme Court to overturn a federal judge's order directing the city to ignore the usual rule, "last hired, first fired," when the city was forced by budget cutbacks to lay off employees.

The contested order was intended to preserve the jobs of recently hired blacks. The whites challenged it as unfair to them and a breach of the immunity the Civil Rights Act of 1964 gave to bona fide seniority systems.

Lee's brief argued that the judge had exceeded his authority and created "a new class of victims, completely innocent of any wrongdoing, by depriving them of their rights under a valid seniority system."

Excluding Evidence. Late in November the Court signaled its readiness to consider modifying the much-criticized exclusionary rule that forbids prosecutors to use evidence that was obtained in violation of a defendant's constitutional rights. In an unusual move, the justices asked for a second round of arguments in *Illinois v. Gates,* directing the parties to argue a new question: Should the exclusionary rule be modified to permit use of evidence taken by police in a search they thought to be constitutional?

The administration, along with numerous conservative and law enforcement groups, suddenly became interested in this case, which had drawn little attention when it was first argued in October 1982. Solicitor General Lee filed a brief in which he argued that "at least in the case of reasonable good-faith violations of the Fourth Amendment, the exclusionary rule is entirely unjustified."

Any "reasoned cost-benefit analysis of the exclusionary rule compels the conclusion that it should no longer be applied" in such situations because it exacts a very high penalty for minor or technical errors on the part of police or the magistrate issuing the warrant, he continued.

Busing. Encouraged by the Court's willingness to add perennial controversy after perennial controversy to its docket, Lee in November asked the Court to add one more — school busing. Pursuing the Reagan administration's effort to shift the nation away from busing and toward a neighborhood school policy, Lee urged the justices to uphold a federal judge's decision permitting black and white elementary school students in Nashville, Tenn., to return to their neighborhood schools, instead of being bused to schools where the racial mix of students might be closer to some ideal balance.

An appeals court overturned that decision; Lee asked the justices to reinstate it. The Supreme Court's own school desegregation decisions, he argued, did not preclude judges from deciding that it was more beneficial for students to attend their neighborhood schools than to be transported to other, more "racially balanced" schools.

Administration Defeats

The year 1983 did not begin well for the administration at the Court. On Jan. 17 the Court denied Lee permission to argue in the Boston affirmative action case or in a case from Nebraska in which the administration seconded the state's defense of the practice of beginning legislative sessions with a prayer by a state-employed chaplain.

A week later, on Jan. 24, the justices refused to review the Nashville busing case. That refusal was only the beginning of a long line of major judicial rebuffs for the administration. On April 20, the Court unanimously upheld a California law imposing a moratorium on the construction of nuclear power plants until a satisfactory federal plan was devised for disposing of nuclear waste. The administration had joined the nuclear power industry in challenging this moratorium as invalid.

A month later the Court dashed hopes that it would limit the use of affirmative action, sending the Boston firefighters case back to a lower court to decide whether it was moot.

In similar fashion, the Court in June sidestepped the exclusionary rule question in *Illinois v. Gates,* deciding the case on another issue. Justice Rehnquist said that "with apologies to all," the Court felt that this was not the case in which to rule on a possible change in that rule.

Tax Exemptions. Then on May 24 the Court administered a stinging rebuke to the administration. By 8-1 the Court upheld the IRS policy of denying tax-exempt status to racially discriminatory private schools. Burger spoke for the majority that flatly rejected the administration's argument that the IRS lacked authority for this policy. Only Rehnquist agreed with the administration position in *Bob Jones University v. United States.*

The long debate was over. There was to be no backing down on the Court's commitment to a national policy of equality. "There can be no doubt as to the national policy" against racial discrimination in education, Burger wrote. "It would be anomalous for the executive, legislative and judicial branches to reach conclusions that add up to a firm public policy on racial discrimination, and at the same time have the IRS blissfully ignore what all three branches of the federal government had declared."

To be eligible for this tax-favored status, he wrote, an institution "must serve a public purpose and not be contrary to established public policy. . . . Whatever may be the rationale for such private schools' policies, and however sincere the rationale may be, racial discrimination in education is contrary to public policy."

The two schools had argued that, by denying them tax-exempt status, the IRS infringed their First Amendment rights, since their discriminatory policies were founded on sincere religious beliefs. Perhaps so, Burger wrote, but the national interest in eliminating racial discrimination in education "substantially outweighs whatever burden denial of tax benefits places on . . . exercise of their religious beliefs."

Abortion. Three weeks later on June 15 the Court, 6-3, administered another blow, reaffirming *Roe v. Wade* and rejecting the administration's invitation to bow out of the abortion controversy altogether.

"Arguments continue to be made . . . that we erred in interpreting the Constitution" in *Roe,* noted Powell, the majority's spokesman in *Akron v. Akron Center for Reproductive Health, Akron Center for Reproductive Health v. Akron.* But *Roe* was now settled precedent, Powell continued, and "the doctrine of stare decisis, demands respect in a society governed by the rule of law."

In a long footnote, Powell said that there were "especially compelling reasons"

for affirming *Roe v. Wade.* "That case was considered with special care," he said, and in the decade since, the Court "repeatedly and consistently has accepted and applied the basic principle that a woman has a fundamental right to make the highly personal choice whether or not to terminate her pregnancy."

In the *Akron* case O'Connor at last revealed her position on abortion. She joined Rehnquist and White, the dissenters from *Roe,* in dissent. They espoused the administration argument that states and cities should be permitted to regulate abortions at any point in pregnancy so long as they did not unduly burden the woman's right to choose to have an abortion.

Deregulation. There was still one more blow to fall on the battered Reagan campaign for change.

On June 24 the Court told the administration it could not deregulate American business by wholesale removal of regulations that had been imposed after careful consideration.

The Court unanimously ruled that the National Highway Transportation Safety Administration had acted arbitrarily and capriciously in 1981 when it simply rescinded a requirement that all cars be equipped with passive safety restraints — air bags or automatic seat belts — by September 1983.

The rescission was part of Reagan's plan to save the ailing auto industry by lightening its burden of federal regulation. In announcing the rescission, agency officials said that the requirement would no longer produce the anticipated safety benefits because the auto industry had chosen to comply by using an automatic seat belt that could easily be detached and rendered useless.

The fact that the industry had decided to use a system that did not meet the safety goals of the regulation was "hardly . . .

cause to revoke the standard itself," White wrote for the Court. Before rescinding a regulation, "the agency must examine the relevant data and articulate a satisfactory explanation for its action, including a 'rational connection between the facts found and the choices made.'" No such analysis or justification occurred in the air bag case, wrote White.

Administration Victories

Apart from these major policy rebuffs, the Reagan administration could claim its share of victories during the October 1982 term. The lion's share of them came in cases where the administration argued the institutional issue, rather than the policy preference.

At the top of this list was the legislative veto ruling. On June 25, just after the abortion decision and air bag defeat, the Court ruled 7-2 that the executive branch was right in its long-held belief that use of the legislative veto violated the separation of powers. Lee had argued the case and hailed the Court's ruling in *Immigration and Naturalization Service v. Chadha* as a major victory.

With the exception of this case, in which the administration asked the Court to strike down an existing device, most of the administration's victories came when it asked the Court to preserve the status quo. For example, in *United States v. Ptasynski,* the Court held constitutional the windfall profits tax that Congress imposed in 1980 on the nation's oil companies.

Reagan opposed the tax and had criticized it during his campaign, but the solicitor general's office was responsible for defending it before the Court. Perhaps because of this division within the administration, Lee did not appear for the government. Lee's deputy, Wallace, argued it and won, 9-0, defending a tax that brought billions into the federal coffers each year.

Lee argued and won the case of *Equal*

Employment Opportunity Commission v. Wyoming, in which the Court, although only by a 5-4 vote, upheld the Age Discrimination in Employment Act. Congress, in this measure, had overridden a state's decision to require some employees to retire early.

Hints of Change

In addition to these institutional victories, several of the other decisions of May and June 1983 contained signs that the Court was not adamantly opposed to some of the changes the Reagan administration proposed.

Tuition and Taxes. On two church-state issues, the Court ruled the way the administration urged — in favor of tuition tax deductions for parents of private and public school children, and in favor of the long-established practice of legislative prayer.

The tuition ruling was a narrow victory, 5-4, but it was a victory for the administration. Although the ruling removed one major obstacle to Reagan's own proposal for a federal tuition tax credit, the majority's reasoning placed another obstacle in its way. The majority emphasized that under Minnesota law patrons of public and private schools could avail themselves of a tax deduction for tuition, transportation and textbook expenses.

In fact, the lion's share of the benefit of the deduction accrued to patrons of private and parochial schools, since most public school students pay no tuition. But the neutral wording of the law saved it, in the eyes of the five justices — Rehnquist, Burger, White, Powell and O'Connor — who formed the majority in the June 29 ruling in *Mueller v. Allen.*

Legislative Prayer. The second victory had more symbolic than actual importance. The Court July 5 upheld, 6-3, the practice of opening sessions of Congress, state legislatures and various courts with a prayer.

Writing for the Court in *Marsh v. Chambers,* Burger noted that the same Congress that approved the First Amendment's guarantees of religious freedom also authorized paying a chaplain to open its sessions with prayer. Furthermore, he wrote, "there can be no doubt that the practice of opening legislative sessions with prayer has become part of the fabric of our society.

"To invoke Divine guidance on a public body entrusted with making the laws is not, in these circumstances, an 'establishment' of religion . . . it is simply a tolerable acknowledgement of beliefs widely held among the people of this country," he concluded.

A New Agenda

Although the Court's position on abortion and tax exemptions seemed well settled by the end of the October 1982 term, the justices appeared ready to reconsider several other issues that were not yet completely resolved.

Even before the air bag decision, the Court put another deregulation case on the docket. It agreed to review efforts by the administration to ease federal air pollution standards by redefining key terms, instead of rescinding standards. The administration successfully sought review of a lower court ruling that blocked this approach to deregulation as inconsistent with congressional intent.

Affirmative action was back on the docket within a month of the Court's inconclusive action on the Boston firefighters' case. Early in June the Court agreed to review *Firefighters Local Union No. 1784 v. Stotts, Memphis Fire Department v. Stotts.* The issue presented in those cases was virtually identical to the one the Court had sidestepped in the Boston case.

Before recessing for the summer, the justices accepted the administration's appeal of another exclusionary rule case. In *United States v. Leon,* the administration again argued that the Court should relax this ban by approving a "good faith" exception in cases where police thought they were seizing evidence in a legal fashion.

Also on the schedule was a case from Pawtucket, in which the city and the Reagan administration invited the justices to sanction action challenged by some as "establishing" religion. At issue in *Lynch v. Donnelly* was the decision of city fathers to include a nativity scene in the city's holiday display. All of these cases would be decided during the Court's next term.

7

Reagan's Other Campaign: 1983-1984

Undaunted by their lack of success with the Court, Solicitor General Rex E. Lee, his deputy, Paul Bator, and the administration team renewed their campaign for change in the October 1983 term. This time their determination, coupled with a new sophistication in presenting arguments, paid off. It seemed a watershed term, with the Court moving into a newly conservative position right in line with the Reagan administration.

In the next term, however, the Court paused. Although the administration continued to urge modification of the law in various significant directions, it focused its energies upon two key issues of church and state — school prayer and parochiaid.

On both, the Court rejected its arguments, reaffirming its traditional view that the First Amendment made it very difficult to approve any form of law permitting prayer in public schools or providing state aid to parochial schools.

Victory: October 1983

By the time the October 1983 term began, the solicitor general's office had already staked out controversial positions on a variety of issues ranging from air pollution control to sex discrimination.

The government had expressed its views to the Court in more than half of the 113 cases already set for argument, including 11 of 15 individual rights disputes. In some cases, the administration was asking the Court once again to uphold its challenged policy initiatives, such as its effort to ease the burden of clean air regulations by redefining key terms in those rules.

In others, Lee was urging the justices to narrow the scope of laws and policies adopted before the Reagan era. Such arguments were being made in cases involving sex bias, exclusion of evidence, access to the courts and the relationship of church and state.

Old Theme, New Key

The administration's arguments for change had a common theme. Each sought a decision that would relax the grip of government on the decisions of employers, educators, administrators and businessmen. The administration's deregulation thrust could be seen in its antitrust and clean air arguments, in its affirmative action and sex bias briefs, in its criminal law arguments and in its view of the proper relationship of church and state.

Supreme Court Schedule

The Supreme Court follows a regular schedule. From the first Monday in October, when the justices open their term with a public session at 10 o'clock, until the end of April of the following year, the Court alternates two weeks of oral argument with two or four weeks of recess.

In each two-week argument period, the Court hears approximately two dozen cases, each for an hour — 30 minutes by each side. Oral arguments are presented from 10-12 a.m. and 1-3 p.m. on Monday, Tuesday and Wednesday.

The cases argued that week are discussed on Thursday and Friday, with only the nine members of the Court in attendance. The chief justice begins the discussion by stating his views of a case, followed by the others, in order of seniority.

When the Court is ready to dispose of a case, the voting begins with the most junior justice and ends with the chief justice. After the result is clear, the chief justice — if he votes with the majority — assigns the task of writing the majority opinion. If the chief justice is in dissent, the most senior member of the majority assigns the opinion.

The Court usually hears arguments in October, November and December; recesses for four weeks over the holiday season; returns for two more weeks of arguments in January and recesses for four more weeks. More cases are argued in February, March and April. Oral arguments usually end by May 1, and, from that point on, the Court meets in public session only to issue opinions.

May and June bring a deluge of decisions, culminating in the last week of June and the week before July 4, when it is not unusual for the Court to issue a number of major decisions every day of the week.

Overall, the tone of the government's arguments was less strident and its positions less extreme than during the previous term. Its reasoning was clearly tailored to the contemporary Court's inclination to take a limited view of the proper role of judicial power in American life.

Instead of asking the Court to withdraw from the abortion debate, to reverse a dozen years of IRS policy, or to permit the wholesale cancellation of government health or safety regulations, the administration argued that activist federal judges had taken liberal laws and precedents just one step too far.

Its arguments appealed to a much broader and more moderate constituency generally. This shift in tone led to some speculation that the most extreme positions of the year before had been taken to fulfill campaign commitments to the more demanding conservative groups and did not, in fact, reflect the administration's own views.

To some degree the more moderate approach of the briefs filed in the October 1983 term also reflected the solicitor general's growing awareness that his primary audience was the nine justices, and that his office would lose the immeasurable litigating advantage built up over years at the Court if it took too many extreme positions too often.

Another factor was Bator, a highly regarded Harvard law professor and legal conservative who had joined the office in December 1982. His appointment was in line with the Reagan administration's policy of having both a department chief and the top assistant chosen and/or approved as ideologically "correct" by the White House.

Bator was a skilled advocate, on paper and on his feet. He argued three cases before the Court during the October 1982 term and won them without a single dissenting vote. In each the Supreme Court agreed to reverse a lower court and affirm the government's position for which Bator argued. None was a major policy matter.

In the October 1983 term, Bator shared with Lee the responsibility of arguing the administration's case for change. Lee argued the Pawtucket crèche case, the affirmative action case, the access to federal courts case and the exclusionary rule case. Bator argued the sex discrimination case and the clean air case, and he successfully defended the administration's crackdown on travel to Cuba and on overnight sleeping in certain national parks.

Crèche and State: The Argument

The day after the term began, Lee argued as a friend of the court in *Lynch v. Donnelly,* in which Pawtucket, R.I., city officials argued that it was constitutional for them to include a nativity scene in their city's annual holiday display. The elaborate presentation included almost all the traditional Christmas symbols.

Lee urged the Court to permit the city fathers to continue in this tradition. The men who wrote the First Amendment did not intend "to require government wholly and rigidly to exclude religion from our public occasions," he argued. Total separation of church and state, Lee continued, "would betoken a systematic hostility to religion — in effect, the establishment of irreligion. But hostility toward religion is as

prohibited by the Constitution as is governmental establishment of religion."

Early in 1984 Attorney General William French Smith expanded on this theme, leaving no doubt that the Reagan administration was committed to convincing the Court to take a softer line on questions of church and state. "We would like to see the Court re-assess the consequences of its own establishment clause precedents and the lower courts' increasing tendency to be hostile toward religion," he said. "If not soon, at some later point, the Court may wish to decide that a subtler analysis of the establishment clause is in order, one that encourages the state to take an attitude of — in the Court's own words — benevolent neutrality toward religion."

Sex Bias: The Argument

Two years earlier Lee had refused to argue for a narrow interpretation of Title IX of the 1972 education act amendments, the law barring sex discrimination by federally funded education programs. At that time, the question before the Court was whether this ban forbade discriminatory treatment of a school's employees or just its students. Lee argued for the broad reading of the law, prohibiting discrimination against employees, and the Court agreed in *North Haven Board of Education v. Bell.*

But in 1983 a different question concerning Title IX was before the Court. In this case Lee took the narrow view, much to the consternation of many members of Congress. The case of *Grove City College v. Bell* presented the Court with several questions about the reach of Title IX, but the key issue on which the administration wished to argue was the reach of the ban within a federally aided institution.

Title IX forbade sex discrimination "under any education program or activity receiving federal financial assistance." Since its enactment, the ban had been consistently interpreted as applying to all

An Officer or an Advocate...

The solicitor general has a dual role, Rex Lee pointed out in a June 1985 interview with National Public Radio. "On the one hand, I am a presidential appointee, a part of the president's team. I very much believe in the president's program and I want to do what I can to help advance it. And there are ways that I can help it by helping to shape and to guide the development of Supreme Court law.

"On the other hand, I am also an officer of the court. And the relationship between the solicitor general and the Supreme Court is one that knows no counterpart."

As officers of the court — and as the government's chief spokesmen before the Supreme Court — Lee and those on his staff sometimes found themselves defending the institutional interest of the government, even when those positions were at odds with the policies of the president.

One notable — and embarrassing — example of the conflict between the solicitor general's dual roles was the *Bob Jones University* case in 1982. The Reagan administration had decided to reverse a decade of executive support for the Internal Revenue Service (IRS) policy of denying tax exempt status to discriminatory private schools.

That White House reversal placed the solicitor general's office in the uncomfortable position of having to abandon both the IRS and a legal argument already before the justices. Ultimately, the Court appointed an outside counsel to defend the IRS. The solicitor general could no longer act as its defense because of the White House about-face. *(Details, p. 106)*

More often than not, however, the institutional interest — the government's traditional position — prevails over a president's policy preferences. For example, although Reagan personally opposed the windfall profits tax on oil and supported some use of the legislative veto, the solicitor general and his deputies argued in the Supreme Court that the tax should be upheld and the veto struck down. The Court agreed.

Throughout the period 1981-1985, there was a constant and unresolved tension between administration views and government interests on the question of federalism —

programs and departments at any school or college accepting any federal aid. The Reagan administration urged the Court to discard this broad ruling and stick to the literal wording of the law, applying the ban only to the particular "program or activity" or department that actually received federal aid.

When the administration's position became known, in the summer of 1983, a storm of protest arose from Capitol Hill. Fifty members of Congress, led by the chairman of the Senate Finance Committee, Robert Dole, R-Kan., and Rep. Claudine Schneider, R-R.I., filed a friend of the court brief arguing that Congress intended Title IX to encompass all programs at any recipient institution.

In November, before Bator argued the case, the House of Representatives voted 414-8 to oppose any attempt to narrow the scope of Title IX. Nevertheless, Bator took the administration line to the Court, arguing that only the particular program benefiting from federal funds is affected by Title IX. That was clearly the common-sense reading of the law, he contended.

During oral argument, Bator implicitly acknowledged that in this case, as in the air

...The Solicitor General's Dual Role

the proper balance between state and federal powers. The Reagan administration was strongly committed to returning power and authority from the federal government to the states. The government, however, is loath to surrender power, no matter who lives in the White House.

So in 1982 Lee argued against the states in the case of *Federal Energy Regulatory Commission v. Mississippi* and won. The Court agreed with the government that a 1978 energy law did not tread too far upon state prerogatives.

And in 1983 Lee again argued the institutional position in the case of the *Equal Employment Opportunity Commission v. Wyoming,* defending the power of Congress to override a state's decision that certain state employees should retire early.

In 1984 Lee argued for federal power and against states' rights in the case of *Garcia v. San Antonio Metropolitan Transit Authority,* defending as appropriate the application of federal law to tell cities how much they must pay employees of a city-owned mass transit system. The Court not only agreed but, to the dismay of the Reagan administration, threw out the major states' rights victory of modern times, overturning its 1976 decision in the case of *National League of Cities v. Usery.*

In that case the Court had told Congress that it could not constitutionally tell states and cities how much to pay their own employees. In arguing the San Antonio case, Lee had contended that it was legally consistent for the Court to require the city-owned transit system to comply with federal wage laws.

The Court changed its mind and, by discarding the 1976 precedent, removed virtually all specific constitutional limits on federal power over the states. Lee described this decision as a "major disappointment."

In mid-1985 Attorney General Edwin Meese pointedly criticized this ruling as "an inaccurate reading of the text of the Constitution," although it was technically a victory for the government. "We hope for a day when the Court returns to the basic principles of the Constitution as expressed in *Usery*," Meese said.

---

bag and clean air cases, the administration was seeking to lighten the hand of government in various areas of life. "The government's current position," he told the Court, "stems from an understanding that Congress intended a more surgical intervention than the ... regulatory overkill previously advocated by the government."

Antitrust: The Arguments

Seeking to lighten government regulation of business in another area, the Reagan administration during the October 1983 term urged the Court to adopt a more flexible interpretation of the nation's antitrust laws, giving business more leeway to use whatever practices are appropriate in a given business situation.

The antitrust laws were enacted in the early part of the 20th century to prevent businesses from conspiring together to reduce competition. The Reagan administration urged change in three key elements of antitrust policy: the ban on resale price maintenance, the general presumption that it is illegal for suppliers to force a consumer who buys one product also to buy the other and the view that it is possible for a company to violate antitrust laws by conspiring with its subsidiary.

In November the administration joined a Louisiana hospital in defending its agreement granting one anesthesiology group practice the privilege of supplying all such services at the hospital, thus requiring patients at the hospital also to "buy" that firm's services.

In December the administration backed Monsanto's appeal of a $10.5 million damage award to a distributor who charged the company with conspiring to fix the retail prices of its products. In its brief in *Monsanto Co. v. Spray-Rite Inc.,* the administration told the Court that "there is no sound basis for assuming . . . that resale price maintenance is so invariably anti-competitive as to justify per se condemnation." In some cases, the government argued, resale price maintenance might actually stimulate competition among brands. Such situations should be judged on a case by case basis, it argued, separating the anti-competitive cases from those in which price maintenance had a competitive effect.

Congress solidly opposed the administration's position and put teeth into its opposition by adding to the Justice Department appropriations bill a rider denying use of any funds in the bill to pursue this policy. In obedience to that order, the Justice Department's antitrust chief, William F. Baxter, did not argue this point when he appeared before the justices Dec. 5.

On the same day, administration attorneys urged the Court to exempt from certain provisions of the antitrust laws concerted action by a parent company and a subsidiary. Commonly controlled corporations should be treated as a single economic entity under the antitrust laws, the government argued in *Copperweld Corp. v. Independence Tube Corp.* They should not be penalized for cooperating in dealing with competitors.

Affirmative Action: The Arguments

On Dec. 6 Lee argued the administration's case against affirmative action for the second time in 1983. *Firefighters Local Union No. 1784 v. Stotts, Memphis Fire Department v. Stotts* brought to the Court the joint claims of judicial overreaching and reverse discrimination.

When a federal judge ordered Memphis in 1981 to carry out budget-dictated layoffs by dismissing senior white firefighters so that more recently hired blacks could keep their jobs, the city and the whites protested. After the appeals court upheld the order, the city took its complaint to the Supreme Court. Its arguments were backed by the administration.

Assistant Attorney General for Civil Rights William Bradford Reynolds, an outspoken foe of affirmative action, joined Lee in the government's friend of the court brief. They argued that the judge's action was illegal. The 1964 Civil Rights Act immunizes good-faith seniority systems against challenge as discriminatory and, by implication, protects them from this sort of judicial tampering — unless they are shown to have been designed to discriminate against minority employees. No such finding was made in this case.

The administration intensified its push to limit the use of affirmative action. Four days before the *Stotts* case was argued, Lee filed another brief urging the Court to hold affirmative action programs unconstitutional when they were adopted to benefit any persons or groups who were not themselves the victims of discrimination.

Lee recommended that the justices hear a case challenging the affirmative action plan voluntarily adopted by Detroit police. Lee wrote: "We have profound doubts whether the Constitution permits governments to adopt remedies involving racial quotas to benefit persons who are not themselves the victims of discrimination." The justices refused to review the case.

Exclusionary Rule: The Arguments

Early in 1984 the administration began a full-court press for relaxation of the rule barring the use of evidence obtained by police in violation of a suspect's rights. On Jan. 17 and 18 the Court heard four cases in which prosecutors appealed rulings excluding evidence for this reason. In all four, the Reagan administration backed the prosecutors' argument that the evidence should be admitted.

The government was a party only to *United States v. Leon,* a narcotics case from California. In this case, a federal judge threw out evidence obtained by federal narcotics agents because the search warrant they used was based on information the judge did not find sufficiently reliable.

The administration made its argument in friend of the court briefs in the other three cases. In a murder case, *Massachusetts v. Sheppard,* a judge had excluded evidence seized by police with a warrant written on the wrong form.

In *New York v. Quarles,* an armed rape case, prosecutors had been forbidden to use as evidence a weapon found in a supermarket, where police had arrested a suspect and asked him, before warning him of his constitutional rights, to show them where he had put the gun.

In *Nix v. Williams,* a murder case from Iowa, the justices were asked to permit the use of evidence that was discovered as a result of police questioning of a suspect in the absence of his lawyer. The state, again backed by the administration, argued for an "inevitable discovery" exception to the exclusionary rule.

In all four cases, the reason for the government's position was the same: the high cost to society of a strict application of the exclusionary rule. It was overkill, argued Lee, to jeopardize a conviction in these cases in order to penalize police for such minor infringements of the constitutional guarantees.

Charles Fried

Clean Air: The Arguments

In February 1984 Bator argued the government's case for deregulation by definition. The case involved clean air regulation, but many saw this approach — redefining key terms in federal regulations — as the alternative avenue to deregulation, which the administration chose after the Court in the 1983 air bag case made outright rescission of regulations difficult. Emphasizing the need to lighten the economic burden that clean air regulations imposed on industry, Bator defended the "bubble concept" of clean air enforcement.

This concept views an entire plant as enclosed in an imaginary bubble, from which a total amount of emissions is permissible. Any change the plant makes in its operation that increases the emissions from that portion of the plant is permissible, if it is offset by a decrease in emissions from some other part. This permits companies to make major changes in existing plants without meeting the Clean Air Act's stiff standards governing new sources of pollution.

During the Carter administration the Environmental Protection Agency (EPA) had considered using this plan but decided against it. In October 1981, however, the Reagan administration revived and adopted the concept as an option for states to use in enforcing the Clean Air Act.

Broad support within the industrial community for the administration's position was evident in the cases of *Environmental Protection Agency v. Natural Resources Defense Council (NRDC), Chevron USA Inc. v. NRDC, American Iron and Steel Institute v. NRDC.* Joining in defense of the bubble concept were Chevron, General Motors, the American Petroleum Institute, the American Iron and Steel Institute, the Chemical Manufacturers Association and the Rubber Manufacturers Association.

In defending this route to deregulation, the administration emphasized that courts should defer to the expertise of the adminstrative agencies. Lee's brief criticized the appeals court ruling rejecting the bubble concept as "an unwarranted usurpation of the authority reserved to" EPA. In his argument, Bator emphasized that this concept gave states more flexibility in enforcing the act and permitted economic development to continue even while progress was made toward cleaner air.

A Winning Streak

In February 1984 the administration's campaign began to produce results. The Court announced its approval for the administration's new narrow reading of the federal law banning sex discrimination in schools and colleges receiving federal aid. A few days later, the Court moved toward the posture of benevolent neutrality on questions of church and state.

By the spring of 1984, Lee and his team had a winning streak under way at last.

Sex Bias: The Decisions

The day before Bator argued the clean air case, he won a major victory in *Grove City College v. Bell.* With a 6-3 vote, the Court Feb. 28 approved the Reagan administration's decision to apply Title IX literally, restricting its scope to the particular program receiving federal aid, not the entire institution.

Even though federal funds awarded to students or to certain programs within a college "ultimately find their way into the College's general operating budget and are used to provide a variety of services to the students ... we have found no persuasive evidence ... that Congress intended that the [Education] Department's regulatory authority follow federally aided students from classroom to classroom, building to building or activity to activity," wrote Justice Byron R. White for the majority.

Justices William J. Brennan Jr., Thurgood Marshall and John Paul Stevens dissented. The decision also generated immediate protest on Capitol Hill. Civil rights groups quickly began work to win passage of legislation overturning the new narrow view of Title IX.

In May, however, the Court unanimously agreed with the administration's unexpectedly liberal position — again argued by Bator — and told law firms that the federal law barring discrimination in the workplace on the basis of sex, race, religion or national origin applied to their decisions about whom to promote to partner.

Writing for the majority in *Hishon v. King & Spalding,* Chief Justice Warren E. Burger demonstrated that the literal approach to statutory interpretation can yield a liberal result as easily as a conservative one. Nothing in the job bias ban of the 1964 Civil Rights Act exempts law firms from its reach, Burger reasoned. "When Congress wanted to grant an employer complete immunity, it expressly did so," he said, and it did not do so for law firms.

Crèche and State: The Decision

A week after its *Grove City* victory, the administration on March 5, 1984, chalked up a second major win. The Court further eased its insistence on separation of church and state, permitting Pawtucket, by a 5-4 vote, to include the nativity scene in its holiday display.

The margin of victory in *Lynch v. Donnelly* was narrow, but the language of the majority was broad. Echoing the administration's arguments, Burger wrote that the Constitution "affirmatively mandates accommodation, not merely tolerance, of all religions, and forbids hostility toward any.

"No significant segment of our society and no institutions within it can exist in a vacuum or in total and absolute isolation from all the other parts, much less from government," Burger continued.

Brennan, Marshall, Stevens and Harry A. Blackmun dissented.

However, this was clearly not the justices' last word on church-state matters. The same day it announced its ruling in the Pawtucket case, the Court agreed to hear an appeal from a ruling that Connecticut's law requiring employers to permit devout workers to take their Sabbath off was in conflict with the First Amendment ban on "establishment" of religion. In *Estate of Thornton v. Caldor Inc.,* the administration defended the law as a permissible "accommodation" of religion.

One month later the Court agreed to hear the first school prayer case in more than two decades. The Court granted the request of the state of Alabama and the Reagan administration that it review a ruling striking down the state's "moment-of-silence" law.

In urging the Court to hear *Wallace v. Jaffree,* Lee described it as "an opportunity for the Court to consider the legitimacy of governmental efforts to accommodate the interests of individuals of religious conviction in the public schools and, by implica-

tion, in other contexts where religious practice may require the permission or cooperation of government."

Even as it accepted the moment-of-silence case for review, the Court reaffirmed its opposition to formal spoken prayer in public schools — the sort of religious observance the Warren Court held unconstitutional in 1962. Without arguments or dissenting vote, the justices affirmed a lower court decision that a second Alabama law — permitting teachers to lead students in prayer at the beginning of class — was a violation of the First Amendment.

Antitrust: The Decisions

After some initial setbacks for the administration early in 1984 in antitrust and attorneys' fee cases, Lee's office could count some notable successes in those areas as well, as the term moved toward its end.

The Court unanimously upheld the damage award against Monsanto, sidestepping the issue of price maintenance on which the administration had intended to argue for change.

In the second antitrust case, *Jefferson Parish Hospital District No. 2 v. Hyde,* the justices agreed with the administration that a hospital could legitimately grant one firm the right to provide all its anesthesiology services.

And the Court accepted the administration's invitation to discard a long-held tenet of antitrust law as it, 5-3, in *Copperweld Corp. v. Independence Tube Corp.,* declared that a corporation and its wholly owned subsidiary could no longer be charged with conspiring to violate certain provisions of the antitrust laws.

On a different subject, the justices unanimously rejected administration arguments that judges should use a lower base rate in calculating fee awards to public interest attorneys than that used in figuring the size of such awards to attorneys in private practice.

Affirmative Action: The Decision

The Court handed the Reagan administration another major victory June 12 when it ruled that the federal judge in Memphis exceeded his powers when he ordered the city to ignore its usual seniority rule of "last hired, first fired," to protect new minority employees from layoffs. Attorney General Smith hailed the ruling as a broad one, denying federal judges the power to use racial quotas in employment.

Lee labeled the decision "one of the greatest victories of all time." And Assistant Attorney General Reynolds said that the Justice Department would begin reviewing all existing affirmative action decrees and agreements involving the federal government with an eye to eliminating all such quotas.

Although the administration clearly chose to read the ruling as a broad denunciation of the use of quotas to remedy discrimination, it was not clear that the Court's ruling was such a sweeping one. Justice White wrote the majority opinion in *Firefighters Local Union No. 1784 v. Stotts.* As he usually does, he tied his opinion closely to the particular facts of this complex case. But his opinion, joined by four other justices, stated that, in enacting the job bias provisions of the 1964 Civil Rights Act, Congress intended to provide particular remedies only to those who had been the actual victims of illegal discrimination.

This was especially true when seniority was at issue, White explained, referring to the law's provisions immunizing good-faith seniority systems from challenge. Just being a member of a group that was the target of discrimination was not enough to win a seniority award, he wrote. "Each individual must prove that the discriminatory practice had an impact on him." No such finding was made in this case, White reasoned, and so there was no justification for the judge to override the seniority system's operations in a layoff context.

Justice Stevens joined the majority, but not White's opinion; Blackmun, Brennan and Marshall dissented.

Clean Air: The Decision

Ten days later, the president's campaign to lighten the regulatory burden on business and industry took a giant step forward as the Court reinstated the bubble concept for clean air enforcement.

By a 6-0 vote — Justices Sandra Day O'Connor, William H. Rehnquist and Marshall not participating — the Court upheld the administration's redefinition of key terms in the clean air law as "a reasonable accommodation of manifestly competing interests."

Writing for the majority in *EPA v. NRDC,* Justice Stevens acknowledged that "an agency to which Congress has delegated policy-making responsibilities may, within the limits of that delegation, properly rely upon the incumbent administration's view of wise policy to inform its judgments." He continued in a surprisingly deferential tone for one who generally took a liberal and expansive view of judicial power. "While agencies are not directly accountable to the people, the chief executive is, and it is entirely appropriate for this political branch of the government to make such policy choices," he said. "In such a case, federal judges — who have no constituency — have a duty to respect legitimate policy choices made by those who do."

Exclusionary Rule: The Decision

On the last day of the term came what Rex Lee would later hail as "the jewel in the crown." After years of hammering at the exclusionary rule, its critics had won a major exception to its sweep.

The Court, 6-3, approved a "good faith" exception to the rule in *United States v. Leon.* The Court held that evidence taken in violation of a defendant's constitutional rights by police with a search warrant could be used in court if police sincerely believed they were acting properly. The Court applied that exception to permit use of the challenged evidence in the companion murder case of *Massachusetts v. Sheppard.*

Earlier in June, it had approved two other exceptions to the exclusionary rule — a "public safety" exception permitting use of the gun as evidence in *New York v. Quarles* and the "inevitable discovery" exception permitting use of evidence in *Nix v. Williams.*

For the majority in *Leon,* Justice White agreed with the administration that a simple cost-benefit analysis of applying the exclusionary rule in such good-faith situations proved that the rule simply "cannot pay its own way." As in the affirmative action case, however, White tied the exception to the facts of this case, limiting its use to situations in which police obtained a warrant and executed the search as it authorized them to do, only to find out later that the warrant was defective.

The dissenters, Brennan, Marshall and Stevens, were distressed. "The Court's victory over the Fourth Amendment is complete," lamented Brennan, predicting that this exception would soon be extended to situations in which police did not even bother to obtain a warrant. Stevens, writing separately, warned that the majority was on the verge of converting "the Bill of Rights into an unenforced honor code."

Citizens' Rights

In its busy final weeks of the term, the Court had still more pleasant news for the administration. In three unrelated cases, the Court upheld the administration's arguments in favor of restricting the individual citizen's freedom.

On June 28 it upheld, 5-4, the administration's 1982 decision to curtail travel by U.S. citizens to Cuba. Writing for the narrow majority in *Regan v. Wald,* Justice Rehnquist was quite definite in reiterating

the view that foreign policy is the province of the president and Congress "largely immune from judicial inquiry."

The following day, the Court, 7-2, upheld the administration's 1982 ban on camping — defined to include sleeping — in certain national parks, including Lafayette Park across from the White House, for years the site of many demonstrations and protests.

Again, Rehnquist spoke to refute the claim that this rule violated the expressive rights of protestors guaranteed by the First Amendment. The regulation was a reasonable way of maintaining that park and other parks in attractive condition, he wrote in *Clark v. Community for Creative Non-Violence.*

And on July 3 the Court, 5-3, held that parents of black public school students lacked legal standing to sue the IRS for being too lenient in granting tax-exempt status to private schools. *Allen v. Wright* was in some ways the inside-out version of the *Bob Jones* case resolved the year before. Here, however, the administration — instead of trying to reverse a long-held national policy of administrative support for the civil rights laws — argued successfully for a limit on the power of federal courts, an argument to which the Court was far more receptive.

Repeating principles set out in the *Valley Forge Christian College* case some two years earlier, Justice O'Connor wrote that the parents claimed no specific personal injury from the allegedly lax enforcement of IRS policy. Therefore they did not have standing to come into federal court with their suit.

Justice Marshall did not participate in the case. Brennan, Stevens and Blackmun dissented. Brennan criticized the majority's "startling insensitivity to the historic role played by the federal courts in eradicating race discrimination from our nation's schools."

A Swing to the Right

As in the previous terms, the solicitor general's office chalked up a number of other major victories in cases in which the government defended existing policy. For example, Lee argued and won a decision approving the federal law denying student aid to young men who did not register for the draft.

But all such institutional matters were overshadowed for the time being by the remarkable string of policy victories for the Reagan administration. The justices had approved the administration's proposals for change in almost every case, a dramatic change from the rejections it administered to the same advocates the year before.

Reagan's victories were the most visible aspect of the most conservative Court term in decades. It looked like a watershed — the October 1983 term in which the Court turned firmly away from the Warren Court brand of judicial activism in defense of individual rights and settled into a new posture of committed conservative restraint.

Lee, as point man for the administration, was delighted with the results of the October 1983 term. By approving the good faith exception to the exclusionary rule, he said in a summer 1984 television appearance, the Court in fact broadened the rights of individuals to be safe and secure against criminals.

Despite his success, Lee was the target of criticism from both right and left. During the term, an article in *Benchmark,* a conservative legal publication, called for Lee's removal from office. It charged him with being too liberal, too hesitant in urging the Court to reverse earlier liberal precedents.

It was time, *Benchmark* said, for the administration to challenge the half-century-long line of rulings that applied the Bill of Rights to the states. That doctrine, the article said, was "the great seedbed of judicial power in the modern Court." On the other hand, Harvard law professor

Laurence Tribe, a frequent and successful advocate before the Court, described some of the administration victories during the term as "shackling" the Statue of Liberty.

Tribe was particularly critical of the Court's balancing of individual rights with the societal cost of ensuring those rights. In a joint appearance with Lee in early July on ABC-TV's "This Week with David Brinkley," Tribe expressed concern that the Court had adopted a new method of decision making, no longer "explaining the underlying constitutional principles," but now "calibrating things on a cost-benefit scale where the government is bound to win more and more often and where fundamental principles — because they're so intangible, because their benefits are so diffuse — are likely to get lost in the bargain."

Lee responded to Tribe's criticism in an August address to the American Bar Association. He again emphasized that the Court's rulings in fact expanded protection for the individual rights of innocent citizens. "Very simply," he said, "crime inhibits freedom. . . . To whatever extent our persons, our homes and our property are more secure, we are also more free."

He also defended the cost-benefit approach. "Considering costs as well as benefits carries no real threat to individual rights and, in fact, permits examination of the individual rights on both sides."

"Neither literally nor symbolically is the Statue of Liberty in shackles," Lee concluded. "It is simply being restored to its original condition."

Pause: October 1984 Term

Buoyed by its success in the October 1983 term, the Reagan administration sought to press its advantage in the term that began Oct. 1, 1984.

Lee urged the Court to ease restrictions on prayer in schools, student searches, use of confessions from unwarned suspects and state aid to students attending parochial schools. He asked the justices to construe broadly the federal ban on age discrimination in the workplace, to give the Justice Department sanction for some "selective prosecution" of draft non-registrants, to give the CIA broad discretion to protect intelligence sources and the EPA permission to ease toxic waste regulations in particular cases.

As the Court added new cases to its docket, Lee kept up the administration's campaign for approval of its policy initiatives. He defended Reagan's exclusion of legal defense funds from the annual charitable fund-raising drive among federal employees. He argued that the Court should back the decision of the National Labor Relations Board (NLRB) to deny unions the power to discipline workers who resign during a strike. And he argued that courts should not interfere with the Reagan administration's policy of detaining "boat people" and other excludable aliens, who arrive on American shores without official permission, while a decision is made on their fate.

Despite the length and breadth of this list, both public attention and administration energies during the term focused on questions of First Amendment freedoms, particularly issues of church and state.

Of 150 cases argued and decided during the term, an unusually high number — 19 — concerned some aspect of this broad guarantee for freedoms of belief and expression.

In the first school prayer case before the Court in 21 years, the Reagan administration sounded the theme of "benevolent neutrality," and urged the Court to moderate its strict ban on classroom prayer by endorsing Alabama's "moment-of-silence" law.

Lee made similar arguments in a pair of parochiaid cases from New York and Michigan and a Sabbath-off case from Connecticut.

The Pendulum's Swing

The administration compiled a mixed record on these issues. It suffered painful defeats on the school prayer, parochiaid and Sabbath-off cases. It won the student search, age discrimination, CIA secrecy, selective prosecution and union powers cases.

All in all, the October 1984 term was a surprisingly moderate term that can be characterized as a breathing space between the conservative shift of the 1983 term and the even more intense debates to be aired in the term that began in October 1985. The Court's apparent moderation was in part the natural result of its being confronted by some rather extreme cases.

When the Court is considered liberal, advocates of individual rights and freedoms are encouraged to ask the justices to reverse conservative decisions and policies. When the Court has a conservative reputation, those who support giving more power and authority to police, prosecutors and government officials generally are encouraged to appeal liberal rulings.

Happily aware of the weight that Justice O'Connor added to the conservative wing of the Court, prosecutors, businesses and conservative groups moved eagerly to appeal adverse rulings from the lower courts, which were, in 1984, dominated by relatively liberal judges appointed by Democratic presidents.

Of the 79 cases set for argument when the Court began the 1984 term, there were twice as many in which the Court was asked to reverse a liberal ruling as there were appeals of conservative rulings. In earlier years, prosecutors and police would not have thought of asking the Court to approve court-ordered surgery to remove evidence from a suspect's body or of asking the Court to approve a state law permitting police to shoot and kill unarmed fleeing suspects.

Without the rulings approving legislative prayer, tuition tax deductions and Pawtucket's crèche, it was also unlikely that a state would have thought it worthwhile to ask the Court to approve a moment-of-silence law to permit voluntary silent prayer in its classrooms.

Church and State

Each of these appeals ended in failure during the 1985 term. The administration's greatest disappointment during the term was the Court's 6-3 decision in June 1985 that Alabama's moment-of-silence law was unconstitutional, an establishment of religion in violation of the First Amendment.

If this were not evidence enough of its refusal to approve any further lowering of the wall of separation between church and state, the Court in July, 5-4, struck down the challenged parochiaid programs and reaffirmed the traditional three-part test that made it unlikely that any law challenged as an establishment of religion could survive.

School Prayer. No modern Court ruling has generated so much controversy for so long a period as the 1962 decision in *Engel v. Vitale.* The Court ruled that New York officials could not require public school students to recite a particular prayer each day. The Warren Court followed that decision the following year with a second ruling in which it declared unconstitutional the practice of daily Bible readings in the public schools. Only one justice dissented in each case.

Despite continuing controversy and tireless efforts by school prayer advocates to persuade Congress to pass a constitutional amendment overturning these decisions, they remained pristine landmarks in 1984. Twenty-three states, however, had passed moment-of-silence laws, which varied in their particulars, but in general permitted teachers to set aside a moment in each public school classroom each day for students to engage in some quiet meditative activity.

When Alabama's moment-of-silence law was challenged, a federal judge, in clear disregard of a half-century of Supreme Court rulings applying the Bill of Rights to the states, upheld it, declaring that the First Amendment did not deny Alabama the power to establish a state religion. An appeals court quickly overturned that ruling and held Alabama's law unconstitutional. With the enthusiastic backing of the Reagan administration, the state appealed to the justices for reversal.

The Court heard arguments in *Wallace v. Jaffree* on Dec. 4, 1984. Deputy Solicitor General Bator argued as a friend of the court, urging the justices to uphold Alabama's law as a permissible state accommodation of personal religious beliefs in a neutral and non-coercive manner.

"The values of pluralism and diversity in our public schools suffer needlessly from a reading of the Establishment Clause that destroys the possibility of accommodating, in a spirit of toleration, voluntary religious practices of the sort involved in this case," he argued.

It was time, Bator continued, for the Court "to take a fresh look at the tests for distinguishing between establishments of religion, on the one hand, and permissible instances of accommodation of and toleration for private religious beliefs and practices, on the other."

Parochiaid. Time gave emphasis to the intensity of the administration's campaign for change in this area of First Amendment law. The day after Bator's arguments in *Wallace v. Jaffree,* Lee was before the Court, arguing in support of New York City's system for delivering Title I services — federally funded remedial and enrichment classes — to eligible children who attended non-public schools.

Since 1966 New York had provided these services to children attending private and parochial schools by sending public school teachers to the non-public schools to conduct the Title I classes during the school day. Congress, which had set up the Title I program for culturally deprived children, intended the aid to go to eligible children, wherever they attended school.

But after 18 years of operation, the New York system was held unconstitutional. The First Amendment, said the appeals court, permits use of public funds for services for non-public school students only if these services are provided at a neutral site — outside the "sectarian" atmosphere of a religious school.

Backed by the Reagan administration, New York parents and school officials sought Supreme Court reversal of that ruling. "Nothing in the Constitution," contended the administration in its brief in *Aguilar v. Felton,* "requires us to adopt the unwelcome rule that Congress and the states are rigidly disabled from rendering secular remedial assistance to educationally deprived children in their own schools."

Sabbaths Off and Other Matters. The justices refused to permit an administration advocate to argue in the Sabbath-off case, *Estate of Thornton v. Caldor, Inc.,* which they heard in November. But the administration made clear in its written friend of the court brief that it felt Connecticut's law, requiring employers to permit devout employees to take their Sabbath off without penalty, should be reinstated.

Such laws, Lee wrote, joined by Bator and Reynolds, "reflect ... an admirable tolerance for the diversity of religious practices in this country and a willingness to enable religious believers — particularly those of minority views — to overcome the burdens their religious observances would otherwise place on them in the workplace."

And Lee filed a friend of the court brief in another crèche case — this one from Scarsdale, N.Y. He urged the Court to affirm a lower court ruling that city officials could not use the Establishment Clause as a reason for refusing to permit a

citizens' group to erect a nativity scene on public property.

Disappointing Decisions

The Court sidestepped the Scarsdale case, dividing 4-4 and sending it back to the lower court. The even split, a result of Justice Powell's absence from the Court following prostate surgery early in January, was in effect a victory for the Reagan administration. A 4-4 split affirms the contested decision, as the administration had suggested the justices do. And it seemed likely, again as the administration had urged, that the decision on whether to permit a crèche in Scarsdale would be left to the local officials.

That was the good news for the administration on the church-state issue for this term.

School Prayer. The bad news began to arrive in June. On June 4 the Court announced that it found the Alabama moment-of-silence law unconstitutional. The administration was especially pained by the 6-3 vote, with Justices O'Connor and Lewis F. Powell Jr. voting against the administration in *Wallace v. Jaffree.*

Each added a concurring opinion making clear that some moment-of-silence laws might be permissible, but both made perfectly plain that the administration had chosen the wrong case to use as its vehicle for changing the Court's mind on school prayer.

O'Connor and Powell emphasized that a neutral moment-of-silence law might be permissible, but not a statute that was clearly a subterfuge for restoring the practice of prescribed prayer to public schools. And here, as the majority noted, the sponsor of the legislation had told the lower court that he had no other purpose in introducing the measure.

For the majority, Justice Stevens seemed to abandon altogether the theme of accommodation. It was an "established principle that the government must pursue a course of complete neutrality toward religion," he declared.

In dissent, Chief Justice Burger charged the majority with hostility toward religion. Justices Rehnquist and White said that it was time for the Court to reassess its precedents on this matter. Rehnquist urged the Court to discard entirely the idea of a wall of separation between church and state.

Sabbaths Off. Three weeks later, Burger and White joined the school prayer majority to strike down Connecticut's Sabbath-off law. "Government must guard against activity that impinges on religious freedom, and must take pains not to compel people to act in the name of any religion," wrote Burger in *Estate of Thornton v. Caldor*.

The Connecticut law flunked the constitutional test, he continued, because it "imposes on employers and employees an absolute duty to conform their business practices to the particular religious practices of the employee." Therefore, Burger concluded, its primary effect was to advance the particular religious practice of Sabbath observance, and thus it breached the necessary neutrality of the state.

Only Justice Rehnquist dissented.

Parochiaid. On July 1 the Court emphatically reaffirmed the view that the First Amendment requires a careful separation of church and state. By a 5-4 vote, the Court held New York City's Title I program and a comparable program in Grand Rapids, Mich., unconstitutional.

As it already had done in the earlier decisions, the Court drew the line against further government "accommodation" of religion. Instead it again stressed the need for "neutrality," saying that government may not act to "promote or hinder a particular faith or faith generally."

Justice Powell was the key vote, joining the more liberal members of the Court — Brennan, Marshall, Blackmun and Stevens — to hold that these programs created an impermissible alliance of church and state.

Brennan, a Warren Court veteran and, as the Court's only Catholic, perhaps more sensitive to this issue than his colleagues, wrote the opinion. "The symbolic union of church and state inherent in the provision of secular, state-provided instruction in the religious school buildings threatens to convey a message of state support for religion to students and the general public," he warned. That the First Amendment did not permit.

"The programs in effect subsidize the religious functions of the parochial schools by taking over a substantial portion of their responsibility for teaching secular subjects," he continued. To approve this was to "let the genie out of the bottle," and permit "ever larger segments of the religious school curriculum to be turned over to the public school system, thus violating the cardinal principle that the state may not in effect become the prime supporter of the religious schools system," Brennan concluded in *School District of the City of Grand Rapids v. Ball*.

Offsetting Victories

Although the fact was overshadowed at the time by the string of defeats on church-state issues, the Reagan administration compiled a long list of victories on other issues.

The Court unanimously approved tough enforcement of the federal ban on age bias in the workplace, a broad discretion for the CIA to protect its sources and the freedom of states to form regional banking networks.

With only two dissenting votes, the Court permitted selective prosecution of draft non-registrants who call attention to their non-compliance through letters to the president or some public protest until a more uniform method of identifying non-registrants was put into effect. The Court also approved the administration's new regulations governing the decision to detain or release excludable aliens in the United States.

By a narrow margin, the administration won approval of its argument that an initial failure of police to warn a suspect of his rights does not bar use of all future confessions from the suspect, obtained after such warnings are given.

By other close votes, the Court upheld the law limiting a veteran's right to pay an attorney for pressing his claim with the government and the administration's exclusion of legal advocacy funds from the annual federal fund-raising drive.

Similar close votes brought the administration the Court's support for the NLRB ruling denying unions the right to discipline workers who violate union agreements by resigning during a strike and EPA power to grant variances from toxic waste pre-treatment standards.

Personnel Changes

Lee and Bator had left the solicitor general's office before the bad news arrived. Bator, nominated by Reagan in the summer of 1984 to a newly created seat on the U.S. Court of Appeals for the District of Columbia Circuit, was hospitalized for treatment of heart disease early in the fall. At his request, his nomination was withdrawn, and in January 1985 he returned to his post at Harvard Law School.

Bator was succeeded as deputy and counselor to the solicitor general by Charles Fried, another Harvard professor with views congenial to those of the Reagan White House.

Lee resigned, effective June 1, to return to the private practice of law as a partner in the Chicago-based firm of Sidley & Austin. He would also resume teaching at Brigham Young University Law School, where he had previously served as dean. He said he felt it was time for him to move on, and he also cited the difficulty of educating his large family of seven children on a government salary, even the solicitor general's $73,600.

Fried, who successfully argued the union powers case twice, was designated acting solicitor general after Lee's departure. In October 1985 Fried was named solicitor general.

In several interviews, Lee provided illuminating glimpses into the interplay between his office and key administration figures such as Attorney General Edwin Meese and Reynolds. Lee frankly acknowledged that he had refused to make some of the more radical conservative arguments that Meese and others had urged upon him. "I'm not the pamphleteer general," he told the Associated Press. "I'm the solicitor general. My audience is not 100 million people; my audience is nine people."

Lee emphasized that these disagreements within the administration during Reagan's first term were disagreements over tactics, not substance. He told National Public Radio's Nina Totenberg: "What the president hired me to do was to make judgments concerning the kinds of arguments that could and could not be successful in the Supreme Court. It is very damaging to the administration's position to make arguments before the Supreme Court that are not likely to succeed."

One such argument, in Lee's view, contends that the Bill of Rights does not apply to states, but only to the action of the federal government. It was reported that Meese and others urged Lee to make that argument in the 1985 school prayer case.

"There is an interesting historical and legal argument that can be made in support of that proposition," Lee told National Public Radio in June 1985. "But as a matter of Supreme Court precedents, the binding quality of the First Amendment on the states is so well established that for me to assert it in a solicitor general's brief would not only mean that I would lose that case but it would also seriously impede my overall effectiveness with the Court. . . .

"When you come to issues like that," Lee summarized, "it's simply a question of 'do you want to blow the bugle, or do you want to win the war?' "

Lee continued, "Credibility is the most important asset that any solicitor general has. . . . One of the worst short-range mistakes that any administration could possibly make would be to jeopardize the most important possible Supreme Court litigating benefit that any administration has and that is that special trust, confidence and credibility that has been built up between these two institutions — the Supreme Court and the solicitor general's office."

A New Hard Line

Lee's words seemed to fall on deaf ears at his old office. Meese and Fried made clear within days of the end of the disappointing October 1984 term that the administration's campaign for change would continue at the Court.

And their words seemed to reflect a hard new line, a tougher approach, in dealing with the Court. "We hope for a day when the Court returns to the basic principles of the Constitution," Meese told the American Bar Association in July. The men who wrote the First Amendment would find "bizarre" the Court's view "that the amendment demands a strict neutrality [of government] between religion and irreligion," he said. "The purpose [of the amendment] was to prohibit religious tyranny, not to undermine religion generally."

Meese said that the Court, in the October 1984 term, "continued to roam at large in a veritable constitutional forest," conjuring up images of nine lost children wandering without a pocketful of precedential breadcrumbs to lead them to judicial truth. Meese promised that the administration would continue to urge the Court to use the original intention of the Framers of the Constitution and the Bill of Rights as the standard for its constitutional decisions.

Soon after Meese's speech, Fried provided a contemporary example of that approach by filing a friend of the court brief urging that the Court overturn *Roe v. Wade*, the 1973 landmark denyings states the power to criminalize abortion. "There is no explicit textual warrant in the Constitution for a right to an abortion."

It was the first time the government had ever asked the Court to take back an individual right it had found to be guaranteed by the Constitution.

8

Looking Ahead

At the end of Ronald Reagan's fifth year in the White House, the future of his efforts for change remained in doubt. Reagan's single skillful appointment and his energetic advocacy of new policy positions *had* made a difference at the Supreme Court. But the president was clearly still finding it more difficult to win votes at the Court than in the country at large.

Focusing public attention on Reagan's campaign for a different brand of justice, Attorney General Edwin Meese expanded the administration's policy arguments into a full-fledged constitutional debate. That debate frames the Court's consideration of major issues for the remaining years of Reagan's presidency.

In many ways the fate of this Reagan campaign depends on his opportunity to appoint at least one more justice. After several years of predicting an imminent vacancy, Court watchers threw up their hands late in 1985 and refused to make any further comments.

Attention turned from the health and hopes of the current justices to the list of potential Reagan choices, should a vacancy occur. There were important differences among the possible choices, but there was little doubt that the primary impact of a second Reagan appointment would be to strengthen the already reinvigorated conservative wing at the Court.

Constitutional Debate

In July 1985 Meese urged the Court to return to a literal view of the Constitution, to abandon what he described as "a jurisprudence of idiosyncrasy" for "a jurisprudence of original intention." In a pair of speeches delivered to the American Bar Association, Meese criticized a number of the Court's decisions in its just-ended term as "more policy choices than articulations of constitutional principle. The voting blocs, the arguments, all reveal a greater allegiance to what the Court thinks constitutes sound public policy than a deference to what the Constitution — its text and intention — may demand."

Enlarging his criticism to include the entire modern era of the Court, Meese declared that "the Bill of Rights, as debated, created and ratified was designed to apply *only* to the national government." The foundation for the last 60 years of decisions applying the Bill of Rights to limit state action was "intellectually shaky," Meese continued.

In October Justices William J. Brennan Jr. and John Paul Stevens responded, defending the liberal tradition of constitutional interpretation.

"We current justices read the Constitution in the only way we can: as Twentieth Century Americans," Brennan said. "The ultimate question must be, what do the words of the text mean in our time. For the genius of the Constitution rests not in any static meaning it might have had in a world that is dead and gone, but in the adaptability of its great principles to cope with current problems and current needs."

Stevens focused his criticism on Meese's view that the Bill of Rights should not apply to the states. Such an argument, Stevens said, "overlooks the profound importance of the Civil War and the post-war amendments on the structure of our government, and particularly upon the relationship between the Federal Government and the separate states."

In the remaining years of the Reagan presidency, these themes will recur as the Court considers cases about state and federal power, abortion, affirmative action, capital punishment, other criminal law matters, and church and state. In resolving these issues, the Supreme Court of the 1980s will reveal whether it endorses the liberal view — or the literal view — of the nation's charter.

The Literal View

The Constitution should be interpreted the way the men who wrote it in 1789 meant it to be, Meese argued. Adherence to such a jurisprudence of original intention would reflect commitment to the idea of democracy, he continued. "The Constitution is the fundamental will of the people; that is why it is the fundamental law. To allow the courts to govern simply by what it views at the time as fair and decent, is a scheme of government no longer popular; the idea of democracy has suffered."

Emphasizing his view of the Constitution as "an external and tangible check on any arbitrary exercise of government power," Meese promised that "in the cases we file and those we join as *amicus*" before the Court "we will endeavor to resurrect the original meaning of constitutional provisions and statutes as the only reliable guide for judgment."

"It is our belief that only 'the sense in which the Constitution was accepted and ratified by the nation,' and only the sense in which laws were drafted and passed provide a solid foundation for adjudication. Any other standard suffers the defect of pouring new meaning into old words, thus creating new powers and new rights totally at odds with the logic of our Constitution and its commitment to the rule of law." *(Text, p. 171)*

Part and parcel of this point of view was the argument, which Meese only initiated in these July speeches and had not yet made at full strength, that the Bill of Rights — the guarantees of free speech and freedom of religion, of fair treatment for criminal suspects and of security against unreasonable searches — should not be applied against state action, but only against the federal government.

The language of the First Amendment clearly forbids *only* Congress to make a law abridging the freedoms guaranteed by the amendment.

And in 1833 Chief Justice John Marshall explicitly held that the Bill of Rights did not apply to states.

But in 1925 the Supreme Court held that the 14th Amendment, ratified 35 years after Marshall's ruling, extended the free speech guarantee of the First Amendment against state as well as federal action. Over the next half century, the Court used this "incorporation" rationale again and again to extend other provisions of the Bill of Rights to protect the individual against state, as well as federal, action.

The Liberal View

Justice Brennan, the Court's senior member and most articulate liberal, stepped forward to present another view. The argument that the only true guide for constitutional interpretation is the intention of the Framers "feigns self-effacing deference to the specific judgments of those who forged our original social compact," Brennan told a symposium at Georgetown University Oct. 12. "But in truth it is little more than arrogance cloaked as humility. It is arrogant to pretend that from our vantage we can gauge accurately the intent of the Framers on application of principle to specific, contemporary questions."

"We are an aspiring people, a people with faith in progress," Brennan continued, "Our amended Constitution is the lodestar for our aspirations.... As augmented by the Bill of Rights and the Civil War Amendments, this text is a sparkling vision of the supremacy of the human dignity of every individual."

In contrast with these aspirations, he declared, this literal approach to constitutional interpretation reflects an "antipathy to claims of the minority to rights against the majority. Those who would restrict claims of right to the values of 1789 ... turn a blind eye to social progress."

Brennan then turned to address the more sophisticated, and more successful, argument that former solicitor general Rex E. Lee and his deputy, Paul Bator, had used — that in a democracy, "substantive value choices" should be made by the elected representatives of the people, the legislature and the executive.

"This view emphasizes not the transcendent historical authority of the Framers but the predominant contemporary authority of the elected branches of government.... Yet it has similar consequences," Brennan explained.

"Unabashed enshrinement of majority will would permit the imposition of a social

Edwin Meese

caste system or wholesale confiscation of property so long as a majority of the authorized legislative body, fairly elected, approved," Brennan warned. "Our Constitution could not abide such a situation. It is the very purpose of a Constitution — and particularly of the Bill of Rights — to declare certain values transcendent, beyond the reach of temporary political majorities."

"Faith in democracy is one thing, blind faith quite another," he added.

Ten days later, Justice Stevens joined the debate on Brennan's side. Speaking at a meeting of the Federal Bar Association in Chicago, Stevens targeted his brief remarks on Meese's criticism of the rulings applying the First Amendment and other guarantees of the Bill of Rights to the states.

"It is possible," he said in concluding this portion of his remarks, "that I have misconstrued the speech given by Attorney General Meese last July and that he did not actually intend his recommended 'Jurisprudence of original intention' as a rejection of the proposition that the Fourteenth Amendment has made the First Amendment applicable to the states. But if there is ambiguity in the message that was conveyed by an articulate contemporary lawyer last July, is it not possible that some uncertainty may attend an effort that equally articulate lawyers were attempting to convey almost two hundred years ago?"

Federalism: The Proper Balance

The balance of power, respect and prerogative between the states and the federal government is affected by almost every Supreme Court decision. When the Court strikes down state laws regulating abortions, permits state agencies voluntarily to adopt affirmative action plans, requires local police to follow certain procedures in dealing with suspects and reviews state laws recognizing the role of religion in American life, it affects this balance.

The liberal members of the Supreme Court believe that the national government is more likely than the state governments to act in line with their ideals. The memories of rampant racial discrimination by states, the stories of the brutality of local police and their disregard for the rights of criminal suspects, the blatant malapportionment that state legislatures perpetuated for half a century — all these work to win their vote for federal power over state prerogatives.

President Reagan, who came to Washington from state government, has much more faith in the ability and integrity of state officials. His administration is philosophically committed to giving states more leeway, permitting them to exercise their authority free of federal statutory, regulatory or constitutional restrictions.

Yet the administration has sometimes found itself divided between the need to defend the institutional interest of the federal government and the desire to implement its philosophical commitment. The current Supreme Court is closely divided

over this matter as well. Three times during the early 1980s, the Court has voted 5-4 to support the extension of federal power into matters which states argued fiercely should be left to them alone to regulate.

Each time the line-up of justices was the same. Supporting the extension of federal power over state decisions concerning energy use, early retirement for state employees and the compensation of employees of publicly owned mass-transit systems, were Justices Byron R. White, Thurgood Marshall, Harry A. Blackmun, Brennan and Stevens. Dissenting were Chief Justice Warren E. Burger and Justices Lewis F. Powell Jr., William H. Rehnquist and Sandra Day O'Connor.

Even the administration's argument that the Bill of Rights should not be applied to state action might find a warmer reception at the Court if Reagan has the opportunity to replace one of the five who espouse federal power with one who does not. As Meese said in July, "Nowhere else has the principle of federalism been dealt so politically violent and constitutionally suspect a blow as by the theory of incorporation," the belief that the 14th Amendment applied the guarantees of the Bill of Rights to the states.

The average citizen is affected far more frequently and directly by the action of his state and local government than by the federal government. If the Supreme Court agreed to lift the restraints the Bill of Rights has imposed on state action since the 1920s and 1930s, that decision would be the most far-reaching reversal in American history and could place at risk many of the rights and freedoms that Americans assume to be secure against government infringement.

Meese criticized the most recent of these 5-4 decisions, a 1985 ruling reversing a 1976 decision that Congress had no business telling states and cities how much to pay their employees. This was "an inaccurate reading of the text of the Constitution and a disregard for the Framers' intention that state and local governments be a buffer against the centralizing tendencies of the national Leviathan," Meese said. "We hope for a day when the Court returns to the basic principles of the Constitution as expressed in *Usery,"* the overturned decision.

Abortion: Unanchored Right

By far the most controversial decision of the 1970s was *Roe v. Wade,* the 1973 ruling legalizing abortion. This decision was grounded in a right of personal privacy that the majority in *Roe v. Wade* found implicit in the Constitution. As Justice Blackmun explained: "This right of privacy, whether it be founded in the 14th Amendment's concept of personal liberty and restrictions upon state action, as we feel it is, or in the Ninth Amendment's reservation of rights to the people, is broad enough to encompass a woman's decision whether or not to terminate her pregnancy."

Roe v. Wade was the immediate target of the administration's argument for a literal reading of the Constitution. In July 1985 Charles Fried, then acting solicitor general, told the justices they should overrule *Roe v. Wade* because "there is no explicit textual warrant in the Constitution for the right to an abortion."

The Akron Case

Just two years earlier, when the Court had reviewed abortion regulations imposed by the city of Akron, Ohio, the administration had been more subtle in its approach. Solicitor General Lee, arguing that the Court should uphold these regulations and leave future regulation of abortion to legislators, added a footnote stating that the government's position on this matter did not indicate that it agreed with *Roe v. Wade.* *(Details, p. 110)*

In the *Akron* case, the Court reaf-

firmed *Roe v. Wade.* In her dissent, Justice O'Connor not only at last revealed her judicial views on abortion, but also showed herself an incisive critic of the framework as well as the foundation of that ruling.

Just two years later, the Court agreed to review procedurally awkward appeals from lower court rulings holding Illinois and Pennsylvania abortion control laws unconstitutional. Surprise at the Court's decision to reconsider this issue so soon led to speculation that one of the justices in the *Akron* majority — perhaps Powell, who had undergone surgery twice in 1985 — was about to retire.

The prospect of Powell's replacement by a Reagan nominee willing to reverse *Roe v. Wade,* the speculation continued, might have encouraged Chief Justice Burger, a reluctant supporter of *Roe v. Wade,* to join the *Akron* dissenters in voting to review the two new cases.

But Powell did not retire, and Blackmun downplayed the significance of the decision to reconsider this issue, telling a meeting of federal judges that "there are always four votes" to hear an abortion case. In that situation, he said, "the other five of us heave a deep sigh and wish we didn't have to go through this traumatic experience again."

The Administration Argument

However, in July, the administration urged the Court to use these new cases — *Thornburgh v. American College of Obstetricians and Gynecologists* and *Diamond v. Charles* — to reverse *Roe v. Wade.* Six months earlier, President Reagan had told a massive rally of anti-abortion forces that "the momentum is with us" to end "the terrible national tragedy of abortion."

Translating that observation into legal terms, Fried told the justices "the textual, historical and doctrinal basis of that decision is so far flawed that this Court should overrule it and return the law to the condition in which it was before that case was decided.

"The key factors in the equation — viability, trimesters, the right to terminate one's pregnancy — have no moorings in the text of our Constitution. . . . Because the parameters of the inquiry are indeterminate, courts are disposed to indulge in a free-ranging, essentially legislative, process of devising regulatory schemes that reflect their notions of morality and social justice," he added.

The Scientific Challenge

Even before such politically potent criticism was directed at the constitutional foundation of *Roe v. Wade,* the justices had already been well aware that scientific advances would soon require the restructuring of its logical framework.

Justice O'Connor had made this point with stinging precision in 1983. Dissenting in the *Akron* case, she wrote that scientific progress in neo-natal care, on the one hand, and abortion procedures, on the other, were placing this framework "on a collision course with itself."

The Court's 1973 ruling permitted regulations designed to protect maternal health throughout pregnancy. But not until the point at which a fetus was viable — that is, able to survive outside the mother's body — could a state prohibit abortion. In 1973 that point was generally considered to be 28 weeks, but no earlier than 24 weeks. Thus it was only in the last three months, or trimester, of pregnancy that abortions could be forbidden.

O'Connor pointed out that the intervening decade had brought technological progress that enabled doctors to keep alive, at least for a brief time, infants born as early as 22 weeks. The point of viability was being moved earlier and earlier in pregnancy — and along with it the point at which a state could ban abortion. At the same time, abortions were becoming safer

for women later and later in pregnancy, making state regulation to protect maternal health less necessary.

By tying the state's power to regulate abortion to the current state of medical technology, O'Connor wrote, the trimester approach to regulating abortion becomes "a completely unworkable method of accommodating the conflicting personal rights and compelling state interests that are involved" in the issue of abortion.

O'Connor said that she believed the state's interest in protecting potential life existed throughout pregnancy. The Court should discard the trimester approach, she said, and permit states to regulate abortion however they wish so long as the regulation does not place an undue burden on the woman's right to seek an abortion.

The Outlook

Although it is considered quite unlikely that the Court would overturn *Roe v. Wade* in the 1985-86 term, the challenge to that ruling seems likely to intensify rather than to moderate. The political pressure has mounted steadily since 1973. Although polls show strong public support for the right to choose abortion, that support is perhaps not as obvious to elected officials as the organized and vocal opposition.

The scientific factor O'Connor has pointed out assures that in time *Roe v. Wade* must at least be restructured to fit with contemporary reality. On this point, a second Reagan nomination to the Court could prove crucial. The *Roe* majority was seven justices; the *Akron* majority was six. If one of those six leaves the bench and Reagan appoints his successor, *Roe v. Wade* could be on its way to the constitutional dustheap.

Civil Rights

The civil rights issues of the 1980s are second- or third-generation cases — the grandchildren of the landmark *Brown* ruling of 1954. There is no question of returning to the days of blatant discrimination; the questions instead focus on the appropriate means for continuing to push toward the ideal of equal opportunity for all.

Affirmative Action

Affirmative action — the use of race as a plus, not a minus in an individual's record — is the major contemporary civil rights issue. Advocates of affirmative action consider it a necessary tool to redress past employment discrimination against women and minorities. They acknowledge that the ultimate goal of the national commitment to civil rights progress is "a color-blind Constitution," but they argue that "race-conscious remedial action is necessary to achieve equal opportunity" first.

Such policies have received general support for more than a decade as they have been employed by governments and private employers, sometimes voluntarily and sometimes under court order, to increase the representation of women and minorities in various professions and positions.

But the Reagan administration firmly opposes affirmative action. Calling for a return to the ideal of the color-blind Constitution, Meese and his colleagues at the Justice Department characterize affirmative action as nothing more than "reverse discrimination" denying white males their rights to equal protection in the same way blacks and women were so long denied equal treatment.

Preliminary Victories. Both sides in this debate can and do point to recent Supreme Court rulings as support for their argument. The Court addressed the issue of affirmative action several times in the 1975-1985 decade. The results were mixed. Twice, in 1978 and 1984, it limited the use of preferential treatment plans. Three times, it upheld such plans.

The Court's first full-scale decision on affirmative action provided ample evidence of the complexity of the issue and the close division within the nine justices over its proper resolution. In the 1978 case of *Regents of the University of California v. Bakke,* the Court held it illegal under the 1964 Civil Rights Act for a state medical school to set aside a specific quota of places in an entering class for blacks and other minorities. That decision was reached by a vote of 5-4.

But in the same case, the Court held that it was constitutionally permissible for admissions officers to consider minority race as a "plus" in weighing an applicant's qualifications. This decision also came by a vote of 5-4. Only one justice — Lewis Powell — agreed with both halves of the decision.

The following year, in the case of *United Steelworkers of America v. Weber,* the Court, 5-2, approved a private employer's voluntary affirmative action plan setting aside for black workers half of the openings in in-plant training programs.

In 1980, in *Fullilove v. Klutznick,* the Court, 6-3, upheld a provision of a 1977 public works law in which Congress set aside for minority contractors 10 percent of the funds authorized under the bill.

When the Court four years later ruled 6-3 that a federal judge was wrong to override seniority rules to protect the jobs of recently hired minority employees, the Reagan administration claimed a sweeping victory. Assistant Attorney General William Bradford Reynolds announced that the Court's ruling in *Firefighters Local Union No. 1784 v. Stotts* barred the use of racial quotas except to benefit the individual victims of bias.

The Justice Department urged 51 cities, counties and states to discard existing affirmative action plans in light of *Stotts.* But that suggestion was rejected by most of those public employers and, to compound the administration's frustration, lower courts applying the *Stotts* ruling uniformly viewed it as a narrow decision lacking the broad sweep the administration claimed for it.

The Administration Argument. Congress intended to protect blacks and whites by approving the 14th Amendment's guarantee of equal protection, the administration argued. Moreover, according to the administration, that amendment forbids all legal distinctions based on race or color. It requires the government to oppose affirmative action in the workplace in 1985 just as staunchly as it opposed racial segregation in public schools in 1954.

Administration officials quote Justice John Harlan's famous dissent from *Plessy v. Ferguson,* the 1896 decision upholding the concept of "separate but equal" facilities for blacks and whites: "Our Constitution is color-blind, and neither knows nor tolerates classes among citizens. In respect of civil rights, all citizens are equal before the law. . . . The law regards man as man, and takes no account of his surroundings or of his color."

Urging the Court to restrict the use of affirmative action to individual cases of discrimination, discarding it as a class or group remedy, Fried told the justices in summer 1985 that in the administration's view, "any governmental action based on race or national origin bears the heaviest possible burden of justification."

He continued, "Racial quotas cannot lighten, much less discharge, this burden of justification by claiming to favor blacks or other disadvantaged groups and therefore claiming to be benign."

Fried coupled this argument from a teacher lay-off case from Michigan, *Wygant v. Jackson Board of Education,* with a second argument, made in a firefighters' promotion case from Cleveland, that many affirmative action plans of this type also

were illegal, in conflict with the provisions of the 1964 Civil Rights Act as interpreted by the Supreme Court in *Stotts.* The Cleveland case, Fried argued, gave the Court an opportunity to "correct" the "series of recent lower court decisions upholding quota relief and giving . . . *Stotts* what we regard as an overly narrow interpretation."

On the first day of the October 1985 term, the Court agreed to hear the case, *Local #93, International Association of Firefighters v. Cleveland and Cleveland Vanguards,* later in the term.

Even as Fried filed these briefs with the Court, a second affirmative action battle was under way within the executive branch over proposals to water down the government's own affirmative action requirements for its contractors, in effect since 1965.

Meese, the leading critic of this program, contended that racially preferential policies are vestiges of slavery. Labor Secretary William E. Brock, who emerged as the leading advocate of affirmative action in the Cabinet, responded that there was a continuing need for such remedial plans.

Busing

Affirmative action leads the list of civil rights issues before the Court, but it is not the only issue on that particular agenda. The Supreme Court has not directly addressed the issue of public school desegregation since 1979, but the administration hopes to bring such a case back to the Court within the next few terms.

Justice Department officials hope to win a ruling that would spell an end to federal court supervision of school desegregation in many cities. Administration attorneys are urging lower court judges to release school boards from court orders requiring busing and other steps toward desegregation once they find that the board has "fully and in good faith" carried out a desegregation plan.

By emphasizing the school board's efforts rather than the actual results, this standard would permit an end to court supervised desegregation, even in school districts where factors such as white flight had made a truly desegregated system impossible.

In early 1985 Justice Department attorneys joined the Norfolk, Va., school board in asking the federal court that had been supervising its 15-year-long desegregation effort to eliminate the current busing plan, return the system to a neighborhood-oriented attendance plan and release the board from existing court orders.

Aid and Bias

The Reagan administration also planned to capitalize on the Court's 1984 decision narrowing the reach of the ban on sex discrimination by federally aided education programs. In *Grove City College v. Bell,* the Court agreed with the administration that Congress intended that only the specific program receiving aid — not the entire institution — came within the bias ban. *(Details, p. 124)*

Legislation to reverse that ruling, which civil rights groups regard as a threat to the sweep of several other federal laws barring discrimination in federally aided programs, has been pending in Congress for almost two years. The administration, which opposes that legislation, pressed ahead in the courts for decisions building on *Grove City.* The Supreme Court late in October 1985 agreed to hear the administration's appeal in such a case, *Department of Transportation v. Paralyzed Veterans of America.*

At issue in this case was the reach of the federal ban on discrimination against handicapped persons, as it affects commercial airlines. Because most commercial airlines do not themselves receive direct government aid, the administration argued that they did not come within the sweep of this ban.

But an appeals court disagreed, ruling that because of the pervasive indirect federal aid airlines receive — through airport subsidies and the use of the federal air traffic control system — the airlines themselves were indeed subject to this ban, which is part of the Rehabilitation Act of 1973. The Supreme Court was expected to hear administration arguments for reversal of that ruling early in 1986.

The Outlook. As the Court's ringing reaffirmation of the national commitment to equality in its *Bob Jones* decision in 1983 demonstrated, the Court still believes firmly that the nation must continue to move in that direction. However, the cases that challenge the use of affirmative action and busing raise an intermediate question, a question of means rather than goals. And on the matter of means, the balance within the Court is now a narrow one.

O'Connor's replacement of Justice Potter Stewart could prove the critical difference in the Court's stance on affirmative action. Stewart generally opposed mandatory quotas but supported voluntary use of affirmative action. If O'Connor opposes the willing adoption of such remedial plans, she could swing a majority of the Court to the administration's position.

O'Connor's position on busing differs little from Stewart's. Late in his career Stewart cast several votes against massive use of busing. O'Connor made clear at her confirmation that as a child who was bused to school for other reasons, she was firmly opposed to long-distance transportation of young school children. In addition, her belief in the authority of local and state governments would tend to favor a policy of neighborhood schools.

Should the Court decide that practical considerations as well as political ones advise a shift away from the drastic measure of busing, it is likely that it will couch its decision carefully to avoid the appearance of retreating from the promise of *Brown v. Board of Education* (1954), perhaps by emphasizing the use of more positive incentive for desegregation, such as magnet schools and specialized high school programs in different areas of a city.

Church and State

Religious freedom in the United States is protected by a constitutional paradox. The First Amendment forbids Congress to make any law prohibiting the free exercise of religion or respecting an establishment of religion.

Until well into the 20th century, neither of these prohibitions curtailed state action. In 1833, with Chief Justice John Marshall as its voice, the Supreme Court declared that the Bill of Rights bound only the federal government, not the states.

But in 1925 all that began to change. The Court looked at the language the 14th Amendment added to the Constitution in 1868. And within the phrase that forbids states to deprive any person of life, liberty or property without due process of law the Court found reason to rule that the First Amendment freedom of speech was now protected against state, as well as federal, action.

In 1934 the Court found that the 14th Amendment also protected an individual's freedom to exercise his religion against state action. And 13 years later the Court applied the ban on establishment of religion to the states as well.

The Wall of Separation?

This "establishment clause" is the constitutional basis for the Court's most controversial church-state rulings. It was the foundation for the Court's decisions in 1962 and 1963 forbidding state officials to prescribe use of prayer and Bible reading in public school classrooms. It was the basis for the Court's rulings of the 1960s and 1970s striking down a variety of state programs aiding parochial schools.

A single metaphor links these rulings. In 1947 Justice Hugo L. Black declared that "in the words of Jefferson, the clause against establishment of religion by law was intended to erect 'a wall of separation between Church and State.'"

The Court's rulings fortifying this wall of separation have been criticized as reflecting a judicial hostility to religion. The First Amendment merely requires government to be evenhanded in dealing with various denominations, critics argue. Despite the view of the majority of the sitting justices, that amendment does not require that the state be neutral in dealing with religious groups on the one hand and non-religious groups on the other.

Meese reflected that point in his July 1985 speeches, declaring that "to have argued, as is popular today, that the amendment demands a strict neutrality between religion and irreligion would have struck the founding generation as bizarre. The purpose was to prohibit religious tyranny, not to undermine religion generally."

The Idea of Accommodation

Early in the 1980s the Court seemed ready to move away from the idea of separation and toward a stance permitting accommodation of the interests of church and state in American life. When the Court in 1984 permitted Pawtucket city officials to include a crèche in their holiday display, Chief Justice Burger declared that the Constitution "affirmatively mandates accommodation, not merely tolerance, of all religions and forbids hostility toward any."

The administration moved quickly to capitalize on this line of reasoning, urging the Court to approve Alabama's moment-of-silence law as an appropriate accommodation of the interests of religious students in the public schools. The administration sounded this same theme in arguing to the

Court that it approve two programs — one in Grand Rapids and the other in New York City — in which publicly paid teachers went into parochial schools to provide special supplementary courses. The Court rejected both arguments, striking down the Alabama law and the Grand Rapids and New York City programs — all as violating the Establishment Clause.

The Divided Court

These mid-1985 decisions illustrate how delicate a balance exists on the Court between those justices who find the administration's arguments persuasive and those who do not. The 1984 Pawtucket crèche case was decided, as the administration wished, in favor of accommodation by a vote of 5-4. The five were Burger, White, Powell, Rehnquist and O'Connor. Dissenting were Brennan, Marshall, Blackmun and Stevens.

But in the 1985 parochiaid cases Justice Powell voted against the Grand Rapids and New York City plans, changing the 5-4 majority for accommodation into a 5-4 majority against. Powell was also part of the 6-3 majority to strike down the moment-of-silence law. The sixth vote was Justice O'Connor, a notable disappointment for the White House.

In that case, *Wallace v. Jaffree,* Justice Stevens told the nation that the Court believed that "government must pursue a course of complete neutrality toward religion. . . . The Court has unambiguously concluded that the individual freedom of conscience protected by the First Amendment embraces the right to select any religious faith or none at all," he continued.

This position was vigorously attacked by the administration, which found ample intellectual support for its view in the dissenting opinion written by Justice Rehnquist. This, according to Attorney General Meese, was the correct historical view of the meaning of the Establishment Clause.

Rehnquist and O'Connor

Rehnquist criticized the "wall of separation" to which Black referred in 1937 as a "misleading metaphor," that encapsulated "a mistaken understanding of constitutional history." He added, "It should be frankly and explicitly abandoned."

Referring to the discussion in the House of Representatives by James Madison and others of the proposed Bill of Rights, Rehnquist contended that Madison designed this clause to prohibit establishment of a national religion, and perhaps to prevent the government from preferring one sect over another, but not to require the government to be neutral between religion and irreligion.

"It would come as much of a shock to those who drafted the Bill of Rights . . . to learn that the Constitution, as construed by the majority, prohibits the Alabama legislature from 'endorsing' prayer. George Washington himself, at the request of the very Congress which passed the Bill of Rights, proclaimed a day of 'public thanksgiving and prayer, to be observed by acknowledging with grateful hearts the many and signal favors of Almighty God.' History must judge whether it was the father of his country in 1789, or a majority of the Court today, which has strayed from the meaning of the Establishment Clause," Rehnquist concluded.

O'Connor, who agreed with the majority that this moment-of-silence law could not pass muster, rejected the majority's emphasis on government neutrality. She saw the solution to the potential conflict between the need to protect the free exercise of religion while avoiding any establishment of religion as lying "not in 'neutrality,' but rather in identifying workable limits to the Government's license to promote the free exercise of religion."

It was difficult to use history as a guide on the matter of school prayer, she pointed out, because "free public education was virtually non-existent" at the time the First Amendment was ratified, and, therefore, "it is unlikely that the persons who drafted the First Amendment . . . anticipated the problems of interaction of church and state in the public schools."

The Outlook

Although the Court had several church-state cases before it in the October 1985 term, none appeared as significant as the moment-of-silence law, the parochiaid questions, or the crèche case. The case of most general interest, *Bender v. Williamsport Area School District,* asked the Court to overturn a school board's decision that the First Amendment required it to deny a student religious group the same access to space and time for meeting at the high school as other student groups have.

The Reagan administration told the Court that it should overturn that decision and permit the students to meet. "Their only request is that the state be neutral toward religion — a request fully in accord with the basic value of the First Amendment," it said.

In one of the other church-state cases set for argument, a blind student asked the Court to hold that a state violated the First Amendment by denying him scholarship aid just because the goal of his studies was the ministry. In the others a Jewish rabbi challenged the military rule forbidding him to wear his yarmulke indoors while on duty and an Indian who believes numbers and computers to be evil sought exemption from the requirement that he obtain a Social Security number for his child.

Most Court observers expected the broader questions — of state laws permitting prayer in schools and of state and local programs aiding parochial as well as public schools — to recur. And, as the disagreement between O'Connor and Rehnquist illustrates, all conservatives do not agree on the proper resolution of these questions. The disagreement between the two youngest and most conservative members of the Court foreshadows continued division within the Court on these questions, even with the addition of other conservative justices.

Criminal Law

In the field of criminal law, the conservative literalism of the Reagan administration has focused primarily upon the exclusionary rule, which denies prosecutors the use of evidence obtained from suspects in violation of their constitutional rights. The exclusionary rule is a Court-made rule, first announced in 1914, designed to prevent or punish police misconduct by denying the state the use of evidence obtained by such behavior.

The rule was first announced to forbid the use of evidence obtained in searches that violated the Fourth Amendment guarantee of security against unreasonable searches, usually understood to be searches not authorized by warrant. And the rule was first applied only in federal courts.

But after the Fourth Amendment, the Fifth, which guarantees freedom from compelled self-incrimination, and the Sixth, which guarantees the aid of a lawyer, were applied against state as well as federal action by the Warren Court, the exclusionary rule was applied in state courts too. In 1964 the Supreme Court applied it against evidence state prosecutors wished to use but which had been obtained through improper searches.

Two years later, in the controversial decision of *Miranda v. Arizona,* the Warren Court forged the exclusionary rule into an affirmative requirement: before a suspect in custody could be interrogated, the Court held, he must be advised of his right to remain silent, of the fact that anything he said could be used against him and of his right to the aid of an attorney.

If the suspect indicated he wished to

remain silent, the police must cease the interrogation; if he indicated he wished his attorney to be present, the police must cease the interrogation until the attorney arrived, the Court declared. And if police did not administer these warnings or if they did not comply with the suspect's wish to exercise these rights, any evidence they obtained from him would be excluded from use in court, the Court held.

The *Miranda* decision immediately drew fire from conservative politicians, police and prosecutors, all of whom criticized it as tying their hands and making the job of apprehending and prosecuting criminals far more difficult. During his 1968 presidential campaign, Richard Nixon criticized *Miranda* and promised to appoint justices who would repudiate it. Nixon was elected; he appointed four justices; *Miranda* remained the law through the 1970s and into the 1980s.

The Administration Attack

The Reagan administration began its attack on the exclusionary rule by having the solicitor general argue for a "good faith" exception to it. As approved in 1984, however, the good faith exception is a fairly narrow one. In the case of *United States v. Leon,* Justice White explained that the Court majority approved use of evidence taken in a search authorized by a warrant and carried out by police who felt they were acting legally — even if the warrant was later shown to be defective.

In 1985 the administration turned its criticism full force on the *Miranda* rule. "The *Miranda* decision was wrong," Attorney General Meese bluntly told *U.S. News & World Report* in October. "Its practical effect is to prevent police from talking to the person who knows the most about the crime — namely, the perpetrator. . . . *Miranda* only helps guilty defendants. Most innocent people are glad to talk to the police. They want to establish their inno-

cence so that they're no longer a suspect."

"You don't have many suspects who are innocent of a crime," Meese added. This comment drew fire from law professors and civil libertarians who criticized it as reflecting a basic misunderstanding of the American system of criminal justice in which a person is presumed innocent until proven guilty.

The *Miranda* decision is involved in a handful of cases that come to the Court each year for full review. The solicitor general was expected to translate Meese's remarks into a legal brief urging the Court to overturn the 1966 ruling. The Court has already made clear its disinclination to expand *Miranda* beyond its current reach.

Public Safety Exception

In 1984 the Court permitted a "public safety" exception to *Miranda,* allowing use in evidence of a gun found in a supermarket, although the police apprehending the suspect in the supermarket asked him where the gun was before giving him his *Miranda* warnings. The majority agreed that in that situation the public safety demanded that police locate the gun first and advise the suspect of his rights second.

Justice O'Connor dissented from that decision, reflecting the traditional conservative's respect for settled precedent and criticizing the majority for blurring the clear mandate of *Miranda,* making the police officer's job again more difficult.

But O'Connor was part of the majority that ruled later in that term that evidence that would inevitably have been discovered independent of any police misconduct could be used even if it was in fact discovered as the result of indirect interrogation of a suspect by police in the absence of his attorney. And she was the author of a 1985 decision, hailed by the administration, in which the Court held that the initial failure of police to warn a suspect of his rights did not so taint all subsequent statements by the suspect, after he was warned, as to render them all inadmissible.

The Future Court

As each justice marks another birthday or anniversary, the speculation about a vacancy on the Supreme Court intensifies. No one knows whether President Reagan will name another member of the Court before he leaves the White House in January 1989.

Bruce Fein, a former administration official and close observer of the Court, said in mid-1985 that he no longer expected any retirements from the Court during Reagan's second term. He predicted that only death or severe physical disability would create a vacancy before 1989. Justice Blackmun reinforced this view, telling the 8th U.S. Judicial Conference in July 1985 that, as far as he knew, none of the justices had any retirement plans.

Should one of the more liberal justices leave the Court during Reagan's tenure, the impact of a second Reagan appointment would be much greater than if one of the more conservative justices left the bench. As the arrival of O'Connor demonstrated, the impact of any single new justice depends to a substantial degree upon the extent to which his or her views and voting record contrast or coincide with those of the departing justice.

O'Connor, a staunch conservative, had more impact on the Court because she replaced a swing vote. A second justice chosen by Ronald Reagan will have a greater influence on the Court if he or she fills the seat now held by Brennan, Marshall, Stevens or Blackmun than if selected to succeed Burger, Rehnquist, Powell or White.

The Candidates

The prime candidates for the next Reagan appointment to the Court are all men.

Having named the first woman justice, it is unlikely that Reagan would name a second woman to the Court.

They are all white. Should Justice Marshall, the only black member of the Court, leave the bench, it is questionable whether he would be replaced with another black. The Reagan administration is philosophically opposed to viewing certain seats on the Court as the property of certain groups — Jews, Catholics or blacks, for example. Meese has said that he is "opposed to quotas even on the Supreme Court."

The candidates fall into two groups: the scholars who are now, by and large, federal judges courtesy of a Reagan appointment, and the political lawyers who are or were part of the Reagan administration. Unless he has the opportunity to fill several seats on the Court, the president is considered more likely to choose one of the scholarly judges than one of his political allies who might encounter more difficulty in winning confirmation.

Robert H. Bork

No one has been mentioned more often than Robert H. Bork as Reagan's next nominee to the Court. In 1982 Reagan appointed Bork, born in 1927, to the U.S. Circuit Court of Appeals for the District of Columbia.

A 1953 graduate of the University of Chicago Law School, Bork practiced in Chicago with the firm of Kirkland and Ellis until 1962 when he joined the faculty of Yale Law School. The association with Yale stretched for almost 20 years, with time out in the 1970s for Bork to serve as solicitor general in the Nixon administration.

As solicitor general he argued a number of important cases before the Court, but he is best known as the man who carried out Richard Nixon's order to fire Watergate Special Prosecutor Archibald Cox in October 1973, after his superiors, Attorney General Elliot Richardson and Deputy Attorney General William Ruckelshaus, resigned rather than carry out that order.

Bork served as solicitor general until 1977, when he returned to Yale. In 1981 he resumed private law practice with Kirkland and Ellis' Washington, D.C., office. He was appointed an appeals court judge on Feb. 12, 1982.

Bork is the leading intellectual advocate of judicial restraint. It is his view that unless a constitutional right clearly has been violated, courts should leave decisions involving policy to the political branches of the state and federal government.

In a 1984 lecture Bork emphasized this point: "In a constitutional democracy the moral content of law must be given by the morality of the framer or the legislator, never by the morality of the judge. The sole task of the latter ... is to translate the framer's or the legislator's morality into a rule to govern unforeseen circumstances. That abstinence from giving his own desires free play, that continuing and self-conscious renunciation of power, that is the morality of the jurist."

One of his most notable opinions from the appeals court demonstrated the application of this view to a particular set of facts. In rejecting the argument that a homosexual man had a constitutional right to remain in the U.S. Navy, Bork declared that "if the revolution in sexual mores that ... [the homosexual man] proclaims is in fact ever to arrive, we think it must arrive through the moral choices of the people and their elected representatives, not through the ukase of this court."

Antonin Scalia

If Bork is the most senior member on the "justice-in-waiting" list, his colleague on the D.C. Circuit Appeals Court, Antonin Scalia, born in 1937, is the brightest star.

Before Reagan appointed him a judge in 1982, Scalia specialized in administrative

Robert H. Bork

law, an academic speciality of far less general interest than constitutional law. Thus his reputation as an academic was not as high as some of the other men on the candidates' list. But that deficiency has been more than remedied by the judicial leadership Scalia has brought to the appeals court. Since the 1960s feuding between key members of the court had created a tense and antagonistic atmosphere there.

Jonathan R. Macey, a law professor at Emory University, wrote in the *Wall Street Journal* that since Scalia's arrival, "not only has the court pulled together and eliminated much of the old rancor, but, more important, he has demonstrated an ability to convince more liberal judges that they should adopt his uniformly conservative legal positions."

Scalia would be the first Italian-American justice. A Catholic from Queens, he has nine children, aged five to 24. He is young, personable, bright and very conservative.

Scalia graduated from Georgetown University and then Harvard Law School in 1960, spent six years practicing law at Jones, Day in Cleveland. He then taught contracts, commercial and comparative law at the University of Virginia Law School.

Scalia, like Bork, stopped teaching in the 1970s to serve in the Nixon administration, first as general counsel of the Office of Telecommunications Policy in the White House, where his interest in administrative law began. In 1972 Scalia became chairman of the Administrative Conference of the United States, a federal interagency think tank. After two years, Nixon named him to head the office of legal counsel in the Justice Department, a job Scalia held through the Ford adminstration.

In 1977 Scalia moved to Chicago to teach at the University of Chicago Law School, maintaining a presence in Washington as an active critic of the legislative veto and as editor of the American Enterprise Institute's *Regulation* magazine.

Richard Posner

Richard Posner, born in 1939, is one of the most original and controversial thinkers in the field of law today. Chief advocate of an economic approach to the law, applying the principles of free-market economics to deciding cases, Posner was a professor at the University of Chicago Law School until Reagan named him to the 7th Circuit Court of Appeals in 1981.

Judges, Posner contends, should apply the "theory of rational choice in a world of limited goods" in making decisions. He uses a cost-benefit analysis, for example, to justify the general approach of judges in construing constitutional provisions more liberally than statutory ones. That distinction was based on "a sound economic principle," he said, because of the "much greater costs of changing the Constitution compared with changing a statute."

Posner, a 1962 graduate of Harvard Law School, clerked for Justice Brennan and later served in the solicitor general's office under Thurgood Marshall. He began his teaching career at Stanford Law School in 1968.

He is a prolific author, having written a dozen books, more than 100 articles and, according to the *Wall Street Journal,* more opinions since his appointment to the bench in 1981 than any other appeals court judge.

Posner is not an advocate of judicial self-restraint. He pointed out in a recent book, *The Federal Courts: Crisis and Reform,* that judicial self-restraint and good judging are not synonymous. If all conservative judges espoused self-restraint and adhered strictly to precedent — much of which is liberal — nothing would change very much.

Posner would discard adherence to precedent as the hallmark of the conservative judge and replace it with what he calls "separation-of-powers restraint," which limits judicial intervention in matters that are properly resolved by the legislature or the executive. Not surprisingly, his appeals court opinions often emphasize deference to administrative and legislative decisions.

Despite his approval of flexibility in constitutional interpretation, Posner himself usually takes a narrow view of constitutional language. As *Benchmark* magazine observed, Posner is "securely within the rank of federal judges who do not accept constitutional questions as invitations to develop individual rights and to reduce the prerogatives of the states or Congress."

Ralph K. Winter Jr.

When he was named by Reagan to the 2nd U.S. Circuit Court of Appeals in 1982, Ralph K. Winter Jr., born 1935, found himself on familiar territory. Twenty years earlier, Winter, a recent graduate of Yale Law School, had clerked for Thurgood Marshall, then a member of that same appeals court.

After his clerkship, Winter joined the faculty of Yale University Law School and became a full professor in 1968. He is a prolific and facile writer and within a year of taking his seat on the appeals court had published 28 opinions, a large number. Winter's opinions reflect a practicality, a close attention to the facts and a concern for the efficient working of the legal and political systems that blur ideological lines.

Winter is cognizant of the limits on judicial power. In 1982 he ruled that Congress, not courts, should choose a way of setting a limit on the liability of airlines for loss or damage to property of passengers. His opinion recognized that only Congress could set a standard that would be uniformly applied. The Supreme Court did not agree.

Although many of his opinions could be described as conservative, he struck down New York's preventive detention law for juveniles as unconstitutional in 1982, basing that decision in part upon the fact that many more juveniles were detained before disposition of the charges against them than afterwards. Winter felt the disparity indicated that the pretrial detention was in fact being used as punishment without due process. The Supreme Court, 6-3, reversed that decision in 1984.

Frank Easterbrook

The youngest man suggested as a Reagan choice for the Court is Frank Easterbrook, born in 1948. A 1973 graduate of the University of Chicago Law School, Easterbrook worked for five years in the solicitor general's office, the last two as deputy solicitor general (1978-1979).

A Posner protégé, he went to Chicago in 1979 to teach securities regulation and antitrust law at the University of Chicago Law School. He and Posner wrote the second edition of a major antitrust law text. President Reagan named him to the 7th Circuit U.S. Court of Appeals in 1984.

Richard A. Posner

Easterbrook argues that judges ought only to apply a law to a given situation if the law explicitly addresses the matter involved, or explicitly grants judges the power to make law to fill in any gaps the legislature did not close. He has suggested that judges should not even try to ascertain what decision would best serve the public interest, but should just enforce whatever bargains were struck in the passage of a particular law.

Easterbrook's approach to statutory matters, however, does not necessarily correlate with a conservative view of the Constitution and the rights it guarantees. In August 1985 he set out a broad view of the freedom protected by the First Amendment, as he wrote for the appeals court to hold unconstitutional an Indianapolis ordinance that was intended to curtail the distribution of material considered pornographic because of its degrading depiction of women.

Easterbrook wrote: "Under the First Amendment the government must leave to

Ripon Society Compiles ...

The Ripon Society, a group of moderate-to-liberal Republicans, set out an alternative list of moderate Court candidates in the July 1985 issue of the *Ripon Forum*. The only candidate on their list who figured on any serious Reagan list was FBI Director William Webster. *(See p. 155)*

The others were:

—Stephen G. Breyer, born in 1938, a federal judge on the 1st U.S. Circuit Court of Appeals. Breyer graduated from Harvard Law School, clerked for Justice Arthur Goldberg, served in the Justice Department and was an assistant special prosecutor during the Watergate scandal. A specialist in administrative law and a foe of regulatory overkill, he was a professor at Harvard Law School for 14 years, during which he also served as chief counsel to the Senate Judiciary Committee during the brief chairmanship of Sen. Edward M. Kennedy, D-Mass.

—John Hart Ely, born in 1938, dean of Stanford Law School. Ely graduated from Yale Law School, clerked for Chief Justice Earl Warren the same year that Breyer clerked for Goldberg. After a stint at the new Department of Transportation, Ely taught first at Yale and then at Harvard Law School before moving to head Stanford's law school in 1982. Ely, a well-known constitutional scholar, is a moderate. He contends that the judiciary should ensure that the procedures through which the legal system operates and through which a democracy functions are fair and equitable.

—William D. Ruckelshaus, born in 1932, of counsel to the Seattle, Wash., law firm, Perkins Coie. He has displayed an uncommon ability to keep his reputation untainted while moving through one political quagmire after another. A graduate of Harvard Law School, Ruckelshaus came to Washington with the Nixon administration, serving as the administrator of the newly created Environmental Protection Agency from 1970 until 1973. He then moved to second in command at the Justice Department, serving as deputy to Attorney General Elliot L. Richardson. Ruckelshaus resigned in October 1973 rather than fire Watergate special prosecutor Archibald Cox.

the people the evaluation of ideas. A belief may be pernicious — the beliefs of the Nazis led to the death of millions, those of the Klan to the repression of millions. A pernicious belief may prevail. One of the things that separates our society from others is our absolute right to propagate opinions that the government finds wrong or even hateful."

Richard Epstein

Richard Epstein, born in 1943, a law professor at the University of Chicago, is conservative, but he has reservations about the economic approach to the law and he is not an advocate of judicial restraint.

A graduate of Yale Law School in 1968, Epstein taught at the University of Southern California before moving to Chicago in 1972.

A philosopher as much as an advocate, Epstein contends that property and economic rights should be accorded more respect by the judiciary than they have been in modern times. Epstein advocates eliminating many laws that infringe on property

...List of Moderate Candidates

Ruckelshaus left the federal government to serve for eight years as senior vice president of Weyerhaeuser Company in Washington State. He returned to government in 1983 to succeed Anne M. Burford as administrator of the Environmental Protection Agency. At that time EPA was suffering severe morale problems because of charges of mismanagement leveled at Burford and criticism of its enforcement of the environmental laws. Ruckelshaus resigned the EPA post early in 1985, after getting the agency back on a "steady course."

—William T. Coleman Jr., born in 1920, probably the nation's most respected black attorney. Currently, he is practicing law in the Washington office of O'Melveny and Myers, a California law firm. Coleman, a graduate of Harvard Law School, was the first black attorney to be a Supreme Court clerk, working for Justice Felix Frankfurter during the 1948-1949 term. Subsequently, he helped draft the brief attacking public school segregation in *Brown v. Board of Education.* After more than 20 years in the private practice of law, during which he also served as counsel to the U.S. Arms Control and Disarmament Agency, Coleman became secretary of transportation in the Ford Administration.

A mark of his standing in the legal community was his selection by the Court to argue the *Bob Jones University* case. Coleman argued for the IRS because the Reagan administration refused to continue defending the denial of tax exemptions to discriminatory private schools. Coleman won the case for the IRS.

—Amalya L. Kearse, born in 1937, named to the 2nd U.S. Circuit Court of Appeals by President Jimmy Carter. A graduate of the University of Michigan Law School, Kearse practiced law in New York City for 17 years before moving to the bench. She was a partner in the Wall Street firm of Hughes, Hubbard & Reed.

Kearse believes that courts should act to ensure that government agencies implement the law properly, but she has written that "the courts . . . are not charged with general guardianship against all potential mischief in the complicated tasks of government."

rights — which the Constitution also protects, he points out. "There are many blatantly inappropriate statutes" like that "that cry out for a quick and easy kill," he has said. He is not a disciple of the Posner approach, declaring instead that "on a case-by-case basis, cost-benefit analysis is a source of intellectual suicide."

It is time, Epstein contends, for courts to resuscitate the clauses of the Constitution that forbid states to pass any law impairing the obligation of contracts or to take private property for public use without just compensation. These provisions should be employed to restrain legislatures from infringing too far on economic liberties.

"I'm against [judicial] activism in the sense that one ought not to push the Constitution beyond what the text requires," the *Legal Times* quoted Epstein, "but I think the text requires a whole lot."

The Political Possibilities

Attorney General Edwin Meese, born 1931; former attorney general William

French Smith, born 1917; and former interior secretary William P. Clark, born 1931, all have been mentioned as possible Reagan choices for the Court, but with every passing day they recede into the long-shot category. Lame-duck presidents rarely succeed in naming their friends to the Court.

Meese's rocky road to confirmation as attorney general makes it unlikely that the Senate would approve his nomination to the Court. Smith has told friends that he considers a judge's job boring. He moved back to California after leaving the Reagan Cabinet in 1985. Clark never graduated from law school, a fact that set off a major confirmation battle when Reagan nominated him to the California Supreme Court. Clark served on the state court for a number of years without particular distinction, although he proved himself as deputy secretary of state, national security adviser and head of the Interior Department during Reagan's first term.

If a Court vacancy occurs in 1987 or 1988, Reagan will have to choose carefully to avoid the "save the seat" syndrome. The Senate began, in the 19th century, denying confirmation to Court nominations made late in a presidential term, hoping to "save the seat" for the new president to fill. Partisan hopes and loyalties play a large role in this syndrome, as the party that does not hold the White House and hopes to capture it in the next election usually can muster the votes to block confirmation of the lame-duck president's choice.

As recently as 1968, the Senate refused to confirm President Lyndon Johnson's nomination of Abe Fortas as chief justice after Senate Republicans mounted a filibuster in opposition. As a result, the new president, Richard Nixon, was able to name his choice as chief justice — Warren Burger — in the first months of his term.

The one sure way to avoid this syndrome, however, is to nominate a member of the Senate to the Court. If Reagan chooses this route, the top two candidates are Orrin G. Hatch, R-Utah., and Paul Laxalt, R-Nev. Not since 1945, when President Harry S Truman selected Sen. Harold H. Burton, R-Ohio, has a sitting senator been named a Supreme Court justice.

Orrin G. Hatch

Orrin G. Hatch, born in 1934, catapulted into national politics in 1976 by upsetting incumbent senator Frank E. Moss. Hatch, who had never held public office, was a graduate of the University of Pittsburgh Law School and practiced in Salt Lake City.

A longtime supporter of Ronald Reagan, Hatch came to Washington with such militant conservative views that he immediately became the favorite of the New Right — and a "near fanatic" in the eyes of some liberals.

A bishop in the Mormon church, he opposes gun control and supports a balanced budget and capital punishment. As chairman of the Senate Judiciary subcommittee on the Constitution, he has been a forceful, although ultimately unsuccessful, proponent of amending the Constitution to limit busing, ban abortion, outlaw affirmative action and return prayer to the schools.

As Hatch came to the end of his first term in the Senate, he moderated his tone, if not his views. That new moderation served him well after he became chairman of the Senate Labor and Human Resources Committee in 1981. One test of his new reasonable approach was his ability to forge an effective working relationship with liberals such as Sen. Edward M. Kennedy, D-Mass., the ranking minority member of that committee, and Rep. Henry A. Waxman, D-Calif., chairman of the House subcommittee on health.

Paul Laxalt

Paul Laxalt, born in 1922, first met Ronald Reagan during the 1964 Goldwater

Paul Laxalt

Orrin G. Hatch

presidential campaign. A few years later, they met again as governors of neighboring states and became close friends. Indeed, Laxalt was known in the early 1980s as "Ronald Reagan's best friend in the Senate," a designation that was reflected in his unofficial role as liaison between the president and the Hill.

Laxalt, a Roman Catholic, graduated from law school in 1949 at the University of Denver and practiced law in Nevada. Entering politics in the 1960s, Laxalt was first lieutenant governor (1963-1967) and then governor (1967-1971) of the state.

He won a Senate seat in 1974 and was easily re-elected in 1980. He served as chairman of Reagan's 1976 and 1980 presidential campaigns and was Reagan's "man in Washington" in the time between the two races. In 1983 he was named general chairman of the Republican National Committee and participated in planning the 1984 GOP presidential and congressional campaigns.

Laxalt is a charming bridge builder who makes clear that he avoids translating political differences into personal animosity. Nevertheless, his voting record shows him to be one of the most consistently conservative members of Congress, supporting deregulation and capital punishment while opposing busing, abortion and the Court decisions barring official prayer from public schools.

Laxalt announced in August 1985 that he would not run for re-election in 1986, a move that dealt a serious blow to Republican hopes of retaining control of the Senate. But Laxalt said he would remain as general chairman of the Republican Party through Reagan's tenure in the White House and would be available for political "troubleshooting."

Webster and Ball

If Reagan chooses to look to government service or the private sector for his next nominee, the most likely candidates are FBI Director William Webster and William Bentley Ball, a leading constitutional advocate who practices law in Harrisburg, Pa. Both are men whose personal views are conservative, but whose integrity and ability is praised even by those who disagree with them.

Webster, born in 1924, has served as FBI director since 1978; his term will expire in 1988. At the time President Carter selected him for the FBI post, Webster had been a federal judge for seven years. President Nixon had named him a district judge in 1971 and to the 8th U.S. Circuit Court of Appeals in 1973.

A graduate of Washington University Law School, Webster had practiced law in Missouri for 20 years before moving to the bench. As a judge, he was known as an evenhanded man who would not penalize police and prosecutors for harmless mistakes, but who would not condone errors that prejudiced a court or a jury against a defendant.

Ball, born in 1916, has won a national reputation for his advocacy of freedom of religion before the Supreme Court, where he has argued seven cases. In the landmark case of *Wisconsin v. Yoder* he won Court approval for the rights of Amish parents to keep their children out of public schools. He also argued the *Bob Jones University* case, which he lost.

Ball graduated from Notre Dame Law School in 1948 and then spent eight years in corporate practice, first with W. R. Grace & Co. and then with Pfizer. He taught constitutional law at Villanova University for five years. In 1960 he became executive director and general counsel of the Pennsylvania Catholic Conference. After eight years in that post, he started his own law firm.

Conclusion

It must be continually held in mind that the most predictable characteristic of the U.S. Supreme Court is its unpredictability. Despite much speculation about the impending retirements from the Court during President Reagan's first term, it came as a complete surprise that the single retirement was that of Justice Potter Stewart, one of the Court's younger members.

Despite predictions that the Court would turn even more sharply conservative in the 1984-85 term, particularly in the area of church-state matters, it did not do so, instead reaffirming its stand against school prayer and for a strict test for practices challenged as entangling church and state.

So far Justice O'Connor seems to have voted almost precisely as Ronald Reagan would have wished her to do — and yet, on the highly visible issue of school prayer, she rejected the administration's argument. Like Justice Blackmun, O'Connor may moderate her votes and her views with time.

Such independence is a major element in the Court's unpredictability. Its members are chosen by presidents and confirmed by senators, but it must not be forgotten that the Supreme Court heads the independent third branch of government, the federal judiciary.

Its uniqueness as an institution is underscored by the fierce independence of its members. Each justice listens to an administration's arguments secure in the knowledge that presidents come and go, but Supreme Court justices hold their seats for life.

Appendix

Constitution of the United States

We the People of the United States, in Order to form a more perfect Union, establish Justice, insure domestic Tranquility, provide for the common defence, promote the general Welfare, and secure the Blessings of Liberty to ourselves and our Posterity, do ordain and establish this Constitution for the United States of America.

Article I

Section 1. All legislative Powers herein granted shall be vested in a Congress of the United States, which shall consist of a Senate and House of Representatives.

Section 2. The House of Representatives shall be composed of Members chosen every second Year by the People of the several States, and the Electors in each State shall have the Qualifications requisite for Electors of the most numerous Branch of the State Legislature.

No Person shall be a Representative who shall not have attained to the age of twenty five Years, and been seven Years a Citizen of the United States, and who shall not, when elected, be an Inhabitant of that State in which he shall be chosen.

[Representatives and direct Taxes shall be apportioned among the several States which may be included within this Union, according to their respective Numbers, which shall be determined by adding to the whole Number of free Persons, including those bound to Service for a Term of Years, and excluding Indians not taxed, three fifths of all other Persons.]¹ The actual Enumeration shall be made within three Years after the first Meeting of the Congress of the United States, and within every subsequent Term of ten Years, in such Manner as they shall by Law direct. The Number of Representatives shall not exceed one for every thirty Thousand, but each State shall have at Least one Representative; and until such enumeration shall be made, the State of New Hampshire shall be entitled to chuse three, Massachusetts eight, Rhode-Island and Providence Plantations one, Connecticut five, New-York six, New Jersey four, Pennsylvania eight, Delaware one, Maryland six, Virginia ten, North Carolina five, South Carolina five, and Georgia three.

When vacancies happen in the Representation from any State, the Executive Authority thereof shall issue Writs of Election to fill such Vacancies.

The House of Representatives shall chuse their Speaker and other Officers; and shall have the sole Power of Impeachment.

Section 3. The Senate of the United States shall be composed of two Senators from each State, [chosen by the Legislature thereof,]² for six Years; and each Senator shall have one Vote.

Immediately after they shall be assembled in Consequence of the first Election, they shall be divided as equally as may be into three Classes. The Seats of the Senators of the first Class shall be vacated at the Expiration of the second Year, of the second Class at the Expiration of the fourth Year, and of the third Class at the Expiration of the sixth Year, so that one third may be chosen every second Year; [and if Vacancies happen by Resignation, or otherwise, during the Recess of the Legislature of any State, the Executive thereof may make temporary Appointments until the next Meeting of the Legislature, which shall then fill such Vacancies.]³

No Person shall be a Senator who shall not have attained to the Age of thirty Years, and been nine Years a Citizen of the United States, and who shall not, when elected, be an Inhabitant of that State for which he shall be chosen.

The Vice President of the United States shall be President of the Senate, but shall have no Vote, unless they be equally divided.

The Senate shall chuse their other Officers, and also a President pro tempore, in the Absence of the Vice President, or when he shall exercise the Office of President of the United States.

The Senate shall have the sole Power to try all Impeachments. When sitting for that Purpose, they shall be on Oath or Affirmation. When the President of the United States is tried the Chief Justice shall preside: And no Person shall be convicted without the Concurrence of two thirds of the Members present.

Judgment in Cases of Impeachment shall not extend further than to removal from Office, and disqualification to hold and enjoy any Office of honor, Trust or Profit under the United States: but the Party convicted shall nevertheless be liable and subject to Indictment, Trial, Judgment and Punishment, according to Law.

Section 4. The Times, Places and Manner of holding Elections for Senators and Representatives, shall be prescribed in each State by the Legislature thereof; but the Congress may at any time by Law make or alter such Regulations, except as to the Places of chusing Senators.

The Congress shall assemble at least once in every Year, and such Meeting shall [be on the first Monday in December],⁴ unless they shall by Law appoint a different Day.

Section 5. Each House shall be the Judge of the Elections, Returns and Qualifications of its own Members, and a Majority of each shall constitute a Quorum to do Business; but a smaller Number may adjourn from day to day, and may be authorized to compel the Attendance of absent Members, in such Manner, and under such Penalties as each House may provide.

Each House may determine the Rules of its Proceedings, punish its Members for disorderly Behaviour, and, with the Concurrence of two thirds, expel a Member.

Each House shall keep a Journal of its Proceedings, and from time to time publish the same, excepting such Parts as may in their Judgment require Secrecy; and the Yeas and Nays of the Members of either House on any question shall, at the Desire of one fifth of those Present, be entered on the Journal.

Neither House, during the Session of Congress, shall, without the Consent of the other, adjourn for more than three days, nor to any other Place than that in which the two Houses shall be sitting.

Section 6. The Senators and Representatives shall receive a Compensation for their Services, to be ascertained by Law, and paid out of the Treasury of the United States. They shall in all Cases, except Treason, Felony and Breach of the Peace, be privileged from Arrest during their Attendance at the Session of their respective Houses, and in going to and returning from the same; and for any Speech or Debate in either House, they shall not be questioned in any other Place.

No Senator or Representative shall, during the Time for which he was elected, be appointed to any civil Office under the Authority of the United States, which shall have been created, or the Emoluments whereof shall have been encreased during such time; and no Person holding any Office under the United States, shall be a Member of either House during his Continuance in Office.

Section 7. All Bills for raising Revenue shall originate in the House of Representatives; but the Senate may propose or concur with amendments as on other Bills.

Every Bill which shall have passed the House of Representatives and the Senate, shall, before it become a Law, be presented to the President of the United States; If he approve he shall sign it, but if not he shall return it, with his Objections to that House in which it shall have originated, who shall enter the Objections at large on their Journal, and proceed to reconsider it. If after such Reconsideration two thirds of that House shall agree to pass the Bill, it shall be sent, together with the Objections, to the other House, by which it shall likewise be reconsidered, and if approved by two thirds of that House, it shall become a Law. But in all such Cases the Votes of both Houses shall be determined by yeas and Nays, and the Names of the Persons voting for and against the Bill shall be entered on the Journal of each House respectively. If any Bill shall not be returned by the President within ten Days (Sunday excepted) after it shall have been presented to him, the Same shall be a Law, in like Manner as if he had signed it, unless the Congress by their Adjournment prevent its Return, in which Case it shall not be a Law.

Every Order, Resolution, or Vote to which the Concurrence of the Senate and House of Representatives may be necessary (except on a question of Adjournment) shall be presented to the President of the United States; and before the Same shall take Effect, shall be approved by him, or being disapproved by him, shall be repassed by two thirds of the Senate and House of Representatives, according to the Rules and Limitations prescribed in the Case of a Bill.

Section 8. The Congress shall have Power To lay and collect Taxes, Duties, Imposts and Excises, to pay the Debts and provide for the common Defence and general Welfare of the United States; but all Duties, Imposts and Excises shall be uniform throughout the United States;

To borrow Money on the credit of the United States;

To regulate Commerce with foreign Nations, and among the several States, and with the Indian Tribes;

To establish an uniform Rule of Naturalization, and uniform Laws on the subject of Bankruptcies throughout the United States;

To coin Money, regulate the Value thereof, and of foreign Coin, and fix the Standard of Weights and Measures;

To provide for the Punishment of counterfeiting the Securities and current Coin of the United States;

To establish Post Offices and post Roads;

To promote the Progress of Science and useful Arts, by securing for limited Times to Authors and Inventors the exclusive Right to their respective Writings and Discoveries;

To constitute Tribunals inferior to the supreme Court;

To define and punish Piracies and Felonies commited on the high Seas, and Offences against the Law of Nations;

To declare War, grant Letters of Marque and Reprisal,and make Rules concerning Captures on Land and Water;

To raise and support Armies, but no Appropriation of Money to that Use shall be for a longer Term than two Years;

To provide and maintain a Navy;

To make Rules for the Government and Regulation of the land and naval Forces;

To provide for calling forth the Militia to execute the Laws of the Union, suppress Insurrections and repel Invasions;

To provide for organizing, arming, and disciplining, the Militia, and for governing such Part of them as may be employed in the Service of the United States, reserving to the States respectively, the Appointment of the Officers, and the Authority of training the Militia according to the discipline prescribed by Congress;

To exercise exclusive Legislation in all Cases whatsoever, over such District (not exceeding ten Miles square) as may, by Cession of Particular States, and the Acceptance of Congress, become the Seat of the Government of the United States, and to exercise like Authority over all Places purchased by the Consent of the Legislature of the State in which the Same shall be, for the Erection of Forts, Magazines, Arsenals, dock-Yards, and other needful Buildings; — And

To make all Laws which shall be necessary and proper for carrying into Execution the foregoing Powers, and all other Powers vested by this Constitution in the Government of the United States, or in any Department or Officer thereof.

Section 9. The Migration or Importation of such Persons as any of the States now existing shall think proper to admit, shall not be prohibited by the Congress prior to the Year one thousand eight hundred and eight, but a Tax or duty may be imposed on such Importation, not exceeding ten dollars for each Person.

The Privilege of the Writ of Habeas Corpus shall not be suspended, unless when in Cases of Rebellion or Invasion the public Safety may require it.

No Bill of Attainder or ex post facto Law shall be passed.

No capitation, or other direct, Tax shall be laid, unless in Proportion to the Census of Enumeration herein before directed to be taken.[5]

No Tax or Duty shall be laid on Articles exported from any State.

No Preference shall be given by any Regulation of Commerce or Revenue to the Ports of one State over those of another; nor shall Vessels bound to, or from, one State, be obliged to enter, clear or pay Duties in another.

No Money shall be drawn from the Treasury, but in Consequence of Appropriations made by Law; and a regular Statement and Account of the Receipts and Expenditures of all public Money shall be published from time to time.

No Title of Nobility shall be granted by the United States: And no Person holding any Office of Profit or Trust under them, shall, without the Consent of the Congress, accept of any present, Emolument, Office, or Title, of any kind whatever, from any King, Prince or foreign State.

Section 10. No State shall enter into any Treaty, Alliance, or Confederation; grant Letters of Marque and Reprisal; coin Money; emit Bills of Credit; make any Thing but gold and silver Coin a Tender in Payment of Debts; pass any Bill of Attainder, ex post facto Law, or Law impairing the Obligation of Contracts, or grant any Title of Nobility.

No State shall, without the Consent of the Congress, lay any Imposts or Duties on Imports or Exports, except what may be absolutely necessary for executing it's inspection Laws: and the net Produce of all Duties and Imposts, laid by any State on Imports or Exports, shall be for the Use of the Treasury of the United States; and all such Laws shall be subject to the Revision and Controul of the Congress.

No State shall, without the Consent of Congress, lay any Duty of Tonnage, keep Troops, or Ships of War in time of Peace, enter into any Agreement or Compact with another State, or with a foreign Power, or engage in War, unless actually invaded, or in such imminent Danger as will not admit of delay.

Article II

Section 1. The executive Power shall be vested in a President of the United States of America. He shall hold his Office during the Term of four Years, and, together with the Vice President, chosen for the same Term, be elected, as follows.

Each State shall appoint, in such Manner as the Legislature thereof may direct, a Number of Electors, equal to the whole Number of Senators and Representatives to which the State may be entitled in the Congress: but no Senator or Representative, or Person holding an Office of Trust or Profit under the United States, shall be appointed an Elector.

[The Electors shall meet in their respective States, and vote by Ballot for two Persons, of whom one at least shall not be an Inhabitant of the same State with themselves. And they shall make a List of all the Persons voted for, and of the Number of Votes for each; which List they shall sign and certify, and transmit sealed to the Seat of the Government of the United States, directed to the President of the Senate. The President of the Senate shall, in the Presence of the Senate and House of Representatives, open all the Certificates, and the Votes shall then be counted. The Person having the greatest Number of Votes shall be the President, if such Number be a Majority of the whole Number of Electors appointed; and if there be more than one who have such Majority, and have an equal Number of Votes, then the House of Representatives shall immediately chuse by Ballot one of them for President; and if no Person have a Majority, then from the five highest on the list the said House shall in like Manner chuse the President. But in chusing the President, the Votes shall be taken by States, the Representation from each State having one Vote; a quorum for this Purpose shall consist of a Member or Members from two thirds of the States, and a Majority of all the States shall be necessary to a Choice. In every Case, after the Choice of the President, the Person having the greatest Number of Votes of the Electors shall be the Vice President. But if there should remain two or more who have equal Votes, the Senate shall chuse from them by Ballot the Vice President.][6]

The Congress may determine the Time of chusing the Electors, and the Day on which they shall give their Votes; which Day shall be the same throughout the United States.

No Person except a natural born Citizen, or a Citizen of the United States, at the time of the Adoption of this Constitution, shall be eligible to the Office of President; neither shall any Person be eligible to that Office who shall not have attained to the Age of thirty five Years, and been fourteen Years a Resident within the United States.

In Case of the Removal of the President from Office, or of his Death, Resignation, or Inability to discharge the Powers and Duties of the said Office,[7] the Same shall devolve on the Vice President, and the Congress may by Law provide for the Case of Removal, Death, Resignation or Inability, both of the President and Vice President, declaring what Officer shall then act as President, and such Officer shall act accordingly, until the Disability be removed, or a President shall be elected.

The President shall, at stated Times, receive for his Services, a Compensation, which shall neither be encreased nor diminished during the Period for which he shall have been elected, and he shall not receive within that Period any other Emolument from the United States, or any of them.

Before he enter on the Execution of his Office, he shall take the following Oath or Affirmation: — "I do solemnly swear (or affirm) that I will faithfully execute the Office of President of the United States, and will to the best ,of my Ability, preserve, protect and defend the Constitution of the United States."

Section 2. The President shall be Commander in Chief of the Army and Navy of the United States, and of the Militia of the several States, when called into the actual Service of the United States; he may require the Opinion, in writing, of the principal Officer in each of the executive Departments, upon any Subject relating to the Duties of their respective Offices, and he shall have Power to grant Reprieves and Pardons for Offenses against the United States, except in Cases of Impeachment.

He shall have Power, by and with the Advice and Consent of the Senate, to make Treaties, provided two thirds of the Senators present concur; and he shall nominate, and by and with the Advice and Consent of the Senate, shall appoint Ambassadors, other public Ministers and Consuls, Judges of the supreme Court, and all other Officers of the United States, whose Appointments are not herein otherwise provided for, and which shall be established by Law: but the Congress may by Law vest the Appointment of such inferior Officers, as they think proper, in the President alone, in the Courts of Law, or in the Heads of Departments.

The President shall have Power to fill up all Vacancies that may happen during the Recess of the Senate, by granting Commissions which shall expire at the End of their next Session.

Section 3. He shall from time to time give to the Congress Information of the State of the Union, and recommend to their Consideration such Measures as he shall judge necessary and expedient; he may, on extraordinary Occasions, convene both Houses, or either of them, and in Case of Disagreement between them, with Respect to the Time of Adjournment, he may adjourn them to such Time as he shall think proper; he shall receive Ambassadors and other public Ministers; he shall take Care that the Laws be faithfully executed, and shall Commission all the Officers of the United States.

Section 4. The President, Vice President and all Civil Officers of the United States, shall be removed from office on Impeachment for, and Conviction of, Treason, Bribery, or other high Crimes and Misdemeanors.

Article III

Section 1. The judicial Power of the United States, shall be vested in one supreme Court, and in such inferior Courts as the Congress may from time to time ordain and establish. The Judges, both of the supreme and inferior Courts, shall hold their Offices during good Behaviour, and

shall, at stated Times, receive for their Services, a Compensation, which shall not be diminished during their Continuance in Office.

Section 2. The judicial Power shall extend to all Cases, in Law and Equity, arising under this Constitution, the Laws of the United States, and Treaties made, or which shall be made, under their Authority; — to all Cases affecting Ambassadors, other public Ministers and Consuls; — to all Cases of admiralty and maritime Jurisdiction; — to Controversies to which the United States shall be a Party; — to Controversies between two or more States; — between a State and Citizens of another State;[8] — between Citizens of different States; — between Citizens of the same State claiming Lands under Grants of different States, and between a State, or the Citizens thereof, and foreign States, Citizens or Subjects.[8]

In all Cases affecting Ambassadors, other public Ministers and Consuls, and those in which a State shall be Party, the supreme Court shall have original Jurisdiction. In all the other Cases before mentioned, the supreme Court shall have appellate Jurisdiction, both as to Law and Fact, with such Exceptions, and under such Regulations as the Congress shall make.

The Trial of all Crimes, except in cases of Impeachment, shall be by Jury; and such Trial shall be held in the State where the said Crimes shall have been committed; but when not committed within any State, the Trial shall be at such Place or Places as the Congress may by Law have directed.

Section 3. Treason against the United States, shall consist only in levying War against them, or in adhering to their Enemies, giving them Aid and Comfort. No Person shall be convicted of Treason unless on the Testimony of two Witnesses to the same overt Act, or on Confession in open Court.

The Congress shall have Power to declare the Punishment of Treason, but no Attainder of Treason shall work Corruption of Blood, or Forfeiture except during the Life of the Person attainted.

Article IV

Section 1. Full Faith and Credit shall be given in each State to the public Acts, Records, and judicial Proceedings of every other State. And the Congress may by general Laws prescribe the Manner in which such Acts, Records and Proceedings shall be proved, and the Effect thereof.

Section 2. The Citizens of each State shall be entitled to all Privileges and Immunities of Citizens in the several States.

A Person charged in any State with Treason, Felony, or other Crime, who shall flee from Justice, and be found in another State, shall on Demand of the executive Authority of the State from which he fled, be delivered up, to be removed to the State having Jurisdiction of the Crime.

[No Person held to Service or Labour in one State, under the Laws thereof, escaping into another, shall, in Consequence of any Law or Regulation therein, be discharged from such Service or Labour, but shall be delivered up on Claim of the Party to whom such Service or Labour may be due.][9]

Section 3. New States may be admitted by the Congress into this Union; but no new State shall be formed or erected within the Jurisdiction of any other State; nor any State be formed by the Junction of two or more States, or Parts of States, without the Consent of the Legislatures of the States concerned as well as of the Congress.

The Congress shall have Power to dispose of and make all needful Rules and Regulations respecting the Territory or other Property belonging to the United States; and nothing in this Constitution shall be so construed as to Prejudice any Claims of the United States, or of any particular State.

Section 4. The United States shall guarantee to every State in this Union a Republican Form of Government, and shall protect each of them against Invasion; and on Application of the Legislature, or of the Executive (when the Legislature cannot be convened) against domestic Violence.

Article V

The Congress, whenever two thirds of both Houses shall deem it necessary, shall propose Amendments to this Constitution, or, on the Application of the Legislatures of two thirds of the several States, shall call a Convention for proposing Amendments, which, in either Case, shall be valid to all Intents and Purposes, as Part of this Constitution, when ratified by the Legislatures of three fourths of the several States, or by Conventions in three fourths thereof, as the one or the other Mode of Ratification may be proposed by the Congress; Provided [that no Amendment which may be made prior to the

Year One thousand eight hundred and eight shall in any Manner affect the first and fourth Clauses in the Ninth Section of the first Article; and][10] that no State, without its Consent, shall be deprived of its equal Suffrage in the Senate.

Article VI

All Debts contracted and Engagements entered into, before the Adoption of this Constitution, shall be as valid against the United States under this Constitution, as under the Confederation.

This Constitution, and the Laws of the United States which shall be made in Pursuance thereof; and all Treaties made, or which shall be made, under the Authority of the United States, shall be the supreme Law of the Land; and the Judges in every State shall be bound thereby, any Thing in the Constitution or Laws of any State to the Contrary notwithstanding.

The Senators and Representatives before mentioned, and the Members of the several State Legislatures, and all executive and judicial Officers, both of the United States and of the several States, shall be bound by Oath or Affirmation, to support this Constitution; but no religious Test shall ever be required as a Qualification to any Office or public Trust under the United States.

Article VII

The Ratification of the Conventions of nine States, shall be sufficient for the Establishment of this Constitution between the States so ratifying the Same. Done in Convention by the Unanimous Consent of the States present the Seventeenth Day of September in the Year of our Lord one thousand seven hundred and Eighty seven and of the Independence of the United States of America the Twelfth In witness whereof We have hereunto subscribed our Names, George Washington, President and deputy from Virginia.

New Hampshire:	John Langdon, Nicholas Gilman.
Massachusetts:	Nathaniel Gorham, Rufus King.
Connecticut:	William Samuel Johnson, Roger Sherman.
New York:	Alexander Hamilton
New Jersey:	William Livingston, David Brearley,

	William Paterson, Jonathan Dayton.
Pennsylvania:	Benjamin Franklin, Thomas Mifflin, Robert Morris, George Clymer, Thomas FitzSimons, Jared Ingersoll, James Wilson, Gouverneur Morris.
Delaware:	George Read, Gunning Bedford Jr., John Dickinson, Richard Bassett, Jacob Broom.
Maryland:	James McHenry, Daniel of St. Thomas Jenifer, Daniel Carroll.
Virginia:	John Blair, James Madison Jr.
North Carolina:	William Blount, Richard Dobbs Spaight, Hugh Williamson.
South Carolina:	John Rutledge, Charles Cotesworth Pinckney, Charles Pinckney, Pierce Butler.
Georgia:	William Few, Abraham Baldwin.

[The language of the original Constitution, not including the Amendments, was adopted by a convention of the states on Sept. 17, 1787, and was subsequently ratified by the states on the following dates: Delaware, Dec. 7, 1787; Pennsylvania, Dec. 12, 1787; New Jersey, Dec. 18, 1787; Georgia, Jan. 2, 1788; Connecticut, Jan. 9, 1788; Massachusetts, Feb. 6, 1788; Maryland, April 28, 1788; South Carolina, May 23, 1788; New Hampshire, June 21, 1788.

Ratification was completed on June 21, 1788.

The Constitution subsequently was ratified by Virginia, June 25, 1788; New York, July 26, 1788; North Carolina, Nov. 21, 1789; Rhode Island, May 29, 1790; and Vermont, Jan. 10, 1791.]

Amendments

Amendment I

(First ten amendments ratified Dec. 15, 1791.)

Congress shall make no law respecting an establishment of religion, or prohibiting the free exercise thereof; or abridging the freedom of speech, or of the press; or the right of the people peaceably to assemble, and to petition the Government for a redress of grievances.

Amendment II

A well regulated Militia, being necessary to the security of a free State, the right of the people to keep and bear Arms, shall not be infringed.

Amendment III

No Soldier shall, in time of peace be quartered in any house, without the consent of the Owner, nor in time of war, but in a manner to be prescribed by law.

Amendment IV

The right of the people to be secure in their persons, houses, papers, and effects, against unreasonable searches and seizures, shall not be violated, and no Warrants shall issue, but upon probable cause, supported by Oath or affirmation, and particularly describing the place to be searched, and the persons or things to be seized.

Amendment V

No person shall be held to answer for a capital, or otherwise infamous crime, unless on a presentment or indictment of a Grand Jury, except in cases arising in the land or naval forces, or in the Militia, when in actual service in time of War or public danger; nor shall any person be subject for the same offence to be twice put in jeopardy of life or limb; nor shall be compelled in any criminal case to be a witness against himself, nor be deprived of life, liberty, or property, without due process of law; nor shall private property be taken for public use, without just compensation.

Amendment VI

In all criminal prosecutions, the accused shall enjoy the right to a speedy and public trial, by an impartial jury of the State and district wherein the crime shall have been committed, which district shall have been previously ascertained by law, and to be informed of the nature and cause of the accusation; to be confronted with the witnesses against him; to have compulsory process for obtaining witnesses in his favor, and to have the Assistance of Counsel for his defence.

Amendment VII

In Suits at common law, where the value in controversy shall exceed twenty dollars, the right of trial by jury shall be preserved, and no fact tried by a jury, shall be otherwise re-examined in any Court of the United States, than according to the rules of the common law.

Amendment VIII

Excessive bail shall not be required, nor excessive fines imposed, nor cruel and unusual punishments inflicted.

Amendment IX

The enumeration in the Constitution, of certain rights, shall not be construed to deny or disparage others retained by the people.

Amendment X

The powers not delegated to the United States by the Constitution, nor prohibited by it to the States, are reserved to the States respectively, or to the people.

Amendment XI *(Ratified Feb. 7, 1795)*

The Judicial power of the United States shall not be construed to extend to any suit in law or equity, commenced or prosecuted against one of the United States by Citizens of another State, or by Citizens or Subjects of any Foreign State.

Amendment XII *(Ratified June 15, 1804)*

The Electors shall meet in their respective states and vote by ballot for President and Vice-President, one of whom, at least, shall not be an inhabitant of the same state with themselves; they shall name in their ballots the person voted for as President, and in distinct ballots the person voted for as Vice-President, and they shall make distinct lists of all persons voted for as President, and of all persons voted for as Vice-President, and of the number of votes for each, which lists they shall sign and certify, and transmit sealed to the seat of the government of the United States, directed to the President of the Senate; — The President of the Senate shall, in the presence of the Senate and House of Representatives, open all the certificates and the votes shall then be counted; — The person having the greatest number of votes for President, shall be the President, if such number be a majority of the whole number of Electors appointed; and if no person have such majority, then from the persons having the highest numbers not exceeding three on the list of those voted for as President, the House of Representatives shall choose immediately, by ballot, the President. But in choosing the President, the votes shall be taken by states, the representation from each state having one vote; a quorum for this purpose shall consist of a member or members from two-thirds of the states, and a majority

of all the states shall be necessary to a choice. [And if the House of Representatives shall not choose a President whenever the right of choice shall devolve upon them, before the fourth day of March next following, then the Vice-President shall act as President, as in the case of the death or other constitutional disability of the President —][11] The person having the greatest number of votes as Vice-President, shall be the Vice-President, if such number be a majority of the whole number of Electors appointed, and if no person have a majority, then from the two highest numbers on the list, the Senate shall choose the Vice-President; a quorum for the purpose shall consist of two-thirds of the whole number of Senators, and a majority of the whole number shall be necessary to a choice. But no person constitutionally ineligible to the office of President shall be eligible to that of Vice-President of the United States.

Amendment XIII *(Ratified Dec. 6, 1865)*

Section 1. Neither slavery nor involuntary servitude, except as a punishment for crime whereof the party shall have been duly convicted, shall exist within the United States, or any place subject to their jurisdiction.

Section 2. Congress shall have power to enforce this article by appropriate legislation.

Amendment XIV *(Ratified July 9, 1868)*

Section 1. All persons born or naturalized in the United States and subject to the jurisdiction thereof, are citizens of the United States and of the State wherein they reside. No State shall make or enforce any law which shall abridge the privileges or immunities of citizens of the United States; nor shall any State deprive any person of life, liberty, or property, without due process of law; nor deny to any person within its jurisdiction the equal protection of the laws.

Section 2. Representatives shall be apportioned among the several States according to their respective numbers, counting the whole number of persons in each State, excluding Indians not taxed. But when the right to vote at any election for the choice of electors for President and Vice President of the United States, Representatives in Congress, the Executive and Judicial officers of a State, or the members of the Legislature thereof, is denied to any of the male inhabitants of such State, being twenty-one years of age,[12] and citizens of the United States, or in any way abridged, except for participation in rebellion, or other crime, the basis of representation therein shall be reduced in the proportion which the number of such male citizens shall bear to the whole number of male citizens twenty-one years of age in such State.

Section 3. No person shall be a Senator or Representative in Congress, or elector of President and Vice President, or hold any office, civil or military, under the United States, or under any State, who, having previously taken an oath, as a member of Congress, or as an officer of the United States, or as a member of any State legislature, or as an executive or judicial officer of any State, to support the Constitution of the United States, shall have engaged in insurrection or rebellion against the same, or given aid or comfort to the enemies thereof. But Congress may by a vote of two-thirds of each House, remove such disability.

Section 4. The validity of the public debt of the United States, authorized by law, including debts incurred for payment of pensions and bounties for services in suppressing insurrection or rebellion, shall not be questioned. But neither the United States nor any State shall assume or pay any debt or obligation incurred in aid of insurrection or rebellion against the United States, or any claim for the loss or emancipation of any slave; but all such debts, obligations and claims shall be held illegal and void.

Section 5. The Congress shall have power to enforce, by appropriate legislation, the provisions of this article.

Amendment XV *(Ratified Feb. 3, 1870)*

Section 1. The right of citizens of the United States to vote shall not be denied or abridged by the United States or by any State on account of race, color, or previous condition of servitude.

Section 2. The Congress shall have power to enforce this article by appropriate legislation.

Amendment XVI *(Ratified Feb. 3, 1913)*

The Congress shall have power to lay and collect taxes on incomes, from whatever source derived, without apportionment among the several States, and without regard to any census or enumeration.

Amendment XVII *(Ratified Apr. 8, 1913)*

The Senate of the United States shall be composed of two Senators from each State, elected by the people thereof, for six years; and each Senator shall have one vote. The electors in each State shall have the qualifications requisite

for electors of the most numerous branch of the State legislatures.

When vacancies happen in the representation of any State in the Senate, the executive authority of such State shall issue writs of election to fill such vacancies: *Provided,* That the legislature of any State may empower the executive thereof to make temporary appointments until the people fill the vacancies by election as the legislature may direct.

This amendment shall not be so construed as to affect the election or term of any Senator chosen before it becomes valid as part of the Constitution.

[Amendment XVIII *(Ratified Jan. 16, 1919)*

Section. 1. After one year from the ratification of this article the manufacture, sale, or transportation of intoxicating liquors within, the importation thereof into, or the exportation thereof from the United States and all territory subject to the jurisdiction thereof for beverage purposes is hereby prohibited.

Section 2. The Congress and the several States shall have concurrent power to enforce this article by appropriate legislation.

Section 3. This article shall be inoperative unless it shall have been ratified as an amendment to the Constitution by the legislatures of the several States, as provided in the Constitution, within seven years from the date of the submission hereof to the States by the Congress.][13]

Amendment XIX *(Ratified Aug. 18, 1920)*

The right of citizens of the United States to vote shall not be denied or abridged by the United States or by any State on account of sex.

Congress shall have power to enforce this article by appropriate legislation.

Amendment XX *(Ratified Jan. 23, 1933)*

Section 1. The terms of the President and Vice President shall end at noon on the 20th day of January, and the terms of Senators and Representatives at noon on the 3d day of January, of the years in which such terms would have ended if this article had not been ratified; and the terms of their successors shall then begin.

Section 2. The Congress shall assemble at least once in every year, and such meeting shall begin at noon on the 3d day of January, unless they shall by law appoint a different day.

Section 3.[14] If, at the time fixed for the beginning of the term of the President, the

President elect shall have died, the Vice President elect shall become President. If a President shall not have been chosen before the time fixed for the beginning of his term, or if the President elect shall have failed to qualify, then the Vice President elect shall act as President until a President shall have qualified; and the Congress may by law provide for the case wherein neither a President elect nor a Vice President elect shall have qualified, declaring who shall then act as President, or the manner in which one who is to act shall be selected, and such person shall act accordingly until a President or Vice President shall have qualified.

Section 4. The Congress may by law provide for the case of the death of any of the persons from whom the House of Representatives may choose a President whenever the right of choice shall have devolved upon them, and for the case of the death of any of the persons from whom the Senate may choose a Vice President whenever the right of choice shall have devolved upon them.

Section 5. Sections 1 and 2 shall take effect on the 15th day of October following the ratification of this article.

Section 6. This article shall be inoperative unless it shall have been ratified as an amendment to the Constitution by the legislatures of three-fourths of the several States within seven years from the date of its submission.

Amendment XXI *(Ratified Dec. 5, 1933)*

Section 1. The eighteenth article of amendment to the Constitution of the United States is hereby repealed.

Section 2. The transportation or importation into any State, Territory or possession of the United States for delivery or use therein of intoxicating liquors, in violation of the laws thereof, is hereby prohibited.

Section 3. This article shall be inoperative unless it shall have been ratified as an amendment to the Constitution by conventions in the several States, as provided in the Constitution, within seven years from the date of the submission hereof to the States by the Congress.

Amendment XXII *(Ratified Feb. 27, 1951)*

Section 1. No person shall be elected to the office of the President more than twice, and no person who has held the office of President, or acted as President, for more than two years of a term to which some other person was elected President shall be elected to the office of the President more than once. But this Article shall not apply to any person holding the office of President when this Article was proposed by the Congress, and shall not prevent any person who may be holding the office of President, or acting as President, during the term within which this Article become operative from holding the office of President or acting as President during the remainder of such term.

Section 2. This Article shall be inoperative unless it shall have been ratified as an amendment to the Constitution by the legislatures of three-fourths of the several States within seven years from the date of its submission to the States by the Congress.

Amendment XXIII *(Ratified March 29, 1961)*

Section 1. The District constituting the seat of Government of the United States shall appoint in such manner as the Congress may direct:

A number of electors of President and Vice President equal to the whole number of Senators and Representatives in Congress to which the District would be entitled if it were a State, but in no event more than the least populous State; they shall be in addition to those appointed by the States, but they shall be considered, for the purposes of the election of President and Vice President, to be electors appointed by a State; and they shall meet in the District and perform such duties as provided by the twelfth article of amendment.

Section 2. The Congress shall have power to enforce this article by appropriate legislation.

Amendment XXIV *(Ratified Jan. 23, 1964)*

Section 1. The right of citizens of the United States to vote in any primary or other election for President or Vice President, for electors for President or Vice President, or for Senator or Representative in Congress, shall not be denied or abridged by the United States or any State by reason of failure to pay any poll tax or other tax.

Section 2. The Congress shall have power to enforce this article by appropriate legislation.

Amendment XXV *(Ratified Feb. 10, 1967)*

Section 1. In case of the removal of the President from office or of his death or resignation, the Vice President shall become President.

Section 2. Whenever there is a vacancy in the office of the Vice President, the President shall nominate a Vice President who shall take office upon confirmation by a majority vote of both Houses of Congress.

Section 3. Whenever the President transmits to the President pro tempore of the Senate and the Speaker of the House of Representatives his written declaration that he is unable to discharge the powers and duties of his office, and until he transmits to them a written declaration to the contrary, such powers and duties shall be discharged by the Vice President as Acting President.

Section 4. Whenever the Vice President and a majority of either the principal officers of the executive departments or of such other body as Congress may by law provide, transmit to the President pro tempore of the Senate and the Speaker of the House of Representatives their written declaration that the President is unable to discharge the powers and duties of his office, the Vice President shall immediately assume the powers and duties of the office as Acting President.

Thereafter, when the President transmits to the President pro tempore of the Senate and the Speaker of the House of Representatives his written declaration that no inability exists, he shall resume the powers and duties of his office unless the Vice President and a majority of either the principal officers of the executive department or of such other body as Congress may by law provide, transmit within four days to the President pro tempore of the Senate and the Speaker of the House of Representatives their written declaration that the President is unable to discharge the powers and duties of his office. Thereupon Congress shall decide the issue, assembling within forty-eight hours for that purpose if not in session. If the Congress, within twenty-one days after receipt of the latter written declaration, or, if Congress is not in session, within twenty-one days after Congress is required to assemble, determines by two-thirds vote of both houses that the President is unable to discharge the powers and duties of his office, the Vice President shall continue to discharge the same as Acting President; otherwise, the President shall resume the powers and duties of his office.

Amendment XXVI *(Ratified July 1, 1971)*

Section 1. The right of citizens of the United States, who are eighteen years of age or older, to vote shall not be denied or abridged by the United States or by any State on account of age.

Section 2. The Congress shall have power to enforce this article by appropriate legislation.

Notes

1. The part in brackets was changed by section 2 of the Fourteenth Amendment.
2. The part in brackets was changed by section 1 of the Seventeenth Amendment.
3. The part in brackets was changed by the second paragraph of the Seventeenth Amendment.
4. The part in brackets was changed by section 2 of the Twentieth Amendment.
5. The Sixteenth Amendment gave Congress the power to tax incomes.
6. The material in brackets has been superseded by the Twelfth Amendment.
7. This provision has been affected by the Twenty-fifth Amendment.
8. These clauses were affected by the Eleventh Amendment.
9. This paragraph has been superseded by the Thirteenth Amendment.
10. Obsolete.
11. The part in brackets has been superseded by section 3 of the Twentieth Amendment.
12. See the Twenty-sixth Amendment.
13. This Amendment was repealed by section 1 of the Twenty-first Amendment.
14. See the Twenty-fifth Amendment.

Source: U.S. Congress, House, Committee on the Judiciary, *The Constitution of the United States of America, As Amended Through July 1971,* H. Doc. 93-215, 93rd Cong., 2nd sess., 1974.

Speeches

Following is the text of a speech by Attorney General Edwin Meese to the American Bar Association, July 9, 1985, in Washington, D.C.:

Welcome to our Federal City. It is an honor to be here today to address the House of Delegates of the American Bar Association. I know the sessions here and those next week in London will be very productive.

It is, of course, entirely fitting that we lawyers gather here in this home of our government. We Americans, after all, rightly pride ourselves on having produced the greatest political wonder of the world — a government of laws and not of men. Thomas Paine was right: "America has no monarch: Here the law is king."

Perhaps nothing underscores Paine's assessment quite as much as the eager anticipation with which Americans await the conclusion of the term of the Supreme Court. Lawyers and laymen alike regard the Court not so much with awe as with a healthy respect. The law matters here and the business of our highest court — the subject of my remarks today — is crucially important to our political order.

At this time of year I'm always reminded of how utterly unpredictable the Court can be in rendering its judgments. Several years ago, for example, there was quite a controversial case, *TVA v. Hill.* This dispute involved the EPA and the now-legendary snail darter, a creature of curious purpose and forgotten origins. In any event, when the case was handed down, one publication announced that there was some good news and some bad news. The bad news in their view was that the snail darter had won; the good news was that he didn't use the 14th Amendment.

Once again, the Court has finished a term characterized by a nearly crushing workload. There were 4,935 cases on the docket this year; 179 cases were granted review; 140 cases issued in signed opinions, 11 were *per curiam* rulings. Such a docket lends credence to Tocqueville's assessment that in America, every political question seems sooner or later to become a legal question. (I won't even mention the statistics of the lower federal courts; let's just say I think we'll all be in business for quite a while.)

In looking back over the work of the Court, I am again struck by how little the statistics tell us about the true role of the Court. In reviewing a term of the Court, it is important to take a moment and reflect upon the proper role of the Supreme Court in our constitutional system.

The intended role of the judiciary generally and the Supreme Court in particular was to serve as the "bulwarks of a limited constitution." The judges, the Founders believed, would not fail to regard the Constitution as "fundamental law" and would "regulate their decisions" by it. As the "faithful guardians of the Constitution," the judges were expected to resist any political effort to depart from the literal provisions of the Constitution. The text of the document and the original intention of those who framed it would be the judicial standard in giving effect to the Constitution.

You will recall that Alexander Hamilton, defending the federal courts to be created by the new Constitution, remarked that the want of a judicial power under the Articles of Confederation had been the crowning defect of that first effort at a national constitution. Ever the consummate lawyer, Hamilton pointed out that "laws are a dead letter without courts to expound and define their true meaning."

The Anti-Federalist *Brutus* took him to task in the New York press for what the critics of the Constitution considered his naivete. That prompted Hamilton to write his classic defense of judicial power in *The Federalist,* No. 78.

An independent judiciary under the Constitution, he said, would prove to be the "citadel of public justice and the public security." Courts were "peculiarly essential in a limited constitution." Without them, there would be no security against "the encroachments and oppressions of the representative body," no protection against "unjust and partial" laws.

Hamilton, like his colleague Madison, knew that *all* political power is "of an encroaching nature." In order to keep the powers created by the Constitution within the boundaries marked out by the Constitution, an independent — but constitutionally bound — judiciary was essential. The purpose of the Constitution, after all, was the creation of limited but also energetic government, institutions with the power to govern, but also with structures to keep the power in check. As Madison put it, the Constitution enabled the government to control the governed, but also obliged it to control itself.

But even beyond the institutional role, the Court serves the American republic in yet another, more subtle way. The problem of any popular government, of course, is seeing to it that the people obey the laws. There are but two ways: either by physical force or by moral force. In many ways the Court remains the primary moral force in American politics.

Tocqueville put it best:

> The great object of justice is to substitute the idea of right for that of violence, to put intermediaries between the government and the use of its physical force. . . . It is something astonishing what authority is accorded to the intervention of a court of justice by the general opinion of mankind. . . .
> The moral force in which tribunals are clothed makes the use of physical force infinitely rarer, for in most cases it takes its place; and when finally physical force is required, its power is doubled by his moral authority.

By fulfilling its proper function, the Supreme Court contributes both to institutional checks and balances and to the moral undergirding of the entire constitutional edifice. For the Supreme Court is the only national institution that daily grapples with the most fundamental political questions — and defends them with written expositions. Nothing less would serve to perpetuate the sanctity of the rule of law so effectively.

But that is not to suggest that the justices are a body of Platonic guardians. Far from it. The Court is what it was understood to be when the Constitution was framed — a political body. The judicial process is, at its most fundamental level, a political process. While not a partisan political process, it is political in the truest sense of that word. It is a process wherein public deliberations occur over what constitutes the common good under the terms of a written constitution.

As a result, as Benjamin Cardozo pointed out, "the great tides and currents which engulf the rest of men do not turn aside in their course and pass the judges by." Granting that, Tocqueville knew what was required.

As he wrote:

The federal judges therefore must not only be good citizens and men of education and integrity ... [they] must also be statesmen; they must know how to understand the spirit of the age, to confront those obstacles that can be overcome, and to steer out of the current when the tide threatens to carry them away, and with them the sovereignty of the union and obedience to its laws.

On that confident note, let's consider the Court's work this past year.

As has been generally true in recent years, the 1984 term did not yield a coherent set of decisions. Rather, it seemed to produce what one commentator has called a "jurisprudence of idiosyncracy." Taken as a whole, the work of the term defies analysis by any strict standard. It is neither simply liberal nor simply conservative; neither simply activist nor simply restrained; neither simply principled nor simply partisan. The Court this term continued to roam at large in a veritable constitutional forest.

I believe, however, that there are at least three general areas that merit close scrutiny: Federalism, Criminal Law, and Freedom of Religion.

Federalism

In *Garcia v. San Antonio Metropolitan Transit Authority,* the Court displayed what was in the view of this Administration an inaccurate reading of the text of the Constitution and a disregard for the Framers' intention that state and local governments be a buffer against the centralizing tendencies of the national Leviathan. Specifically, five Justices denied that the 10th Amendment protects states from federal laws regulating the wages and hours of state or local employees. Thus the Court overruled — but barely — a contrary holding in *National League of Cities v. Usery.* We hope for a day when the Court returns to the basic principles of the Constitution as expressed in *Usery;* such instability in decisions concerning the fundamental principle of federalism does our Constitution no service.

Meanwhile, the constitutional status of the states further suffered as the Court curbed state power to regulate the economy, notably the professions. In *Metropolitan Life Insurance Co. v. Ward,* the Court used the Equal Protection Clause to spear an Alabama insurance tax on gross premiums preferring in-state companies over out-of-state rivals. In *New Hampshire v. Piper,* the Court held that the Privileges and Immunities Clause of Article IV barred New Hampshire from completely excluding a nonresident from admission to its bar. With the apparent policy objective of creating unfettered national markets for occupations before its eyes, the Court unleashed Article IV against any state preference for residents involving the professions or service industries. *Hicklin v. Orbeck* and *Baldwin v. Montana Fish and Game Commission* are illustrative.

On the other hand, we gratefully acknowledge the respect shown by the Court for state and local sovereignty in a number of cases, including *Atascadero State Hospital v. Scanlon.*

In *Atascadero,* a case involving violations of § 504 of Rehabilitation Act of 1973, the Court honored the 11th Amendment in limiting private damage suits against states. Congress, it said, must express its intent to expose states to liability affirmatively and clearly.

In *Town of Hallie v. City of Eau Claire,* the Court found that active state supervision of municipal activity was not required to cloak municipalities with immunity under the Sherman Act. And, states were judged able to confer Sherman Act immunity upon private parties in *Southern Motor Carrier Rate Conference v. U.S.* They must, said the Court, clearly articulate and affirmatively express a policy to displace competition with compelling anticompetitive action so long as the private action is actively supervised by the state.

And, in *Oklahoma City v. Tuttle,* the Court held that a single incident of unconstitutional and egregious police misconduct is insufficient to support a Section 1983 action against municipalities for allegedly inadequate police training or supervision.

Our view is that federalism is one of the most basic principles of our Constitution. By allowing the states sovereignty sufficient to govern we better secure our ultimate goal of political liberty through decentralized government. We do not advocate states' rights; we advocate states' responsibilities. We need to remember that state and local governments are not inevitably abusive of rights. It was, after all, at the turn of the century the states that were the laboratories of social and economic progress — and the federal courts that blocked their way. We believe that there is a proper constitutional sphere for state governance under our scheme of limited, popular government.

Criminal Law

Recognizing, perhaps, that the nation is in the throes of a drug epidemic which has severely increased the burden borne by law enforcement officers, the Court took a more progressive stance on the Fourth Amendment, undoing some of the damage previously done by its piecemeal incorporation through the 14th Amendment. Advancing from its landmark *Leon* decision in 1984 which created a good-faith exception to the Exclusionary Rule when a flawed warrant is obtained by police, the Court permitted

warrantless searches under certain limited circumstances.

The most prominent among these Fourth Amendment cases were:

New Jersey v. T.L.O., which upheld warrantless searches of public school students based on reasonable suspicion that a law or school rule has been violated; this also restored a clear local authority over another problem in our society, school discipline;

California v. Carney, which upheld the warrantless search of a mobile home;

U.S. v. Sharpe, which approved on-the-spot detention of a suspect for preliminary questioning and investigation;

U.S. v. Johns, upholding the warrantless search of sealed packages in a car several days after their removal by police who possessed probable cause to believe the vehicle contained contraband;

U.S. v. Hensley, which permitted a warrantless investigatory stop based on an unsworn flyer from a neighboring police department which possessed reasonable suspicion that the detainee was a felon;

Hayes v. Florida, which tacitly endorsed warrantless seizures in the field for the purpose of fingerprinting based on reasonable suspicion of criminal activity;

U.S. v. Hernandez, which upheld border detentions and warrantless searches by customs officials based on reasonable suspicion of criminal activity.

Similarly, the Court took steps this term to place the *Miranda* ruling in proper perspective, stressing its origin in the court rather than in the Constitution. In *Oregon v. Elstad,* the Court held that failure to administer *Miranda* warnings and the consequent receipt of a confession ordinarily will not taint a second confession after *Miranda* warnings are received.

The enforcement of criminal law remains one of our most important efforts. It is crucial that the state and local authorities — from the police to the prosecutors — be able to combat the growing tide of crime effectively. Toward that end we advocate a due regard for the rights of the accused — but also a due regard for the keeping of the public peace and the safety and happiness of the people. We will continue to press for a proper scope for the rules of exclusion, lest truth in the fact-finding process be allowed to suffer.

I have mentioned the areas of Federalism and Criminal Law, now I will turn to the Religion cases.

Religion

Most probably, this term will be best remembered for the decisions concerning the Establishment Clause of the First Amendment. The Court continued to apply its standard three-pronged test. Four cases merit mention.

In the first, *City of Grand Rapids v. Ball,* the Court nullified Shared Time and Community Education programs offered within parochial schools. Although the programs provided instruction in non-sectarian subjects, and were taught by full-time or part-time public school teachers, the Court nonetheless found that they promoted religion in three ways: the state-paid instructors might wittingly or unwittingly indoctrinate students; the symbolic union of church and state interest in state-provided instruction signaled support for religion; and, the programs in effect subsidized the religious functions of parochial schools by relieving them of responsibility for teaching some secular subjects. The symbolism test proposed in *Ball* precludes virtually any state assistance offered to parochial schools.

In *Aguilar v. Felton,* the Court invalidated a program of secular instruction for low-income students in sectarian schools, provided by public school teachers who were supervised to safeguard students against efforts of indoctrination.

With a bewildering Catch-22 logic, the Court declared that the supervisory safeguards at issue in the statute constituted unconstitutional government entanglement: "The religious school, which has as a primary purpose the advancement and preservation of a particular religion, must endure the ongoing presence of state personnel whose primary purpose is to monitor teachers and students in an attempt to guard against the infiltration of religious thought." Secretary of Education William Bennett has suggested logic may reveal a "disdain" for education as well as religion.

In *Wallace v. Jaffree,* the Court said in essence that states may set aside time in public schools for meditation or reflection so long as the legislation does not stipulate that it be used for voluntary prayer. Of course, what the Court gave with one hand, it took back with the other; the Alabama moment of silence statute failed to pass muster.

In *Thornton v. Caldor,* a 7-2 majority overturned a state law prohibiting private employees from discharging an employee for refusing to work on his Sabbath. We hope that this does not mean that the Court is abandoning last term's first but tentative steps toward state accommodation of religion in the Creche case.

In trying to make sense of the religion cases — from whichever side — it is important to remember how this body of tangled case law came about. Most Americans forget that it was not until 1925, in *Gitlow v. New York,* that *any* provision of the Bill of Rights was applied to the states. Nor was it until 1947 that the Establishment Clause was made applicable to the states through the 14th Amendment. This is striking because the Bill of Rights, as debated, created and ratified was designed to apply *only* to the national government.

The Bill of Rights came about largely

as the result of the demands of the critics of the new Constitution, the unfortunately misnamed Anti-Federalists. They feared, as George Mason of Virginia put it, that in time the national authority would "devour" the states. Since each state had a bill of rights, it was only appropriate that so powerful a national government as that created by the Constitution have one as well. Though Hamilton insisted a Bill of Rights was not necessary and even destructive, and Madison (at least at first) thought a Bill of Rights to be but a "parchment barrier" to political power, the Federalists agreed to add a Bill of Rights.

Though the first ten amendments that were ultimately ratified fell far short of what the Anti-Federalists desired, both Federalists and Anti-Federalists agreed that the amendments were a curb on national power.

When this view was questioned before the Supreme Court in *Barron v. Baltimore* (1833), Chief Justice Marshall wholeheartedly agreed. The Constitution said what it meant and meant what it said. Neither political expediency nor judicial desire was sufficient to change the clear import of the language of the Constitution. The Bill of Rights did not apply to the states — and, he said, that was that.

Until 1925, that is.

Since then a good portion of constitutional adjudication has been aimed at extending the scope of the doctrine of incorporation. But the most that can be done is to expand the scope; nothing can be done to shore up the intellectually shaky foundation upon which the doctrine rests. And nowhere else has the principle of federalism been dealt so politically violent and constitutionally suspect a blow as by the theory of incorporation.

In thinking particularly of the use to which the First Amendment has been put in the area of religion, one finds much merit in Justice Rehnquist's recent dissent in *Jaffree*. "It is impossible," Justice Rehn-

quist argued, "to build sound constitutional doctrine upon a mistaken understanding of constitutional history." His conclusion was bluntly to the point: "If a constitutional theory has no basis in the history of the amendment it seeks to interpret, it is difficult to apply and yields unprincipled results."

The point, of course, is that the Establishment Clause of the First Amendment was designed to prohibit Congress from establishing a national church. The belief was that the Constitution should not allow Congress to designate a particular faith or sect as politically above the rest. But to have argued, as is popular today, that the amendment demands a strict neutrality between religion and irreligion would have struck the founding generation as bizarre. The purpose was to prohibit religious tyranny, not to undermine religion generally.

In considering these areas of adjudication — Federalism, Criminal Law, and Religion — it seems fair to conclude that far too many of the Court's opinions were, on the whole, more policy choices than articulations of constitutional principle. The voting blocs, the arguments, all reveal a greater allegiance to what the Court thinks constitutes sound public policy than a deference to what the Constitution — its text and intention — may demand.

It is also safe to say that until there emerges a coherent jurisprudential stance, the work of the Court will continue in this ad hoc fashion. But that is not to argue for *any* jurisprudence.

In my opinion a drift back toward the radical egalitarianism and expansive civil libertarianism of the Warren Court would once again be a threat to the notion of limited but energetic government.

What, then, should a constitutional jurisprudence actually be? It should be a Jurisprudence of Original Intention. By seeking to judge policies in light of principles, rather than remold principles in light of policies, the Court could avoid both the charge of incoherence *and* the charge of being either too conservative or too liberal.

A jurisprudence seriously aimed at the explication of original intention would produce defensible principles of government that would not be tainted by ideological predilection.

This belief in a Jurisprudence of Original Intention also reflects a deeply rooted commitment to the idea of democracy. The Constitution represents the consent of the governed to the structures and powers of the government. The Constitution is the fundamental will of the people; that is why it is the fundamental law. To allow the courts to govern simply by what it views at the time as fair and decent, is a scheme of government no longer popular; the idea of democracy has suffered. The permanence of the Constitution has been weakened. A Constitution that is viewed as only what the judges say it is, is no longer a constitution in the true sense.

Those who framed the Constitution chose their words carefully; they debated at great length the most minute points. The language they chose meant something. It is incumbent upon the Court to determine what that meaning was. This is not a shockingly new theory; nor is it arcane or archaic.

Joseph Story, who was in a way a lawyer's Everyman — lawyer, justice, and teacher of law — had a theory of judging that merits reconsideration.

Though speaking specifically of the Constitution, his logic reaches to statutory construction as well.

In construing the Constitution of the United States, we are in the first instance to consider, what are its nature and objects, its scope and design, as apparent from the structure of the instrument, viewed as a whole and also viewed in its component parts. Where its words are plain, clear and determinate, they require no interpretation. . . . Where the words admit of two senses, each of which is confirmable to general usage, that sense is to be adopted, which without departing from the literal import of the words, best harmonizes with the nature and objects, the scope and design of the instrument.

A Jurisprudence of Original Intention would take seriously the admonition of Justice Story's friend and colleague, John Marshall, in *Marbury* that the Constitution is a limitation on judicial power as well as executive and legislative. That is what Chief Justice Marshall meant in *McCulloch* when he cautioned judges never to forget it is a constitution they are expounding.

It has been and will continue to be the policy of this administration to press for a Jurisprudence of Original Intention. In the cases we file and those we join as *amicus,* we will endeavor to resurrect the original meaning of constitutional provisions and statutes as the only reliable guide for judgment.

Within this context, let me reaffirm our commitment to pursuing the policies most necessary to public justice. We will continue our vigorous enforcement of civil rights laws; we will not rest till unlawful discrimination ceases. We will continue our all out war on drugs — both supply and demand; both national and international in scope. We intend to bolster public safety by a persistent war on crime. We will endeavor to stem the growing tide of pornography and its attendant costs, sexual and child abuse. We will be battling the heretofore largely ignored legal cancer of white collar crime; and its cousin, defense procurement fraud. And finally, as we still reel as a people, I pledge to you our commitment to fight terrorism here and abroad. For as long as the innocent are fair prey for the barbarians of this world, civilization is not safe.

We will pursue our agenda within the

context of our written Constitution of limited yet energetic powers. Our guide in every case will be the sanctity of the rule of law and the proper limits of governmental power.

It is our belief that only "the sense in which the Constitution was accepted and ratified by the nation," and only the sense in which laws were drafted and passed provide a solid foundation for adjudication. Any other standard suffers the defect of pouring new meaning into old words, thus creating new powers and new rights totally at odds with the logic of our Constitution and its commitment to the rule of law.

Thank you.

Following is the text of a speech by Attorney General Edwin Meese to the American Bar Association, July 17, 1985, in London:

Last Saturday representatives of the American Bar Association gathered at Runnymede with a group of our British hosts to commemorate the origin of the Magna Carta.

Last May 1 — Law Day in the United States — I was privileged to participate in a ceremony at the National Archives building in which one of the copies of the Magna Carta was received for permanent display in the United States.

What is it that makes this charter more than just a famous historical document? Why is it that a compact written in Latin and inscribed over 760 years ago has become the lodestar for lawyers, judges, statesmen and all those who love liberty?

I would suggest that the great achievement of the Magna Carta lay not in the particular remedies granted by a king to a group of barons in that feudal age, but in the great and general principle it established: the principle of freedom under law. It is that principle that guides us still and which is the basis for the system of laws that is venerated on both sides of the Atlantic.

As those of us whose business is the law gather here in this ancient land from which the seeds of our own political order came, it is appropriate to reflect on the debt we Americans owe to those who fought the hard constitutional battles on this soil so long ago. For it is from the English tradition of the rule of law that our own constitutionalism grew.

It seems safe to say that without the enlightened political philosophers this land produced — most prominently Thomas Hobbes and John Locke in England, and David Hume and Adam Smith in Scotland — and without the great English jurists — among them Christopher St. Germain, Sir Edward Coke, Sir Francis Bacon, and Sir William Blackstone — the creation of the American republic, in the manner we know it, would not have been possible.

The most important point in the development of the idea of the rule of law came from a uniquely English commitment. That commitment was to the idea of securing individual rights against arbitrary political power.

From England came the two primary roots of the theory of individual rights. From English philosophers came the theory of *natural* rights; from English jurists came the theory of *legal* rights. Together these ideas formed the matrix of an emerging jurisprudence of liberty.

When Thomas Jefferson wrote "that all men ... are endowed by their Creator with certain inalienable Rights," and "that among these are Life, Liberty and the Pursuit of Happiness," he was restating the American variation of the philosophic themes of English liberalism.

These rights derived from nature, not from law. They were *natural* rights, not a matter of class benevolence or legislated privilege.

But what rights nature gave, nature

also left insecure. It was up to mankind to institute governments to secure those rights. And while the forms of a government might be mutable — a democracy, a republic, or a mixed form — the legitimate basis for any government was not mutable. Government — any form of government — to be legitimate was understood to derive its just powers *only* from the consent of the governed. Any powers not so derived were deemed *by the laws of nature* to be illegitimate and unjust.

This truly radical philosophy of government provided the backdrop for the formulation of British law and institutions over several centuries.

The American sequel was a *written* constitution. The preservation of liberty required a document of clear and common language that created limited powers. Such a document would be the only way to enable fundamental principle to curb political power. A *written* constitution was to serve as an external and tangible check on any arbitrary exercise of governmental power.

Thomas Jefferson proclaimed a written constitution to be "our peculiar security"; John Marshall considered it nothing less than "the greatest of all improvements on political institutions."

But too often there is the temptation for well-intentioned but short-sighted courts, legislatures, and law schools to move away from the wisdom of Jefferson and Marshall.

It was not long ago when constitutional interpretation was understood to move between the poles of "strict construction" and "loose construction." Today, it is argued that constitutional interpretation moves between "interpretive review" and "noninterpretive review." As one observer has pointed out, under the old system the question was *how* to read the Constitution; under the new approach, the question is *whether* to read the Constitution. The very fact that such a question has come to be

posed — and seriously debated — raises serious questions about current concepts of limited constitutional government.

The result is that some judges and academics feel free (to borrow the language of Chancellor James Kent) to "roam at large in the trackless fields of their own imaginations."

This is not to suggest that the American Constitution and the institutions it creates and empowers are to be morally neutral or philosophically idle; it is only that in attributing to judges a special rationality to discover and apply hidden values, the great achievement of the Constitution is forgotten: Namely, its check upon *all* political power — judicial as well as executive and legislative. To allow constitutional text and the intentions of the framers to be nudged aside by the moral speculations of judges and advocates is to acquiesce in the misguided notion that a written Constitution can somehow be made viable only by ignoring or supplanting it.

John Marshall, in what is arguably our most famous Supreme Court opinion, *Marbury v. Madison,* reminded our still new nation that the Constitution limits the powers of the judicial branch no less than the legislative. Returning to the same theme in *McCulloch v. Maryland,* he argued eloquently that judges must never forget it is a constitution they are expounding.

But some judges and more than a few lawyers sometimes seem inclined to forget it is a constitution they are expounding.

As a result, many lawsuits have become "sprawling enterprises" wherein vast arrays of competing legal interests and political perspectives vie for victory. In such lawsuits lawyers become ideological lobbyists and the judges too often become political decision makers.

The focus of too many cases is now the determination of moral values or a political and social program that attempts to invoke what one writer has called "a vision of society as it is and as it might be."

The danger inherent in transforming the meaning of the Constitution and loosening its strictures in the name of some supposedly more benevolent and modern vision is that such tampering inevitably increases the power of government. For make no mistake, judicial power is governmental power, and it also must be subject to the restraining impact of the Constitution.

John Stuart Mill knew this well. "The disposition of mankind," he said, "whether as rulers or as fellow citizens, to impose their own opinions and inclinations as a rule of conduct on others, is so energetically supported by some of the best and some of the worst feelings incident to human nature, that it is hardly ever kept under restraint by anything but want of power." Tyranny imposed out of benevolence is tyranny still.

Under the mandate of the Framers the courts were to be the "bulwarks of a limited constitution," as Alexander Hamilton put it in *The Federalist*. Indeed, Hamilton argued, an independent judiciary was "peculiarly essential under a limited constitution." The purpose of judicial power was to curb the pretentions of power in the other branches and to keep political power fenced in by fundamental constitutional principles.

That the courts were *not* presumed to exercise legitimately either force or will, goes almost without saying; they were to exercise "merely judgment." They were not to be policymakers. As Nathaniel Gorham pointed out in the Federal Convention, "judges . . . are not presumed to possess any peculiar knowledge of the mere policy of public measures." James Madison, considered by many the Father of the Constitution, agreed. Judges, Madison argued in *The Federalist*, "by the mode of their appointment, as well as by the nature and permanency of it, are too far removed from the people to share much in their prepossession."

The federal judiciary, as Hamilton so famously phrased it in *The Federalist,* No. 78, would always be, from the nature of its functions, the branch of the federal government "least dangerous to the political rights of the Constitution; because it will be least in a capacity to annoy or injure them."

The judges, he argued, would have no influence over either the sword or the purse of the nation. And the courts were empowered to take "no active resolution whatever." For only by placing the courts a safe distance from the political passions that would blow through society and the representative bodies would it be likely that the judiciary could resist those popular impulses and fulfill their necessary duty as the "faithful guardians of the constitution."

Of course, it did not escape the notice of some that this independent judicial power created by the new Constitution might lend itself to political abuse. The fact was, as one critic saw it, that the courts under the Constitution would likely endeavor to "explain the constitution according to the reasoning spirit of it, without being confined to the words or letter." Yet another critic was even more blunt: "We are more in danger of sowing the seeds of arbitrary government in this branch than in any other."

In response to these concerns, the friends of the Constitution made a promise. There would be no danger of government by an unfettered judiciary. To avoid arbitrary discretion in the courts, the Constitution provided that they would be "bound down by strict rules"; the judicial tradition promised they would be hedged in by the common law regard for precedent.

In recent years, however, regard for these promises has sometimes been eroded. We have come to see examples of sound precedent giving way to "arbitrary discretion" in some of our courts of law. Freed from the statutory shackles of strict rules and from the institutional restraints making for stability in the law, too many courts have become more policy planners than interpreters of the law.

The animating sentiment of this new view of judicial power is that the Constitution is a "transitional" document that takes its meaning from the circumstances of each age. It is argued — and taught — and decreed — that in order to keep the Constitution viable its language and original meaning must often be ignored or blatantly changed by judicial opinion. This is an understanding of constitutional interpretation completely at odds with the Constitution itself.

To those who created our Constitution its principles were intended to be enduring not transitory. During the Convention of 1787 and afterward during the ratification struggle, it was frequently asserted that the Constitution was being created "for future generations, and not merely for the peculiar circumstances of the moment."

The main point of such a Constitution was that its meaning was not to be changed by ordinary interpretation. There was a provision in the Constitution to keep the Constitution in step with the times. That is the Amendment Process. To the Framers the process of altering the Constitution had to be difficult lest the Constitution be rendered "too mutable." The only legitimate means of Constitutional change was to be by the "solemn and authoritative act" of formal amendment. Indeed this process has been utilized 26 times in the more than two centuries of our history.

As members of the Bar — as advocates and teachers and judges — we have a special responsibility to the Constitution. We must dedicate ourselves to take it seriously, to understand it, and to perpetuate it. We must move away from the belief that it is nothing more than what we can make it through shrewd arguments and bold decrees.

As we convene here where our constitutionalism began, I urge that we dedicate ourselves anew to the great principles and purposes of our Constitution. These principles and purposes are as much alive today as they were two centuries ago.

I know that it is sometimes said that the problems of our time, of 1985, are complex — far more complex than the problems of 1787. The issue of terrorism in our peculiar, as Paul Johnson might say, "modern times"; the matter of abortion in contemporary society; the divisions of responsibility between federal and state governments — these are among the issues thought by some to be more complicated and by implication more difficult than those faced by Americans living in the final quarter of the 18th century. And it is in light of these ostensibly very different circumstances that some would urge us to relax our commitment to the principles of our two hundred year old Constitution.

The problem with this line of thought is two-fold. First, there is more than a hint of chronological snobbery here; the idea that our times are more vexing than previous ones appeals to the ego inside all of us. Yet surely the problems facing our forebears two centuries ago seemed every bit as complicated to them. If there is a difference, perhaps it lies in their more humble approach to the issues of their times.

The second problem is fundamental. It is, simply, that the principles which informed the writing of our Constitution were not conceived in an afternoon in Philadelphia. As we are reminded afresh by our visit this week, those principles were the product of several centuries of experience. They were tried principles. They were tested principles. The idea of limited government, of checking arbitrary power, and of a criminal justice system that is fair both to the accused and to those against whom crimes are committed — these were among the seasoned principles that our forebears sought to apply amid the circumstances they uniquely faced. And these principles are no less applicable in our times, however unique we think our times to be.

Today we, along with other nations, including the United Kingdom, face the modern horror of international terrorism. In combatting terrorism, we must not lose sight of the fundamental principles of the criminal law. We must, as Prime Minister Margaret Thatcher so eloquently stated on Monday, remember that those who commit such heinous crimes are indeed criminals, and that the full weight of the law must be brought to bear against them. Further, as she also said, we must never yield, we must never acquiesce to the demands of the terrorists. Whoever does yield, yields not only to a particular demand, but also yields the very principles which distinguish the rule of law from the reign of terror. We must never conform our principles to our circumstances.

In America, we face the difficult question of abortion. It is a question made more difficult by the entry of the federal judiciary into an area once clearly reserved, under our Constitution, for the states themselves to decide. We know there are fervently held opposing views about abortions. It is our responsibility and practical task to dedicate ourselves to the principles and purposes of our Constitution, particularly in areas of great controversy. This week the United States filed as an amicus in the Supreme Court a brief arguing that the Court should return the law to the condition in which it was before the 1973 case, *Roe v. Wade,* was decided. The responsibility of the Justice Department to urge that constitutionally wrong decisions be overruled is no less strong today in this case than it was in 1954 in *Brown v. Board of Education.*

In seeking to carry out the original intentions of the Framers of the Constitution and to make sure that its great principles and purposes endure for the ages, it is fitting that we note the words of James Madison, written nearly forty years after the creation of the Constitution, a time when circumstances had already substantially changed.

Wrote Madison:

I entirely concur in the propriety of resorting to the sense in which the Constitution was accepted and ratified by the nation. In that sense alone it is the legitimate Constitution. And if that be not the guide in expounding it, there can be no security for a consistent and stable, more than for a faithful, exercise of its powers.

To do anything less is to risk the very idea of limited *constitutional* government.

The concern of our Constitution, like that of the Magna Carta, is to reduce the chance of that governmental power will be wielded according to personal whim rather than according to political principles. To make certain the ideal of the rule of law is given practical effect, the law must be fixed and known.

Uncertainty in the law undermines that stability in government that is so necessary to the preservation of liberty, and to the safety and happiness of the people. Arbitrary power is the very definition of tyranny; power controlled is the first step toward freedom.

Constitutional principles are neither liberal nor conservative. Preserving the basic tenets of the Founding Fathers is not simply a conservative notion. Indeed, the purpose of the Constitution and the Bill of Rights was a demonstration of classical English liberalism — to protect individual liberty against an all powerful central government.

We must remember, on the one hand, that adhering to the principles of the Constitution must never become a pretext for denying the civil rights of anyone. At the same time, some nebulous concept of enhancing the general welfare cannot justify usurpation of the traditional authority of the states or the confiscation of the personal liberty, including economic liberty, of individuals.

As lawyers, judges and public officials, we have the responsibility to see current controversies in the light of historical perspective and to preserve our heritage of ordered liberty under the protection of an enduring Constitution. We can have no greater responsibility.

Thank you.

Following is the text of an address by Associate Justice William J. Brennan Jr. Oct. 12, 1985, at Georgetown University, Washington, D.C.:

I am deeply grateful for the invitation to participate in the "Text and Teaching" symposium. This rare opportunity to explore classic texts with participants of such wisdom, acumen and insight as those who have preceded and will follow me to this podium is indeed exhilarating. But it is also humbling. Even to approximate the standards of excellence of these vigorous and graceful intellects is a daunting task. I am honored that you have afforded me this opportunity to try.

It will perhaps not surprise you that the text I have chosen for exploration is the amended Constitution of the United States, which, of course, entrenches the Bill of Rights and the Civil War amendments, and draws sustenance from the bedrock principles of another great text, the Magna Carta. So fashioned, the Constitution embodies the aspiration to social justice, brotherhood, and human dignity that brought this nation into being. The Declaration of Independence, the Constitution and the Bill of Rights solemnly committed the United States to be a country where the dignity and rights of all persons were equal before all authority. In all candor we must concede that part of this egalitarianism in America has been more pretension than realized fact.

But we are an aspiring people, a people with faith in progress. Our amended Constitution is the lodestar for our aspirations. Like every text worth reading, it is not crystalline. The phrasing is broad and the limitations of its provisions are not clearly marked. Its majestic generalities and ennobling pronouncements are both luminous and obscure. This ambiguity of course calls forth interpretation, the interaction of reader and text. The encounter with the Constitutional text has been, in many senses, my life's work.

My approach to this text may differ from the approach of other participants in this symposium to their texts. Yet such differences may themselves stimulate reflection about what it is we do when we "interpret" a text. Thus I will attempt to elucidate my approach to the text as well as my substantive interpretation.

Perhaps the foremost difference is the fact that my encounters with the constitutional text are not purely or even primarily introspective; the Constitution cannot be for me simply a contemplative haven for private moral reflection. My relation to this great text is inescapably public. That is not to say that my reading of the text is not a personal reading, only that the personal reading perforce occurs in a public context, and is open to critical scrutiny from all quarters.

The Constitution is fundamentally a public text — the monumental charter of a government and a people — and a Justice of the Supreme Court must apply it to resolve public controversies. For, from our beginnings, a most important consequence of the constitutionally created separation of powers has been the American habit, extraordinary to other democracies, of casting social, economic, philosophical and political questions in the form of law suits, in an attempt to secure ultimate resolution by the Supreme Court. In this way, important aspects of the most fundamental issues confronting our democracy may finally arrive in the Supreme Court for judicial determination. Not infrequently, these are the issues upon which contemporary society is most deeply divided. They arouse our deepest emotions. The main burden of my twenty-nine Terms on the Supreme Court has thus been to wrestle with the Constitution in this heightened public context, to draw meaning from the text in order to resolve public controversies.

Two other aspects of my relation to this text warrant mention. First, constitutional interpretation for a federal judge is, for the most part, obligatory. When litigants approach the bar of court to adjudicate a constitutional dispute, they may justifiably demand an answer. Judges cannot avoid a definitive interpretation because they feel unable to, or would prefer not to, penetrate to the full meaning of the Constitution's provisions. Unlike literary critics, judges cannot merely savor the tensions or revel in the ambiguities inhering in the text — judges must resolve them.

Second, consequences flow from a Justice's interpretation in a direct and immediate way. A judicial decision respecting the incompatibility of Jim Crow with a constitutional guarantee of equality is not simply a contemplative exercise in defining the shape of a just society. It is an order — supported by the full coercive power of the State — that the present society change in a fundamental aspect. Under such circumstances the process of deciding can be a lonely, troubling experience for fallible human beings conscious that their best may not be adequate to the challenge. We Justices are certainly aware that we are not final because we are infallible; we know that we are infallible only because we are final. One does not forget how much may depend on the decision. More than the litigants may be affected. The course of vital social, economic and political currents may be directed.

These three defining characteristics of my relation to the constitutional text — its public nature, obligatory character, and consequentialist aspect — cannot help but influence the way I read that text. When Justices interpret the Constitution they speak for their community, not for themselves alone. The act of interpretation must be undertaken with full consciousness that it is, in a very real sense, the community's interpretation that is sought. Justices are not platonic guardians appointed to wield authority according to their personal moral predelictions. Precisely because coercive force must attend any judicial decision to countermand the will of a contemporary majority, the Justices must render constitutional interpretations that are received as legitimate. The source of legitimacy is, of course, a wellspring of controversy in legal and political circles. At the core of the debate is what the late Yale Law School professor Alexander Bickel labeled "the counter-majoritarian difficulty." Our commitment to self-governance in a representative democracy must be reconciled with vesting in electorally unaccountable Justices the power to invalidate the expressed desires of representative bodies on the ground of inconsistency with higher law. Because judicial power resides in the authority to give meaning to the Constitution, the debate is really a debate about how to read the text, about constraints on what is legitimate interpretation.

There are those who find legitimacy in fidelity to what they call "the intentions of the Framers." In its most doctrinaire incarnation, this view demands that Justices discern exactly what the Framers thought about the question under consideration and simply follow that intention in resolving the case before them. It is a view that feigns self-effacing deference to the specific judgments of those who forged our original social compact. But in truth it is little more than arrogance cloaked as humility. It is arrogant to pretend that from our vantage we can gauge accurately the intent of the Framers on application of principle to specific, contemporary questions. All too often, sources of potential enlightment such as records of the ratification debates provide sparse or ambiguous evidence of the original intention. Typically, all that can be gleaned is that the Framers themselves did not agree about the application or meaning of particular constitutional provisions, and hid their differences in cloaks of generality. Indeed, it is far from clear whose intention is relevant — that of the drafters, the congressional disputants, or the ratifiers in the states? — or even whether the idea of an original intention is a coherent way of thinking about a jointly drafted document drawing its authority from a general assent of the states. And apart from the problematic nature of the sources, our distance of two centuries cannot but work as a prism refracting all we perceive. One cannot help but speculate that the chorus of lamentations calling for interpretation faithful to "original intention" — and proposing nullification of interpretations that fail this quick litmus test — must inevitably come from persons who have no familiarity with the historical record.

Perhaps most importantly, while proponents of this facile historicism justify it as a depoliticization of the judiciary, the political underpinnings of such a choice should not escape notice. A position that upholds constitutional claims only if they were within the specific contemplation of the Framers in effect establishes a presumption of resolving textual ambiguities against the claim of constitutional right. It is far from clear what justifies such a presumption against claims of right. Nothing intrinsic in the nature of interpretation — if there is such a thing as the "nature" of interpretation — commands such a passive approach to ambiguity. This is a choice no less political than any other; it expresses antipathy to

claims of the minority to rights against the majority. Those who would restrict claims of right to the values of 1789 specifically articulated in the Constitution turn a blind eye to social progress and eschew adaptation of overarching principles to changes of social circumstance.

Another, perhaps more sophisticated, response to the potential power of judicial interpretation stresses democratic theory: because ours is a government of the people's elected representatives, substantive value choices should by and large be left to them. This view emphasizes not the transcendent historical authority of the Framers but the predominant contemporary authority of the elected branches of government. Yet it has similar consequences for the nature of proper judicial interpretation. Faith in the majoritarian process counsels restraint. Even under more expansive formulations of this approach, judicial review is appropriate only to the extent of ensuring that our democratic process functions smoothly. Thus, for example, we would protect freedom of speech merely to ensure that the people are heard by their representatives, rather than as a separate, substantive value. When, by contrast, society tosses up to the Supreme Court a dispute that would require invalidation of a legislature's substantive policy choice, the Court generally would stay its hand because the Constitution was meant as a plan of government and not as an embodiment of fundamental substantive values.

The view that all matters of substantive policy should be resolved through the majoritarian process has appeal under some circumstances, but I think it ultimately will not do. Unabashed enshrinement of majority will would permit the imposition of a social caste system or wholesale confiscation of property so long as a majority of the authorized legislative body, fairly elected, approved. Our Constitution could not abide such a situation. It is the very purpose of a

Constitution — and particularly of the Bill of Rights — to declare certain values transcendent, beyond the reach of temporary political majorities. The majoritarian process cannot be expected to rectify claims of minority right that arise as a response to the outcomes of that very majoritarian process. As James Madison put it:

> The prescriptions in favor of liberty ought to be levelled against that quarter where the greatest danger lies, namely, that which possesses the highest prerogative of power. But this is not found in either the Executive or Legislative departments of Government, but in the body of the people, operating by the majority against the minority.

Faith in democracy is one thing, blind faith quite another. Those who drafted our Constitution understood the difference. One cannot read the text without admitting that it embodies substantive value choices; it places certain values beyond the power of any legislature. Obvious are the separation of powers; the privilege of the Writ of Habeas Corpus; prohibition of Bills of Attainder and ex post facto laws; prohibition of cruel and unusual punishments; the requirement of just compensation for official taking of property; the prohibition of laws tending to establish religion or enjoining the free exercise of religion; and since the Civil War, the banishment of slavery and official race discrimination. With respect to at least such principles, we simply have not constituted ourselves as strict utilitarians. While the Constitution may be amended, such amendments require an immense effort by the People as a whole.

To remain faithful to the content of the Constitution, therefore, an approach to interpreting the text must account for the existence of these substantive value choices, and must accept the ambiguity inherent in the effort to apply them to modern circumstances. The Framers discerned fundamental principles through struggles against particular malefactions of the Crown; the struggle shapes the particular contours of the articulated principles. But our acceptance of the fundamental principles has not and should not bind us to those precise, at times anachronistic, contours. Successive generations of Americans have continued to respect these fundamental choices and adopt them as their own guide to evaluating quite different historical practices. Each generation has the choice to overrule or add to the fundamental principles enunciated by the Framers; the Constitution can be amended or it can be ignored. Yet with respect to its fundamental principles, the text has suffered neither fate. Thus, if I may borrow the words of an esteemed predecessor, Justice Robert Jackson, the burden of judicial interpretation is to translate "the majestic generalities of the Bill of Rights, conceived as part of the pattern of liberal government in the eighteenth century, into concrete restraints on officials dealing with the problems of the twentieth century."

We current Justices read the Constitution in the only way that we can: as Twentieth Century Americans. We look to the history of the time of framing and to the intervening history of interpretation. But the ultimate question must be, what do the words of the text mean in our time. For the genius of the Constitution rests not in any static meaning it might have had in a world that is dead and gone, but in the adaptability of its great principles to cope with current problems and current needs. What the constitutional fundamentals meant to the wisdom of other times cannot be their measure to the vision of our time. Similarly, what those fundamentals mean for us, our descendants will learn, cannot be the measure to the vision of their time. This realization is not, I assure you, a novel one of my own creation. Permit me to quote from one of the opinions of our Court, *Weems* v.

United States, written nearly a century ago:

> Time works changes, brings into existence new conditions and purposes. Therefore, a principle to be vital must be capable of wider application than the mischief which gave it birth. This is peculiarly true of constitutions. They are not ephemeral enactments, designed to meet passing occasions. They are, to use the words of Chief Justice John Marshall, "designed to approach immortality as nearly as human institutions can approach it." The future is their care and provision for events of good and bad tendencies of which no prophesy can be made. In the application of a constitution, therefore, our contemplation cannot be only of what has been, but of what may be.

Interpretation must account for the transformative purpose of the text. Our Constitution was not intended to preserve a preexisting society but to make a new one, to put in place new principles that the prior political community had not sufficiently recognized. Thus, for example, when we interpret the Civil War Amendments to the charter — abolishing slavery, guaranteeing blacks equality under law, and guaranteeing blacks the right to vote — we must remember that those who put them in place had no desire to enshrine the status quo. Their goal was to make over their world, to eliminate all vestige of slave caste.

Having discussed at some length how I, as a Supreme Court Justice, interact with this text, I think it time to turn to the fruits of this discourse. For the Constitution is a sublime oration on the dignity of man, a bold commitment by a people to the ideal of libertarian dignity protected through law. Some reflection is perhaps required before this can be seen.

The Constitution on its face is, in large measure, a structuring text, a blueprint for government. And when the text is not prescribing the form of government it is limiting the powers of that government. The original document, before addition of any of the amendments, does not speak primarily of the rights of man, but of the abilities and disabilities of government. When one reflects upon the text's preoccupation with the scope of government as well as its shape, however, one comes to understand that what this text is about is the relationship of the individual and the state. The text marks the metes and bounds of official authority and individual autonomy. When one studies the boundary that the text marks out, one gets a sense of the vision of the individual embodied in the Constitution.

As augmented by the Bill of Rights and the Civil War Amendments, this text is a sparkling vision of the supremacy of the human dignity of every individual. This vision is reflected in the very choice of democratic self-governance: the supreme value of a democracy is the presumed worth of each individual. And this vision manifests itself most dramatically in the specific prohibitions of the Bill of Rights, a term which I henceforth will apply to describe not only the original first eight amendments, but the Civil War amendments as well. It is a vision that has guided us as a people throughout our history, although the precise rules by which we have protected fundamental human dignity have been transformed over time in response to both transformations of social condition and evolution of our concepts of human dignity.

Until the end of the nineteenth century, freedom and dignity in our country found meaningful protection in the institution of real property. In a society still largely agricultural, a piece of land provided men not just with sustenance but with the means of economic independence, a necessary precondition of political independence and expression. Not surprisingly, property relationships formed the heart of litigation and of legal practice, and lawyers and judges tended to think stable property relationships the highest aim of the law.

But the days when common law property relationships dominated litigation and legal practice are past. To a growing extent economic existence now depends on less certain relationships with government — licenses, employment contracts, subsidies, unemployment benefits, tax exemptions, welfare and the like. Government participation in the economic existence of individuals is pervasive and deep. Administrative matters and other dealings with government are at the epicenter of the exploding law. We turn to government and to the law for controls which would never have been expected or tolerated before this century, when a man's answer to economic oppression or difficulty was to move two hundred miles west. Now hundreds of thousands of Americans live entire lives without any real prospect of the dignity and autonomy that ownership of real property could confer. Protection of the human dignity of such citizens requires a much modified view of the proper relationship of individual and state.

In general, problems of the relationship of the citizen with government have multiplied and thus have engendered some of the most important constitutional issues of the day. As government acts ever more deeply upon those areas of our lives once marked "private," there is an even greater need to see that individual rights are not curtailed or cheapened in the interest of what may temporarily appear to be the "public good." And as government continues in its role of provider for so many of our disadvantaged citizens, there is an even greater need to ensure that government act with integrity and consistency in its dealings with these citizens. To put this another way, the possibilities for collision between government activity and individual rights will increase as the power and authority of government itself expands, and this growth, in turn,

heightens the need for constant vigilance at the collision points. If our free society is to endure, those who govern must recognize human dignity and accept the enforcement of constitutional limitations on their power conceived by the Framers to be necessary to preserve that dignity and the air of freedom which is our proudest heritage. Such recognition will not come from a technical understanding of the organs of government, or the new forms of wealth they administer. It requires something different, something deeper — a personal confrontation with the well-springs of our society. Solutions of constitutional questions from that perspective have become the great challenge of the modern era. All the talk in the last half-decade about shrinking the government does not alter this reality or the challenge it imposes. The modern activist state is a concomitant of the complexity of modern society; it is inevitably with us. We must meet the challenge rather than wish it were not before us.

The challenge is essentially, of course, one to the capacity of our constitutional structure to foster and protect the freedom, the dignity, and the rights of all persons within our borders, which it is the great design of the Constitution to secure. During the time of my public service this challenge has largely taken shape within the confines of the interpretive question whether the specific guarantees of the Bill of Rights operate as restraints on the power of State government. We recognize the Bill of Rights as the primary source of express information as to what is meant by constitutional liberty. The safeguards enshrined in it are deeply etched in the foundation of America's freedoms. Each is a protection with centuries of history behind it, often dearly bought with the blood and lives of people determined to prevent oppression by their rulers. The first eight Amendments, however, were added to the Constitution to operate solely against federal power. It was not until the Thirteenth and Fourteenth Amendments were added, in 1865 and 1868, in response to a demand for national protection against abuses of state power, that the Constitution could be interpreted to require application of the first eight amendments to the states.

It was in particular the Fourteenth Amendment's guarantee that no person be deprived of life, liberty or property without process of law that led us to apply many of the specific guarantees of the Bill of Rights to the States. In my judgment, Justice Cardozo best captured the reasoning that brought us to such decisions when he described what the Court has done as a process by which the guarantees "have been taken over from the earlier articles of the federal bill of rights and brought within the Fourteenth Amendment by a process of absorption . . . [that] has had its source in the belief that neither liberty nor justice would exist if [those guarantees] . . . were sacrificed." But this process of absorption was neither swift nor steady. As late as 1922 only the Fifth Amendment guarantee of just compensation for official taking of property had been given force against the states. Between then and 1956 only the First Amendment guarantees of speech and conscience and the Fourth Amendment ban of unreasonable searches and seizures had been incorporated — the latter, however, without the exclusionary rule to give it force. As late as 1961, I could stand before a distinguished assemblage of the bar at New York University's James Madison Lecture and list the following as guarantees that had not been thought to be sufficiently fundamental to the protection of human dignity so as to be enforced against the states: the prohibition of cruel and unusual punishments, the right against self-incrimination, the right to assistance of counsel in a criminal trial, the right to confront witnesses, the right to compulsory process, the right not to be placed in jeopardy of life or limb more than once upon accusation of a crime, the right not to have illegally obtained evidence introduced at a criminal trial, and the right to a jury of one's peers.

The history of the quarter century following that Madison Lecture need not be told in great detail. Suffice it to say that each of the guarantees listed above has been recognized as a fundamental aspect of ordered liberty. Of course, the above catalogue encompasses only the rights of the criminally accused, those caught, rightly or wrongly, in the maw of the criminal justice system. But it has been well said that there is no better test of a society than how it treats those accused of transgressing against it. Indeed, it is because we recognize that incarceration strips a man of his dignity that we demand strict adherence to fair procedure and proof of guilt beyond a reasonable doubt before taking such a drastic step. These requirements are, as Justice Harlan once said, "bottomed on a fundamental value determination of our society that it is far worse to convict an innocent man than to let a guilty man go free." There is no worse injustice than wrongly to strip a man of his dignity. And our adherence to the constitutional vision of human dignity is so strict that even after convicting a person according to these stringent standards, we demand that his dignity be infringed only to the extent appropriate to the crime and never by means of wanton infliction of pain or deprivation. I interpret the Constitution plainly to embody these fundamental values.

Of course the constitutional vision of human dignity has, in this past quarter century, infused far more than our decisions about the criminal process. Recognition of the principle of "one person, one vote" as a constitutional one redeems the promise of self-governance by affirming the essential dignity of every citizen in the right to equal participation in the democratic process. Recognition of so-called "new property" rights in those receiving government entitlements affirms the essential dignity of the least fortunate among us by demanding that government treat with decency, integrity and consistency those dependent on its benefits for their very survival. After all, a legislative majority initially decides to create governmental entitlements; the Constitution's Due Process Clause merely provides protection for entitlements thought necessary by society as a whole. Such due process rights prohibit government from imposing the devil's bargain of bartering away human dignity in exchange for human sustenance. Likewise, recognition of full equality for women — equal protection of the laws — ensures that gender has no bearing on claims to human dignity.

Recognition of broad and deep rights of expression and of conscience reaffirm the vision of human dignity in many ways. They too redeem the promise of self-governance by facilitating — indeed demanding — robust, uninhibited and wide-open debate on issues of public importance. Such public debate is of course vital to the development and dissemination of political ideas. As importantly, robust public discussion is the crucible in which personal political convictions are forged. In our democracy, such discussion is a political duty; it is the essence of self government. The constitutional vision of human dignity rejects the possibility of political orthodoxy imposed from above; it respects the right of each individual to form and to express political judgments, however far they may deviate from the mainstream and however unsettling they might be to the powerful or the elite. Recognition of these rights of expression and conscience also frees up the private space for both intellectual and spiritual development free of government dominance, either blatant or subtle. Justice Brandeis put it so well sixty years ago when he wrote: "Those who won our independence believed that the final end of the State was to make men free to develop their faculties; and that in its government the deliberative forces should prevail over the arbitrary. They valued liberty both as an end and as a means."

I do not mean to suggest that we have in the last quarter century achieved a comprehensive definition of the constitutional ideal of human dignity. We are still striving toward that goal, and doubtless it will be an eternal quest. For if the interaction of this Justice and the constitutional text over the years confirms any single proposition, it is that the demands of human dignity will never cease to evolve.

Indeed, I cannot in good conscience refrain from mention of one grave and crucial respect in which we continue, in my judgment, to fall short of the constitutional vision of human dignity. It is in our continued tolerance of State-administered execution as a form of punishment. I make it a practice not to comment on the constitutional issues that come before the Court, but my position on this issue, of course, has been for some time fixed and immutable. I think I can venture some thoughts on this particular subject without transgressing my usual guideline too severely.

As I interpret the Constitution, capital punishment is under all circumstances cruel and unusual punishment prohibited by the Eighth and Fourteenth Amendments. This is a position of which I imagine you are not unaware. Much discussion of the merits of capital punishment has in recent years focused on the potential arbitrariness that attends its administration, and I have no doubt that such arbitrariness is a grave wrong. But for me, the wrong of capital punishment transcends such procedural issues. As I have said in my opinions, I view the Eighth Amendment's prohibition of cruel and unusual punishments as embodying to a unique degree moral principles that substantively restrain the punishments our civilized society may impose on those persons who transgress its laws. Foremost among the moral principles recognized in our cases and inherent in the prohibition is the primary principle that the State, even as it punishes, must treat its citizens in a manner consistent with their intrinsic worth as human beings. A punishment must not be so severe as to be utterly and irreversibly degrading to the very essence of human dignity. Death for whatever crime and under all circumstances is a truly awesome punishment. The calculated killing of a human being by the State involves, by its very nature, an absolute denial of the executed person's humanity. The most vile murder does not, in my view, release the State from constitutional restraints on the destruction of human dignity. Yet an executed person has lost the very right to have rights, now or ever. For me, then, the fatal constitutional infirmity of capital punishment is that it treats members of the human race as nonhumans, as objects to be toyed with and discarded. It is, indeed, "cruel and unusual." It is thus inconsistent with the fundamental premise of the Clause that even the most base criminal remains a human being possessed of some potential, at least, for common human dignity.

This is an interpretation to which a majority of my fellow Justices — not to mention, it would seem, a majority of my fellow countrymen — does not subscribe. Perhaps you find my adherence to it, and my recurrent publication of it, simply contrary, tiresome, or quixotic. Or perhaps you see in it a refusal to abide by the judicial principle of *stare decisis,* obedience to precedent. In my judgment, however, the unique interpretive role of the Supreme Court with respect to the Constitution demands some flexibility with respect to the call of *stare decisis.* Because we are the last word on the meaning of the Constitution, our views must be subject to revision over time, or the Constitution falls captive, again, to the anachronistic views of long-gone generations. I mentioned earlier the judge's role in seeking out the community's interpretation of the Constitutional text. Yet, again in my judgment, when a Justice perceives an interpretation of the text to have departed so far from its essential meaning, that Justice is bound, by a larger constitutional duty to the community, to expose the departure and point toward a different path. On this issue, the death penalty, I hope to embody a community striving for human dignity for all, although perhaps not yet arrived.

You have doubtless observed that this description of my personal encounter with the constitutional text has in large portion been a discussion of public developments in constitutional doctrine over the last quarter century. That, as I suggested at the outset, is inevitable because my interpretive career has demanded a public reading of the text. This public encounter with the text, however, has been a profound source of personal inspiration. The vision of human dignity embodied there is deeply moving. It is timeless. It has inspired Americans for two centuries and it will continue to inspire as it continues to evolve. That evolutionary process is inevitable and, indeed, it is the true interpretive genius of the text.

If we are to be as a shining city upon a hill, it will be because of our ceaseless pursuit of the constitutional ideal of human dignity. For the political and legal ideals that form the foundation of much that is best in American institutions — ideals jealously preserved and guarded throughout our history — still form the vital force in creative political thought and activity within the nation today. As we adapt our institutions to the ever-changing conditions of national and international life, those ideals of human dignity — liberty and justice for all individuals — will continue to inspire and guide us because they are entrenched in our Constitution. The Constitution with its Bill of Rights thus has a bright future, as well as a glorious past, for its spirit is inherent in the aspirations of our people.

Supreme Court Biographies

Warren Earl Burger

in St.
fourth
erman
from
ship to
enough
would
he next
during
s, first
then at

aude in
vith one
came a
married
net as a
n, a son

ing law,
s, work-
is guber-
ccessful,
mination

In that 1948 effort, Burger met Herbert E. Brownell, who became attorney general during the Eisenhower administration. Brownell brought Burger to Washington in 1953 to become assistant attorney general in charge of what is now the Civil Division.

In 1956 Eisenhower named Burger to the U.S. Court of Appeals for the District of Columbia Circuit, where he quickly developed a reputation as one of that court's most conservative members. President Nixon named him chief justice, announcing that nomination May 21, 1969. Burger was confirmed by a 74-3 vote June 9 and assumed his new position on June 23.

William Joseph Brennan Jr.

William J. Brennan Jr. was the first man born in the 20th century to be named to the Supreme Court. Born April 25, 1906, in Newark, N.J., Brennan was the second of eight children of Irish parents who had emigrated to the United States in 1890.

An outstanding student, Brennan won academic honors at the University of Pennyslvania's Wharton School of Finance, from which he graduated in 1928, and at Harvard Law School, from which he received his law degree in 1931.

Brennan, who had married Marjorie Leonard in 1928, began the practice of law in Newark with an established firm. The Brennans had three children, two sons and a daughter. Brennan specialized in labor matters in his practice, making partner in 1937. Except for a brief period of service during World War II as a troubleshooter for the War Department in Washington, Brennan practiced law until 1949.

That year, he was named to a judicial post on a new state court created as the result of a judicial reform movement that he had helped lead. Three years later, he was named to the New Jersey Supreme Court.

Eisenhower named Brennan to the Supreme Court Oct. 16, 1956, during a congressional recess. He began serving immediately and was formally nominated Jan. 14, 1957. He was confirmed by voice vote on March 19, 1957.

In 1982 Marjorie Brennan died after a long battle with cancer. The following year, Brennan married his longtime secretary, Mary Fowler.

Byron Raymond White

Byron R. White was born June 8, 1917, in Fort Collins, Colo. He grew up in the small town of Wellington, Colo., where his father was the mayor.

A scholar and a fine athlete, White won a scholarship to the University of Colorado from which he graduated first in his class in 1938. In addition to a Phi Beta Kappa key, White won a total of 10 varsity letters in football, basketball and baseball; the nickname "Whizzer," a one-year contract with the Pittsburgh Pirates professional football team and a Rhodes scholarship.

White played the 1938 season with the Pirates, for which he was paid $15,000, then the highest salary ever paid a professional football player. He spent the first half of 1939 at Oxford University, returning to enter Yale Law School in the fall of that year. After one year at Yale, he returned to his pro football career, playing the 1940-41 season with the Detroit Lions.

After the United States entered World War II, White served in the Navy for four years in the South Pacific where he renewed his acquaintance with John Kennedy, also a Navy man. The two had met

earlier in England, where Kennedy's father was serving as U.S. ambassador.

After the war White married Marion Stearns, whom he had met in college, and returned to Yale for the remainder of his legal education. He graduated with honors in 1946, clerked the following year for Chief Justice Fred M. Vinson and in 1947 joined a law firm in Denver. The Whites had a son and a daughter.

In 1960, when John Kennedy ran for president, White joined the campaign. Kennedy named White deputy attorney general; from that post, in 1962, he promoted him to the Supreme Court. White was only 44 when Kennedy nominated him on March 30, 1962. He was confirmed by voice vote April 11. He took his seat on the Court April 16.

Thurgood Marshall

Thurgood Marshall was born on July 2, 1908, in Baltimore, Md., the son of a school teacher and a club steward. Marshall worked his way through all-black Lincoln University in Chester, Pa., graduating with honors in 1930. He studied law at Howard University Law School, from which he graduated first in his class in 1933. In 1929 he had married Vivian Burey, and they had two sons.

Marshall had already developed a strong interest in civil rights by the time he graduated from law school. While he was establishing a law practice in Baltimore, he served as counsel to the local branch of the National Association for the Advancement of Colored People (NAACP). In 1936 he moved to New York to become an assistant to NAACP special counsel Charles H. Houston, whom Marshall had met at Howard when Houston was vice dean of the law school.

Two years later Marshall became special counsel and in 1939, when the litigating arm of the NAACP split off as the NAACP

Legal Defense and Education Fund, Marshall became its executive director and general counsel. He held that post for more than 20 years, coordinating the fund's attack on segregation in voting, housing, public accommodations and education.

The culmination of his service in this position came in 1954 when he argued the case of *Brown v. Board of Education* and won the Supreme Court decision outlawing racially segregated public schools.

The following year Vivian Marshall died; Marshall married Cecelia Suryat in December 1955.

In 1961 President Kennedy named Marshall to the U.S. Court of Appeals for the 2nd Circuit. Opposition from Southern senators blocked his confirmation for almost a year. In 1966 President Johnson chose Marshall to serve as solicitor general, the first black to hold that post. On June 13, 1967, Johnson named Marshall the first black member of the Supreme Court. He was confirmed Aug. 30 by a vote of 69-11. He took his seat on the bench Oct. 2.

Harry Andrew Blackmun

Harry A. Blackmun was born Nov. 12, 1908, in Nashville, Ill. His family soon moved to the Minneapolis-St. Paul area where, in grade school, Blackmun met Warren E. Burger, with whom he would later serve on the Supreme Court.

Demonstrating an early aptitude for mathematics, Blackmun won a scholarship to Harvard University where he majored in math and considered going to medical school. Instead, after graduating with highest honors in 1929, he worked his way through Harvard Law School, tutoring in math and driving the launch for the Harvard crew team. He graduated from law school in 1932.

Blackmun clerked for Judge John B. Sanborn, a member of the 8th U.S. Circuit Court of Appeals, whom Blackmun would

later succeed. In 1934 he joined the Minneapolis law firm with which he would practice for 16 years. In 1941 he married Dorothy E. Clark; they had three daughters.

In 1950 Blackmun accepted the position of house counsel for the Mayo Clinic in Rochester, Minn., a post he held until 1959 when President Eisenhower named him to the 8th U.S. Circuit Court of Appeals. After a decade on that bench, Blackmun was selected by President Nixon as an associate justice. He was nominated April 14, 1970, and confirmed May 12, by a 94-0 vote.

Lewis Franklin Powell Jr.

Lewis F. Powell Jr. was born Sept. 19, 1907, in Suffolk, Va. He graduated from Washington and Lee University in 1929, earning a Phi Beta Kappa key, and two years later from that university's law school. After a year at Harvard for post-graduate study in the law, Powell returned to Virginia to join one of the state's oldest and most prestigious law firms.

For almost 40 years, Powell practiced law in Richmond, where he and Josephine Rucker, whom he had married in 1936, made their home with their four children, three daughters and a son. During World War II Powell served as an Air Force intelligence officer. He had an extensive practice; his firm represented many well-known companies and corporations.

But Powell also made time for public and community service. In the stormy years following the *Brown v. Board of Education* ruling of 1954, Powell served as president of the Richmond school board (1952-61), consistently opposing intense pressure for "massive" resistance to desegregation. He continued as a member of that board until 1969. He also served on the state board of education in the 1960s.

He was president of the American Bar Association (1964-65) and president of the

American College of Trial Lawyers (1968-69). From those national posts, Powell gained recognition as a moderate who supported the creation of a legal services program for the poor but denounced civil disobedience. As a member of the President's Crime Commission in 1966, Powell criticized Supreme Court rulings intended to safeguard the rights of criminal suspects.

President Nixon nominated Powell Oct. 21., 1971, as an associate justice of the Supreme Court. He was confirmed Dec. 6 by a vote of 89-1

William Hubbs Rehnquist

William H. Rehnquist was born Oct. 1, 1924, in Milwaukee, Wis., where he spent his childhood. After serving in the Air Force during World War II, he went to Stanford University, from which he received a college degree "with great distinction," a master's degree in 1948 and a law degree in 1952. He earned another master's degree in political science from Harvard. One of his classmates at Stanford Law School was Sandra Day, who eventually joined him on the Supreme Court.

After finishing law school, Rehnquist from 1952 to 1953 year clerked for Justice Robert H. Jackson. In 1953 he married Natalie Cornell and moved to Phoenix, Ariz. The Rehnquists had a son and two daughters. In addition to his law practice, Rehnquist was active in Republican politics. He was a charter member of the most conservative wing of the state Republican Party and, in 1957, won notice for a speech denouncing the liberal rulings of the Warren Court.

During the 1964 presidential campaign, Rehnquist worked for the GOP presidential candidate, Arizona senator Barry Goldwater, and met Richard G. Kleindienst, another Arizonan active in Republican politics. Five years later, after Richard Nixon was elected president, Kleindienst,

then deputy attorney general, asked Rehnquist to head the office of legal counsel in the Justice Department.

In this position Rehnquist served as one of the administration's chief spokesmen on Capitol Hill during a time of great legislative activity on matters ranging from wiretapping to the rights of the accused. In 1971 Nixon nominated Rehnquist as an associate justice of the Supreme Court. The nomination was announced Oct. 21, and Rehnquist was confirmed, 68-26, Dec. 10.

John Paul Stevens

John Paul Stevens was born April 20, 1920, to a prominent Chicago family. His father owned and managed the city's largest hotel. He attended school in his hometown, graduating from the University of Chicago, Phi Beta Kappa, in 1941.

Stevens married Elizabeth Jane Sheeren in 1942 and went into the Navy for the remaining years of World War II, earning a Bronze Star. After the war he entered Northwestern University Law School, graduating first in his class in 1947. Stevens then clerked for Justice Wiley B. Rutledge, returning to Chicago in 1948 to practice law.

Stevens developed a reputation as a preeminent antitrust lawyer and eventually formed his own law firm. He also taught part-time at Northwestern and the University of Chicago law schools. The Stevens had four children, a son and three daughters.

Stevens served as minority counsel to a House subcommittee studying monopoly power in 1951 and a member of the attorney general's committee to study antitrust law, 1953-1955.

In 1970 President Nixon named Stevens to the U.S. Court of Appeals for the 7th Circuit, where he served until President Ford chose him as a member of the Supreme Court. He was nominated Nov. 18,

1975, and confirmed, 98-0, Dec. 17.

Stevens was divorced in 1979 and in 1980 married Maryan Mulholland Simon.

Sandra Day O'Connor

Sandra Day was born in El Paso, Texas, on March 26, 1930. After a childhood divided between summers on her family's ranch in southeastern Arizona and winters with her grandparents in El Paso, where she attended school, Sandra entered college at the age of 16.

In 1950 she received a degree in economics from Stanford University and in 1952 her law degree, both with high honors. Despite her obvious achievements, she had difficulty finding a job as a lawyer and worked for several months as a deputy county attorney. In December 1952 she married a classmate, John J. O'Connor, and they moved to Germany where he served in the Army and she worked as a civilian attorney for the Army.

In 1957 they moved back to Arizona, settling in Phoenix, where their three sons were born, and where they would remain until 1981.

O'Connor spent several years in private practice, then several more years as full-time mother and community volunteer — a role that included active participation in local Republican politics. In 1965 she resumed her legal career as assistant attorney general for the state, a post from which she was appointed to the state Senate in 1969. She was elected to two terms in the Arizona Senate and in 1972 was chosen its majority leader, the first woman in the nation to hold such a post.

In 1974 O'Connor left the legislature, winning a seat on the county superior court, where she served for five years before being named to the Arizona Court of Appeals in 1979. From that post, President Reagan chose her in 1981 to become the first woman Supreme Court justice. Her nomination was sent to the Senate Aug. 19; she was confirmed by a 99-0 vote on Sept. 21 and seated Sept. 25.

Selected Readings

Agresto, John. *The Supreme Court and Constitutional Democracy*. Ithaca and London: Cornell University Press, 1984.

Blasi, Vincent, ed. *The Burger Court: The Counter-Revolution That Wasn't*. New Haven and London: Yale University Press, 1983.

Choper, Jesse H. *Judicial Review and the National Political Process: A Functional Reconsideration of the Role of the Supreme Court*. Chicago: University of Chicago Press, 1980.

Cord, Robert. *Separation of Church and State: Historical Fact and Current Fiction*. New York: Lambeth Press, 1982.

Friedman, Leon, and Fred L. Israel, eds. *The Justices of the United States Supreme Court 1789-1969: Their Lives and Major Opinions*. New York and London: R. R. Bowker Co., 1969 and 1978.

Galloway, Russell W. *The Rich and the Poor in Supreme Court History*. Greenbrae, Calif.: Paradigm Press, 1982.

Halpern, Stephen C., and Charles M. Lamb, eds. *Supreme Court Activism and Restraint*. Lexington, Mass., and Toronto: D.C. Heath & Co., 1982.

Jackson, Robert H. *The Struggle for Judicial Supremacy*. New York: Alfred A. Knopf, 1941.

McGuigan, Patrick B., and Randall R. Rader, eds. *A Blueprint for Judicial Reform*. Washington, D.C.: Free Congress Research and Education Foundation, 1981.

Perry, Michael J. *The Constitution, the Courts and Human Rights*. New Haven and London: Yale University Press, 1982.

Pfeffer, Leo. *Religion, State and the Burger Court*. Buffalo: Prometheus Books, 1984.

Posner, Richard A. *The Federal Courts: Crisis and Reform*. Cambridge, Mass., and London: Harvard University Press, 1985.

Schwartz, Bernard. *Super Chief: Earl Warren and His Supreme Court, A Judicial Biography*. New York and London: New York University Press, 1983.

Tribe, Laurence H. *God Save This Honorable Court*. New York: Random House, 1985.

Warren, Charles. *The Supreme Court in United States History*, rev. ed., 2 vols. Boston: Little, Brown & Co., 1922, 1926.

Witt, Elder, ed. *Guide to the U.S. Supreme Court*. Washington, D.C.: Congressional Quarterly Inc., 1979.

Index